Library and Archives Canada Cataloguing in Publication

Prototyping Architecture / edited by Michael Stacey.

Includes essays by international leaders in contemporary architectural prototyping and design and documents the exhibition Prototyping Architecture, which was inaugurated at Wolfson Hall, University of Nottingham, 2012, and then shown at the London Building Centre Gallery, 2013, where it was accompanied by the international conference Prototyping Architecture. The final stage of the exhibition is at Design at Riverside, University of Waterloo, 2013 for the ACADIA 2013 Adaptive Architecture international conference, Cambridge, Ontario.

Includes bibliographical references and index.
Issued in print and electronic formats.
ISBN 978-1-926724-25-6 (pbk.).--ISBN 978-1-926724-33-1 (pdf).--ISBN 978-1-926724-34-8 (epub).--ISBN 978-1-926724-35-5 (mobi)

1. Architectural design--Exhibitions. 2. Prototypes, Engineering--Exhibitions. I. Stacey, Michael, writer of added commentary, editor of compilation II. Design at Riverside, host institution III. ACADIA (Conference) (33rd : 2013 : Cambridge, Ont.)

NA2728.P76 2013 729.074 C2013-906305-6
C2013-906304-8

Prototyping Architecture

Published by Riverside Architectural Press

The Architecture & Tectonics Research Group at the University of Nottingham with The Building Centre Trust, London and Cambridge Galleries and Waterloo Architecture are pleased to present this book, which explores the importance of prototypes in the delivery of high quality contemporary architecture - performative architecture that is inventive, purposeful and beautiful. Maximising the effective use of materials and resources whilst delivering environments that facilitate human well-being. This book accompanies and records the Prototyping Architecture Exhibitions in Nottingham, London and Cambridge, Ontario. This set of exhibitions has evolved venue to venue for site specific reasons.

1007361142.

Editor + Author:	Michael Stacey
Book Design:	Laura Gaskell, Jennifer Grewcock, Benjamin Stanforth and Andrew Tindale
Editorial Advice:	Andrew King, Laura Gaskell, Jennifer Grewcock and Benjamin Stanforth
Cover Image:	The perfomative skin of the SmartWrap Pavilion, architect KieranTimberlake

Prototyping Architecture Exhibition

17 October to 7 December, 2012
Wolfson Prototying Hall,
Nottingham, UK

10 January to 15 March, 2013
The Building Centre,
London, UK

17 October to 17 December, 2013
Cambridge Galleries,
Ontario, Canada

Curator
Michael Stacey
Michael Stacey Architects
+
University of Nottingham

Foreword

Spencer de Grey[1]

This book, appropriately digital, has been prepared to accompany the *Prototyping Architecture* exhibition at the Building Centre, London. On the 10 January 2013, I was delighted to open this exhibition in my role as Chairman of The Building Centre Trust. For me, this is an incredibly important exhibition, prototyping and research has been at the heart of everything we've done in the office and it's wonderful to see so many interesting, innovative and exploratory ideas assembled here. Some of the technologies and techniques an architecture or engineer can take away and use tomorrow in practice, others will stimulate our intellect and our desire to progress in months and years to come. It's a very interesting cross section of a wide range of different ideas and approaches, so I think it is an extraordinarily interesting array of different components and materials. These have been sourced from the leading edge of world architecture, situated both in practice and in university research teams. Components in this exhibition will challenge perceived ideas about material science, others present the potential for the printing of metal components, Additive Manufacturing to transform construction.

Mike Stacey has been at the centre of arranging and putting on this exhibition, it started at Nottingham University where he is Professor. Mike worked with us back in the 80's in particular on the HongKong Bank, Renault Centre and Stanstead Airport - so it's very nice to renew our relationship once again with him. This quality of exhibition and the related conferences; TEST conference for teachers and researchers in Architecture, particularly Technology, Environmental Design & Sustainability [TEST] and the Prototyping Architecture International Conference helps to place The Building Centre at the heart of contemporary discourse on construction and architecture.

Notes

1   Spencer de Grey Head of Design at Foster + Partners and
     Chairman, The Building Centre Trust.

INTRODUCTION

Introduction

Michael Stacey

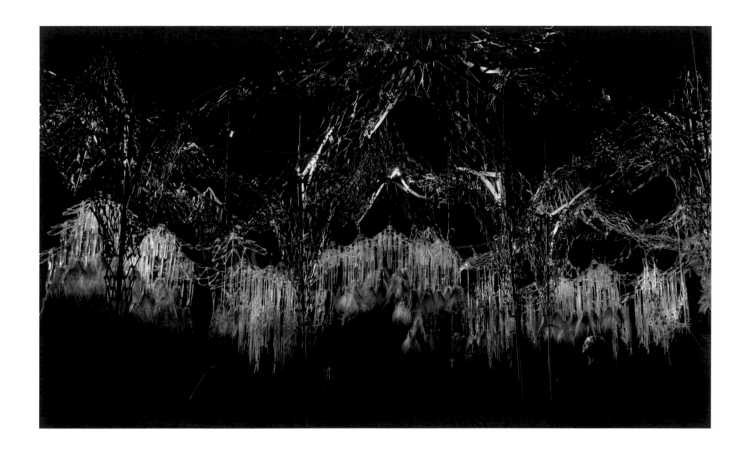

'Work stops at sunset. Darkness falls over the building site. The sky is filled with stars. "There is the blueprint," they say.'

Italo Calvino, *Invisible Cities*[1]

This book explores the importance of prototypes in the delivery of high quality contemporary architecture - performative architecture that is inventive, purposeful and beautiful. Focusing on construction that is informed by aspiration, knowledge and material culture. Written to accompany the *Prototyping Architecture Exhibition* in Nottingham, London and Cambridge, Ontario, 2012-13. *Prototyping Architecture* places a particular emphasis on research and experimentation showing how trial assemblies can inform architecture. In post-digital design practice the prototype remains a vital means of design development. Setting out impending systems and material futures, with the potential for technology transfer from other industries. It highlights the role of low carbon architecture and offsite manufacturing in maximising the effective use of materials and resources, whilst delivering environments that facilitate human well-being.

Fig. 1.1 Protocell Mesh, Philip Beesley Architect Inc, at *Prototyping Architecture*, Nottingham, 2012

Fig. 1.2 Great Workroom of the Johnson Wax Administration Building, Frank Lloyd Wright, completed in 1939

David Leatherbarrow in *Uncommon Ground,* 2000, mourns the death of design perhaps particularly in North America, charting the retreat of architectural practice, "the increased and increasing use of ready made solutions largely transforms design invention into choice, converting creativity into selection."[2] Thus diminishing the cultural value of architecture.[3] *Prototyping Architecture* demonstrates that inventiveness has not been lost within architecture. Both architecture and technology are malleable in the hands of a well-informed architect. *Prototyping Architecture* illustrates the role of models, prototypes and the printed components in the design of architecture and the built environment, with a particular focus on architecture that is assembled from prefabricated components, where prototyping has particular relevance.

The making of architecture is dependent on ideas and the communication of ideas. If we examine the etymology of *'prototype'* we find that it addresses the very core of architecture as generated by typologies.[4]

n 1. An original thing or person of which or whom copies or improved forms, etc. are made.

2. A trial model or preliminary version of a vehicle, machine etc.

Fig. 1.3 Structural arrangement of the Great Workroom of the Johnson Wax Administration Building

Fig. 1.4 Frank Lloyd Wright witnessing the load testing a prototype concrete column for the Johnson Wax Administration Building

From the Greek **Prototupos. Protos** – first, original. **Typos** – impression, figure, type[5]

Whereas if we look at *'innovation'* an overused word of contemporary life, we find the etymology to be:

v 1. bring in new methods, ideas, etc.

2. make changes.
From the Latin **innovatus** 'altered'[6]

Although the definition of innovation contains the notion of new ideas it is much more about transfer or borrowing. There is no need for the original and perhaps this is why governments find it easier to demand. In my view invention, to create by thought, is much more important.[7]

Primo Levi in his novel *The Wench* eloquently describes the creative impulse that resides within construction.

'We agreed then on the good things we have in common. On the advantage of being able to test yourself in your work, not depending on others in test, reflecting yourself in your work. On the pleasure of seeing your creature grow, beam after beam, bolt after bolt, solid, necessary, symmetrical, suited to its purpose and when it's finished you look at it and you think that it will live longer than you, and perhaps it will be use to someone you don't know, who does not know you. Maybe, as an old man, you'll be able to come back and look at it, and it will be beautiful, and it doesn't really matter so much that it will seem beautiful only to you, and you can say to yourself "maybe another man wouldn't have brought it off"'[8]

He captures the essence of the maker, of testing ones tectonic ideas. Is it the prototype or its author who is tested within the experimental process of research design and development? Prototypes are a clear demonstration of the iterative process that is essential when designing. Architects and Engineers develop constructional prototypes for six main reasons, to:

- test new ideas as part of an experimental practice;

- extend the boundaries of the known, [including working beyond current regulations and standards];

- test new holistic assemblies of many parts and components – researching and generating robust constructional technology;

- test scale and to manifest ideas

- focus cross disciplinary collaboration;

- deliver quality.

The first three types of prototypes fully embrace an empirical scientific method and encompass the potential of failure, which is the failure of the prototype and is the basis of the success of the process. This is a process of prototyping and testing, a process of trial and error. However, within the realm of professional practice there is little scope for failure and it is the duty of 'an experimental' architect to return his or her work to the certain and risk free. Even within the experimental practice of Philip Beesley his work is constrained by the inhabitation of the gallery based installations. Although clearly metaphoric provocations of future action and future architecture, works of architecture that are comparable to the creation of literature, his installations including *Protocell Mesh*, remain constrained by many considerations including health & safety. However, all experimentation is now constrained by regulation respecting the health and welfare of the participants.

Examples of prototyping that were essential to realising the proposed architecture include the dendriform or tree-like concrete columns of The Great Workroom of the Johnson Wax Administration Building, completed in 1939 by Frank Lloyd Wright, and Tim Macfarlane's work with Steve Jobs and Seele on the glass stairs and structural glass enclosures of the worldwide Apple stores. Although separated in time by over 60 years both are examples of architects and engineers working beyond the current norms of building regulations and constructional standards. The dendriform columns were outside the building regulations of Wisconsin in the 1930's therefore the structural testing of a prototype column was essential. Robert McCarter records, 'as was typical of Wright's structural innovations, professional engineers and inspectors not only did not understand these columns, they felt that they did not possess the necessary formulas necessary to calculate the indeterminate loads. They therefore opposed [the use of the Lillie columns] when Wright submitted the construction drawings to obtain a building permit in 1937 the Wisconsin State Building Commission was utilising a building code that could not be applied to Wright's design. As a compromise Wright proposed casting and testing a single column.'[19] On 4 June 1937 when the cast concrete was only one week old, not fully cured, the load test was carried with a test load of twelve tons, twice the design load. This was successfully achieved, characteristically Wright had the test continued and the column sustained sixty tons, over ten times the design load.

The prototyping and testing of structural glass components often remains essential, as this practice, although now well established and dating back to pioneering work in the 1980's, is still in advance of agreed Euro Codes. Although EUR 22856 EN set out a strategy for the development of new Euro Codes for the use of glass products in construction in 2007, it is estimated that this new Euro Code is still a further four years away from publication. The design of load bearing glass elements, such as glass floors or glass stair treads is based on operative redundancy, in which layers of glass within a laminated component can break without causing total failure of the component. A key advance was the development of ionoplast interlayers, such as Sentryglas® by Dupont. Sentryglas® interlayer it is considerably stiffer and stronger, when compared to more conventional polyvinyl butyral interlayers, and retains these properties up to temperatures of 70°C. Its higher strength allows it to play an effective role in supporting glass floor panels even after all the glass layers in a composite panel have failed. Tim Macfarlane worked closely with Seele in 2000 to develop the first all glass Apple staircase in New York. Seele undertook the testing programme for a 4-ply 50mm thick tread spanning 2400mm. The testing involved applying a point load of 2.0kN in the centre of the tread span. All four of the glass plies were then intentionally cracked and the load was successfully left in place for a period of 24 hours. These treads are proving durable in use, however, they are meticulously cleaned and maintained by Apple.

A contemporary example of prototyping to test a new and inventive constructional idea is the dynamic solar shades of Ocean One, the Theme Pavilion of Yeosu Expo, South Korea, designed by Austrian architects, soma. Fabricated in South Korea from glass fibre reinforced polymer [GFRP] this biomimetic solar shading opens by the twisting of the GFRP blades. Although inspired by Bird of Paradise Flowers the GFRP solar shading has a gill like quality as it transforms from a curved apparently solid surface to a series of tall vertical doubly curved slits. Soma worked with Jan

Fig. 1.5   The first all glass Apple staircase, New York, 2000

Fig. 1.6   Load testing a 2400mm spanning 4 ply 50mm laminated glass stair tread

Fig. 1.7   Stainless steel pig nose detail securing a tread to the structural glass balustrade

Knippers to develop this dynamic façade. He considered the key design 'question that arises for the Theme Pavilion in Yeosu is how the morphological form and principles of nature can be used for a kinetic façade with the aim of increasing adaptability and energy efficiency, as well as reducing weight and maintenance costs?'[10] He continues 'how can the mechanical complexity of kinetic systems for the façade of the Theme Pavilion in Yeosu be reduced?'[11]

Soma exploited the material qualities of GFRP, its flexibility, to minimise the moving parts in the dynamic and adaptive façade. The idea was first modelled by soma using ordinary sheets of paper. Torsion is applied to deflect each blade by an electrical servomotor. 'The driving power is converted into elastic energy

Fig. 1.8   The adaptive gill like solar shading of Ocean One, architects soma

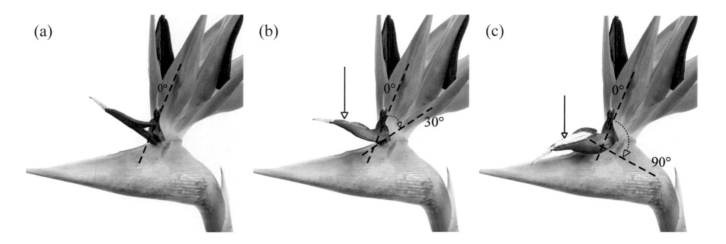

Fig. 1.9   Elastic deformation of the Bird of Paradise Flower – when a bird lands on the petal, the perch bends down, the sheath opens and the pollen is exposed

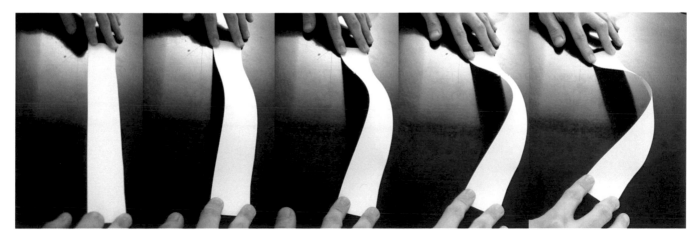

Fig. 1.10   Soma's paper model illustrating the movement idea for the louvers

stored in the deformed louvers.'[12] This simple and elegant assembly was tested by the construction of a 14 metre high prototype.

The first use of carbon fibre in new build construction will be realised by Rogers Stirk Harbour + Partners to form the structure of the entrance canopy of the Berkeley Hotel, London. This is an example of innovative technology transfer from automobile racing and aerospace, where carbon fibre is the material of choice to form the monocoque structures of Formula One racing cars and the cutting edge construction of civilian aircraft, such as the Boeing 787 Dreamliner. The initial ideas for this canopy were developed with Expedition Engineering. Rogers Stirk Harbour

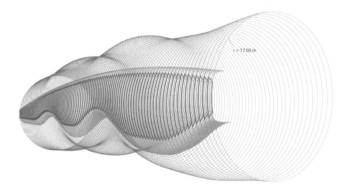

Fig. 1.11 Exploration of the radial geometry of the louvers within the overall form of Ocean One by soma

Fig. 1.12 The testing of the 14 metre high solar shaping prototype of Ocean One

Fig. 1.13 Ocean One, Theme Pavilion, Yeosu Expo 2012, viewed from the shoreline

Fig. 1.14 Prototype carbon fibre beam for entrance canopy of Berkeley Hotel, London

Fig. 1.15 Sectional drawings of the carbon fibre beams for the entrance canopy of the Berkeley Hotel, London by Rogers Stirk Harbour + Partners for the Entrance Canopy of Berkeley Hotel, London

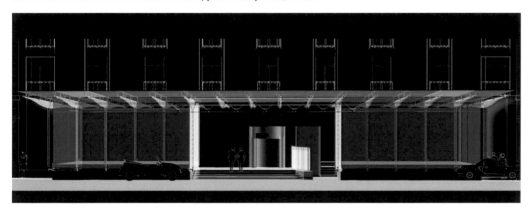

Fig. 1.16 The load testing of the prototype carbon fibre beam

+ Partners then worked closely with specialist manufacturing teams; Bellapart; Nexus Technologies; and Mira Technologica; to design, prototype and test this structure. Dirk Krolikowski of Rogers selected carbon fibre for this structure because 'carbon fibre monocoques are about 3 times lighter and 4 times stiffer than conventional construction methods, which results in a superior rigidity to weight ratio.'[13] The beams are ten metres long and have a self-weight of only 70kg. It was essential to prototype and load test groundbreaking construction. The carbon fibre components have been fabricated and tested and a window of opportunity in the schedule of this busy London hotel is required for assembly.

Bob Sheil part of sixteen*(makers)[14] suggests 'the architectural drawing altered its role as a carrier of design information, so too has the architectural model, the prototype and the speculative construct. The neat divisions that once commissioned, sequenced and qualified these key productions are converging, and the degree of cross-fertilisation between each mode of representation provided by digital tooling has generated a turbulent network of information flux.'[15] Whereas Philip Beesley observes "new architectural prototypes show a kind

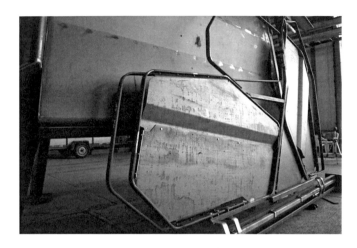

Fig. 1.17 The Rehearsal - sixteen*(makers) Shelter 55/02, Kielder, Northumberland, prototype or trail assembly in Stahlbogen GmbH's factory eastern Germany

Fig. 1.18 The Performance - Shelter 55/02 [right]

Fig. 1.19 The Record - a three-dimensional scan of
Shelter 55/02

of promiscuous exchange between widely varying sources, sweeping away traditional divisions between machine and hand crafts, and between nature and technology.'[16]

Standardisation was a key paradigm of twentieth century architecture, which was never achieved. Even for readily available components batch production remained the norm. Perhaps the nearest components produced from the construction industry that came to mass production was hot rolled steel sections, including I-beams and circular hollow sections. Many advocates see digital fabrication as the manufacturing of the bespoke, the tailoring of architecture to the specific geographic situation and the needs of the users and inhabitants. Barkow Leibinger have taken a different approach in designing CNC machined stainless steel components, which they characterfully describe as 'bones'. Standard stainless steel circular hollow sections have been refabricated by CNC machining producing organic components that have almost no visual link to the original standard components.[17]

Stephen Groák in the *Idea of Building* recorded the need for robust technology with which to construct architecture and that robust technology is based on invention, prototyping and testing, rather than selected from catalogues.[18] He also observes that

Fig. 1.20 Barkow Leibinger's Nomadic Garden- a thicket of CNC machined stainless steel 'bones' at the Venice Biennale, 2008

Fig. 1.21 A CNC machined stainless steel 'bones' - from Barkow Leibinger's Atlas of Fabrication

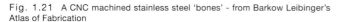

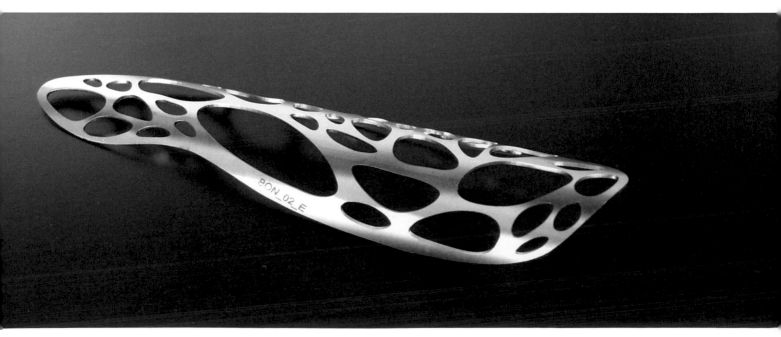

this need for a sophisticated understanding or architecture and construction 'will lead to a greater need for research literacy on the part of all practitioners throughout the professional building industries', suggesting that the role of practitioner-researcher will develop.[19]

The route to achieving robust constructional technology is to design, prototype and holistically test a proposed new and inventive assembly. The design and development of a new composite and integrated cladding assembly for RVP on Merseyside in 1984 is a good example of this process. Based on established manufacturing technology, metal folding, then used to make filing cabinets and monobloc steel partitions, for RVP I designed and tested a new composite cladding panel capable of providing a low U-value combined with a clear span of 4 meters. The system was prototyped in house with George Beardsworth and successfully tested to BS 5368 Parts 1-3, a British Standard Weather Test, at BSI Hemel Hempstead. A wide range of architects including Arup Associates and BDP specified this cladding system; it was first used on an ICI Pharmaceutical Production Facility, which was producing a cancer inhibitor.

Fig. 1.23 An integrated composite panel system, designed by Michael Stacey, undergoing a weather and load test to BS 5368 Parts 1-3 [bottom left]

Fig. 1.22 Composite Metal Panel Prototype at RVP, Merseyside, 1984, designed by Michael Stacey and manufactured by George Beardsworth for RVP

Fig. 1.24 QbissAir - transparent, translucent and opaque cladding system [bottom left]

Fig. 1.25 refabricating architecture, 2003

QbissAir cladding system, although much more technologically advanced than RVP's laminated composite metal panels, appropriately as almost 30 years of technological development has occurred, demonstrates a direct intellectual and technological lineage with this early integrated cladding system. A carrier of this continuity is Ron Fitch, then Technical Director of RVP and now Design Manager of Trimo; the researchers and manufacturers of QbissAir.

The Loblolly House Prototype is exhibited in Europe for the first time in the first two stages of *Prototyping Architecture*. Intriguingly the use of an extruded aluminium frame to structure the Loblolly House by KieranTimberlake is an outcome of their recent body of work, both theoretical and practice based. They first identify the Bosch Rexroth structural system whilst researching mass production for their book *refabricating architecture* 2003.[20] This system of aluminium extrusions is

Fig. 1.26 The perfomative skin of the SmartWrap Pavilion, architect KieranTimberlake, 2004

Fig. 1.27 SmartWrap Pavilion, architect KieranTimberlake, 2004 [right]

Fig. 1.28 Cellophane House, architect
KieranTimberlake, at Home Delivery,
MOMA, New York, 2008

Fig. 1.29 Loblolly House Prototype, at
Prototyping Architecture, Nottingham

typically used to assemble production lines. The practice first prototyped an extruded aluminium frame on the SmartWrap Pavilion, New York, 2004.[21] Subsequently the same system was used to prefabricate the Cellophane House, 2008.[22] This represents a body of work, possibly more like art practice; it also illustrates the strong component and research culture of KieranTimberlake's practice.

Amanda Levete, Director of A_LA, observes there is a myth about architects being individualistic fundamentalists. 'Actually architecture is a very collaborative discipline. On a big project, there can be a cast of thousands: the job of the architect is not only to create, but to get everybody on board. In that sense, it's very consensual.' Lighting engineer Rogier van-der-Hiede, then with Arup and now with Philips, whilst presenting at Nottingham with Richard MacCormac highlighted the

Fig. 1.30 The Timber Wave designed by A_LA with Arup, outside the Victoria and Albert Museum, London 2011

importance of physical models and prototypes in the design and development of both daylit and artificial lighting proposals. Although a realm where one could expect digital modelling such as Radiance to take over, Rogier emphasised the importance of physical models and prototypes as a mode of collaboration for a multi-disciplinary design team.[23] Sadly the Urban Cyclorama of the extension of the BBC's Broadcasting House, a layered and curved façade creating an urban public cinema, which formed the core of this presentation, will remain an unrealised dream following the inappropriate removal of Richard MacCormac's practice MJM from the delivery of this project. The Nasher Sculpture Center in Huston, Texas, is a collaboration between Arup and Renzo Piano Building Workshop a key component of which is the cast aluminium sunshades that bathe these galleries in natural light whilst protecting the exhibits and the visitors form the harsh Texan sun.

Fig. 1.31   Renzo Piano Building Workshop's cross-section through a galley of the Nasher Sculpture Center, Huston, Texas

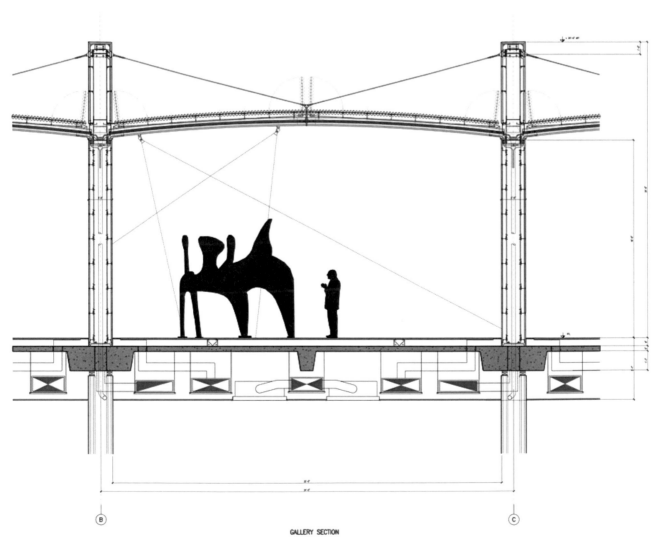

GALLERY SECTION

Fig. 1.32 Nasher Sculpture Center multi-jet wax rapid prototypes of the sun shading produced by Arup for Renzo Piano Building Workshop

Fig. 1.33 The cast aluminium sun shading the of Nasher Sculpture Center

Fig. 1.34 The interior of the Nasher Sculpture Center bathed in daylight, architect Renzo Piano Building Workshop, engineers Arup

Prototyping Architecture encompasses projects where the lead researchers are based in an academic context, for example the Passive Evaporative Downdraft Cooling [PEDC] research led by Professor Brain Ford at The University of Nottingham. Or situated in industry, as is the case with the design of the TRADA Pavilion, by engineers Ramboll. This pavilion has an ingeniously simple construction of flat planes of birch plywood linked with standard hinges to form a complex geometry. The pavilion presents a form-found surface, based on a mathematical idealisation in the tradition of Gaudi or Frei Otto but modified to a more readily achievable form using practice based research. Academia and industry are not two worlds, in the PEDC project, led by The University of Nottingham, the main industrial collaborators are Frialia SRL and Ingeniatrics Tecnologias.[24] This pioneering cooling technique was demonstrated on the Nottingham House, the United Kingdom's entry into Solar Decathlon 2010 in Madrid. The Nottingham House was researched, designed and built by students, architects and engineers based at The University of Nottingham, Department of Architecture & Built Environment.

Fig. 1.36 Nottingham House at the Solar Decathlon Madrid, 2010, it has now been reassembled on University Park, Nottingham

Fig. 1.35 Passive Evaporative Downdraft Cooling System in the Nottingham House.

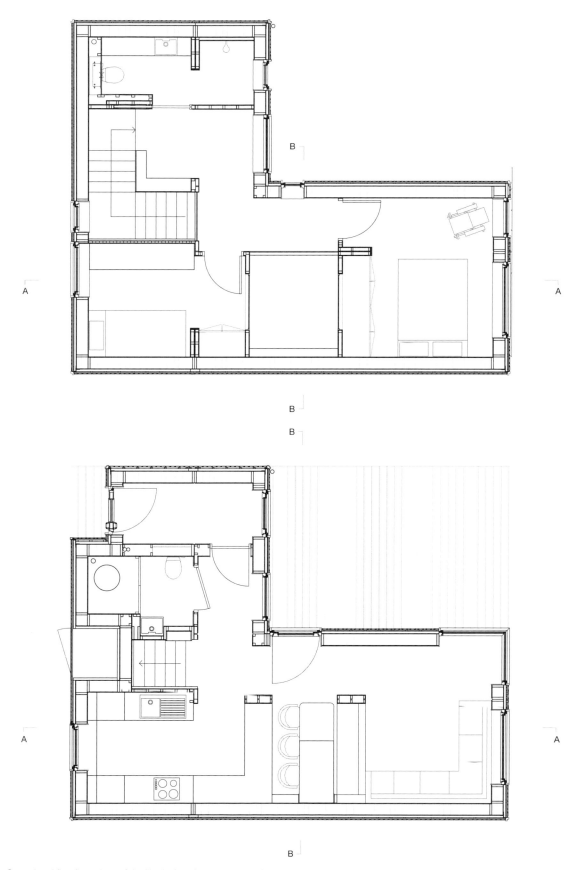

Fig. 1.37 Ground and first floor plans of the Nottingham House designed by
Rachel Lee, Christopher Dalton and Ben Hopkins

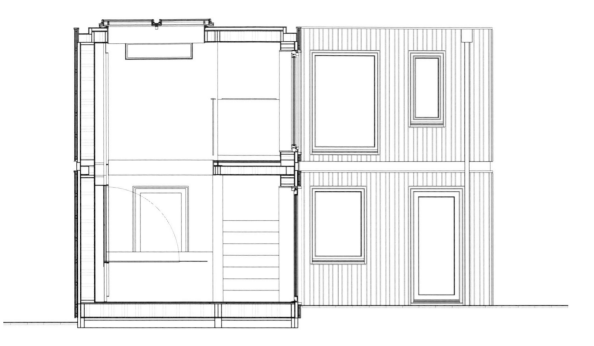

Fig. 1.38 Section BB of the Nottingham House designed by
Rachel Lee, Christopher Dalton and Ben Hopkins

Fig. 1.39 Section AA of the Nottingham House designed by
Rachel Lee, Christopher Dalton and Ben Hopkins

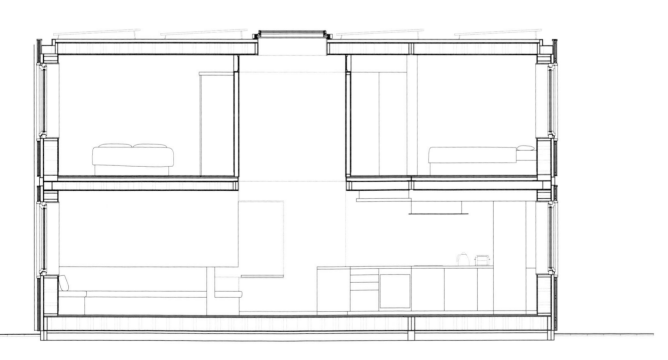

Fig. 1.40   Detail of the completed Nottingham House

Fig. 1.41   TRADA Pavilion by Ramboll

Fig. 1.42   ROC van Twente, Hengelo by IAA Architecten

Prototyping Architecture

The Wolfson Prototyping Hall at The University of Nottingham has been conceived and designed as a place of collaboration, researching tectonics, prototyping and testing architecture. Enabling the Architecture and Built Environment Department to create a new 'Bauhaus' in the heart of England, as a venue for global research collaboration.

Scale

A key reason to prototype a component or assembly is to test the scale, to establish whether the form and proportions shown on the drawings or three-dimensional digital file are appropriate. IAA Architecten were commissioned to transform the derelict Transformer Factory in Hengelo into a Regional Community College – ROC van Tewente. Project Director Harry Abels decided that the eight-metre columns at the new entrance should be cast in iron, in honour of his late father who was a Foundry Man in this works. Michael Stacey Architects worked with IAA and ABT to realise these cast iron columns, which are believed to be the first new cast iron columns in contemporary architecture for over 100 years. Cast in the Netherlands, it proved necessary to cast them in two four-metre sections to avoid distortion. In essence the eight-metre long casting cooled to unreformable banana shapes. The two halves of the column are joined on site

Fig. 1.43 Harry Abels holding the quarter size timber prototype machined on a CNC lathe.

Fig. 1.44 Michael Stacey next to the quarter size timber prototype machined on a CNC lathe.

with an internal concrete plug. This worked well as the columns are primarily in compression. To test the form and proportion of these columns, a quarter size timber prototype was machined on a CNC lathe. Both the tall Dutch Architect and the short Welsh Architect thought the form worked well from their rather diverse eye lines. The internal columns of Tewente ROC, Hengelo are cast is concrete with a similar form.

With some prototypes, when checking for proportion and scale, it is necessary to replicate the material qualities and colour, which is why products such as Alumide® (aluminium filled polyamide) were developed to prototype metal based component. This was used on the Additive Manufactured Violin, see Figure 1.73.

Within Fine Art the question of scale shifts into a more cerebral dimension. In Fine Art scale is not a literal question of dimension, it is more about the intellectual ambition or power of a work of art. To take a Renaissance example Piero della Francesca's,[25]

portraits of Duke and Duchess of Urbino, now housed in the Uffizi, Florence, are arguably more commanding and captivating than Michelangelo's physically larger painting Doni Tondo, which is in the adjacent wing of this gallery.[26] This concept of scale does apply to architecture, as well demonstrated by the book Phyllis Richardson and Lucas Dietrich *XS, Big Idea, Small Projects*.[27]

Fig. 1.45 The Geraedts Foundry, Netherlands

Fig. 1.46 Cast iron column at ROC van Twente, Hengelo by IAA Architecten

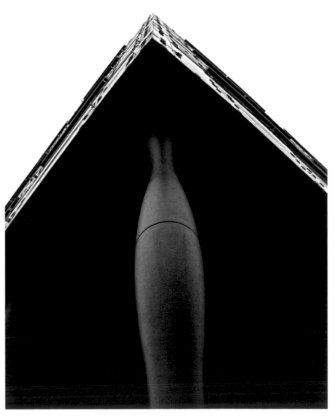

Fig. 1.47   Portraits of Duke and Duchess of Urbino by Piero della Francesca
now housed in the Uffizi, Florence

Prototyping for Quality

Throughout my career as an architect I have observed that prototyping is a key means of achieving high quality construction, not only are ideas tested, a physical focus of collaboration is established and importantly an unambiguous quality standard is set for the contract. I first experienced this whilst working on the Renault Centre, Swindon, 1982 with Norman Foster.[28] All the concrete assemblies were prototyped by the specialist subcontract Cementation and inspected and agreed by Bovis, Arup and Foster Associates. The quality of delivery was so high - that I thought that in situ concrete was a 'simple' technology, only to learn the hard way with other contractors on later projects. Recent examples of prototyping for quality include the in situ concrete external walls of Hepworth Wakefield, 2011, by Chipperfield Architects. Careful control of this pigmented smooth and articulated bolt marked concrete was essential.[29] It is interesting to note that the main contractor chose not to use PERI formwork and developed its own site-based approach. This necessitated a second trail assembly, which was inspected and agreed by Chipperfield. However, the first wall cast was unsatisfactory and with agreement of the client was demolished and built again.

Fig. 1.48   Prototype in situ concrete walls for Hepworth Wakefield, 2011, by Chipperfield Architects

Fig. 1.49   Hepworth Wakefield, 2011, by Chipperfield Architects

For the Royal Playhouse, Copenhagen, 2008, Lundgaard & Tranberg Arkitekter sought a longer brick that linked to ancient tectonic traditions, however, the immediate inspiration came from the long format bricks that architect Peter Zumthor developed in collaboration with Petersen Tegl, for the Kolumba Art Museum in Köln, which opened in 2007.[30] Lundgaard & Tranberg considered the brick for the Kolumba Art Museum too uniform in terms of texture and colour. For the theatre they wanted an even slimmer brick with a greater colour variation and a more rustic

character. Test walls were built on the quayside by Petersen Tegl from Denmark and Wienerberger from Austria, however, this competition was won by Petersen Tegl as its prototypical wall of brickwork fulfilled the architect's technical requirements and aesthetic aspirations. Petersen Tegl is a family run brickmaker that was founded in 1791. To achieve the rich red brown colour of the bricks Petersen Tegl bought English Clay from Baggeridge Bricks. These prototype walls enabled the appropriate supplier to be selected, material qualities to be determined, tectonic details to be agreed and the quality standard set.

Technology Transfer

It is possible to learn from other industries, to practice technology transfer, however architects and engineers should not allow the instruction they received in their schools of architecture and engineering to dominate their thinking. Material science generates material possibilities that defy old rules of thumb. For example, architects will allow for the thermal expansion of metals when detailing, aluminium and glass works well together as they have a similar rate of thermal expansion. Metals typically expand

Fig. 1.50   Trial brickwork prototypes for the Royal Playhouse, Copenhagen

Fig. 1.51   Royal Playhouse, Copenhagen, 2008, Lundgaard & Tranberg Arkitekter

on heating because it is a mutable material, with a crystalline structure. However, to survive the extreme heat of jet engines, Rolls-Royce has developed high pressure turbine blades cast and 'grown' as a single nickel alloy crystal, which exhibit no thermal expansion. Turbine blade research and development is focused on increasing temperature capabilities and its evolution illustrates the hand in hand advancement of materials and manufacturing techniques. Operating in the extreme environment of a jet engine makes severe demands on both the mechanical properties and environmental stability of the blade system and is only possible through the close integration of design, materials and manufacturing. A steep change in temperature capability was realised through the introduction of directional solidification, eliminating transverse grain boundaries, a source of weakness in a creep-dominated application. Manufactured in a vacuum, as an inverse investment or lost wax casting, the nickel alloy is fed in via a spiral 'gateway', which allows only one metal crystal to enter the mould. Rolls-Royce jet engines are guaranteed for 50 years based on its ongoing monitoring and maintenance of each engine.[31]

Within architecture and the built environment beauty is a vital route to a low carbon future. Jonathan Ive, lead designer at Apple, considers 'beauty is a very difficult word to define, certainly in terms of what we do and the way that we work. There is incredible beauty in a very efficiently and elegantly built product....And of course there is beauty based on form, proportion, on material, finish and colour.'[32] By design it is possible to combine improved performance, improved user experience whilst reducing the energy in use and the embodied energy needed to provide comfort within architecture. Collectively humankind needs to develop low carbon products that help to tackle climate change. However, this will only be achieved with designs and technology that humankind wants to appropriate [Feenberg 1999]. Designs, products and architecture, which people want to buy and invest in. Therefore empathy for the user and a striving for excellence and beauty are essential. Three examples of this within *Prototyping Architecture* are: the Plumen Bulbs, the Cantifix Transparent Double/Triple Glazed Corner and the Range Rover 2012. Demonstrating the opposite of a moralist hair shirt approach to sustainability. Particularly within architecture historical precedent shows that it is performance, excellence and beauty that sustains buildings through time, making architecture some of the most durable artefacts of material culture.

The Plumen 001 is the world's first designer energy saving light bulb. The energy saving light bulb is a neglected, yet inspiring invention. It uses 80% less energy than the traditional incandescent light bulb, keeps down electricity bills and is better for the environment. It also lasts around 8 times longer. Despite this, we tend to buy them out of moral obligation. To some, the

Fig. 1.52 A nickel alloy high-pressure turbine blade, researched and manufactured by Rolls-Royce

Fig. 1.53 Plumen 001 the world's first designer low energy light bulb

problem is the light they give off, to others it is the way they look. Both can be solved. The answer is in the design. Make the bulb attractive and people will spend a bit more to enjoy a better quality of light and a design they appreciate every day. Testing shows that Plumen 001 Bulbs will operate for 8000 hours. Glass tubes can be bent in many different shapes, so why are there thousands of manufacturers but only three designs? Plumen aims to address this problem. The excellence and elegance of the Plumen 001 Bulb was recognised by the Award of Brit Insurance Design of the Year 2011. The Plumen 001 is the first of many products that will show light bulbs can be efficient and beautiful at the same time.

Cantifix has developed an all-transparent double glazed corner unit. Where the energy performance at the corner is, in essence, the same as the mid pane of the glass. By using UV curing glue the corner becomes a rigid continuous glass corner. This junction has no extrusions intruding into the view, nor carefully installed sealants. Creating a fully transparent 'Invisible Corner'. This provides transparency and consistent low energy performance of at least 1.5 W/m2/K; the U-value is dependent on the specification of the multi-glazed unit. These units can be more rapidly installed and completed in comparison to previous glazing and curtain walling corner units. The development of glass technology is a particular success of the construction industry, led by research practitioners, working with manufacturers and specialist

Fig. 1.54 An all-transparent double glazed corner unit developed by Cantifix, providing transparency and continuity of thermal performance

subcontractors, prototyping for specific projects and building on technological break throughs such as the Float Process, developed by Pilkington in St Helens, England in the 1950s.[33] The all glass corner has assured the future of transparency within architecture, allowing freedom of design and creating striking and technically beguiling enclosures and façades.

Architecture and the Built Environment can learn from the very significant Research and Development investment in other industries, for example Jaguar Land Rover spent over £900,000,000 annually on R&D.[34] In particular, the realms of science, digital technology, transportation and aerospace. One limitation experienced in architecture is that it remains fundamentally linked to the human scale of spatial enclosure. Architects and engineers can learn from other industries - it is obsolete to think of technology as being specific to a particular industry. The essence of technological development is not high or low technology. Technological development is characterised by the layering of technologies. One technology informing another, for example Perspex or Plexiglas is manufactured on acid etched glass. An iPhone or smart phone can incorporate up to 10,000 patented items.

The all aluminium body shell of the Range Rover 2012 is an excellent example of focused Research and Development expertise and teamwork. Jaguar Land Rover [JLR] has built on its own past experience of developing all aluminium body structures, including the XJ Jaguar, the first volume-production car to use an all-aluminium monocoque chassis, in 2003. The Range Rover 2012 has been designed and fabricated with an all-aluminium body. This is JLR's third generation of lightweight body architecture. Designed and engineered in Britain, it is the world's first SUV with a lightweight all-aluminium body. It was launched by JLR in September 2012 and exhibited in Nottingham from October of that year. The all-new Range Rover achieves a weight saving of 420kg when compared with the previous model, which is the equivalent to the weight of five average adults. This third generation of JLR's lightweight vehicle architecture combined with improved aerodynamics, results in an increase in fuel efficiency of over 20%, significantly reducing the carbon footprint of owning a SUV. The development of the new Range Rover took significant R&D investment by JLR. The use of virtual testing reduced the R&D carbon footprint by 320kg of CO_2 by saving 750 miles of testing, however, over 300 physical prototypes were produced in the development of the new Range Rover. A key part of its material resourcefulness is the use of 50% recycled aluminium. The Range Rover 2012 is a high-profile example of potential technology transfer from other industries.[35]

There is a competitive EU road map for carbon reduction in the European Car Industry, Mark White observes 'in Europe there is

Fig. 1.55 XJ Jaguar, the first volume-production car to use an all-aluminium monocoque chassis

Fig. 1.56 The Range Rover 2012 – a mimetic design that is 420kg lighter than the previous model

now an agreed [car] industry roadmap to reduce emissions by 3% per year over the next 20 years'.[36] This is undertaken collaboratively with outcomes being shared by the major car manufacturers but is competitive since the methods used to generate the achieved savings remain specific to each manufacturer. Perhaps this is a better model for the construction industry rather than the narrow prescriptions of Code for Sustainable Homes or Passivhaus standards. Thus the construction industry can learn from both the processes and products of other industries.

Age of Resourcefulness

In the second decade of the twenty-first century humankind is entering an age of resourcefulness. The excesses of the consumer society that started in the explosive growth of North America after the Second World War is coming to an end. Bill Bryson observed that 'by 1955 the typical American teenager had as much disposable income as the average family of four had enjoyed fifteen years earlier.'[37] Although progress to resourcefulness is not a simple or linear process it is can be characterised by a paradigm clash between market preconceptions and more responsible modes of procurement, combined with intelligent design and manufacturing practices.

Body Complete: Material Breakdown

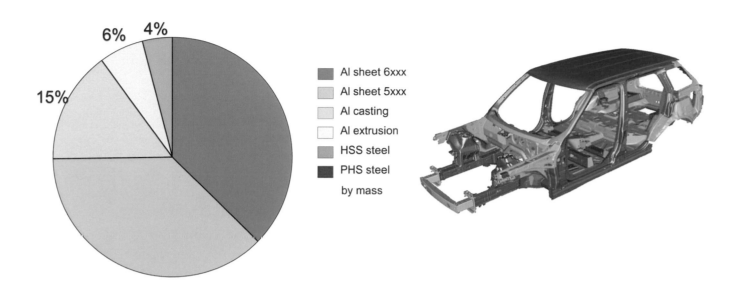

Fig. 1.57 The composition of the aluminium body shell of the Range Rover 2012

Fig. 1.58 A prototype all aluminium body shell of the Range Rover 20132 at Prototyping Architecture, Nottingham

Such resourcefulness, combined with intelligent design and manufacturing practices, is demonstrated in Loblolly House designed by KieranTimberlake, Philadelphia based architects. Unusually, for an architecture practice, they have an in-house research group, KTRG. This team undertakes both project based R&D and one-off or blue sky research.

Loblolly House is located on a barrier island off the coast of Maryland's Chesapeake Bay, the design seeks to deeply fuse the natural elements of its site to architectural form. Positioned between a dense grove of loblolly pines and a lush foreground of saltmeadow cordgrass and the bay, the architecture is formed about and within the elements of trees, tall grasses, the sea, the horizon, the sky and the western sun that define the place of the house. Timber foundations minimise the footprint and provide savannah-like views of the trees and the bay, and the staggered boards of the east facade evoke the solids and voids of the forest.

Loblolly House proposes a new, more efficient method of building through the use of building information modelling (BIM) and integrated component assemblies. The frame comprises Bosch Rexroth aluminium framing and bolted together as opposed to welded, creating a structural system for the house, which can be disassembled without affecting the capacity of beam and column components to be reconnected. The bolted scaffold serves as a frame into which off-site fabricated kitchen; bathroom; and mechanical blocks; and floor and wall cartridges are inserted without the use of permanent fasteners or wet connections. Upon disassembly cartridges and blocks are removed as whole units and column/beam scaffold sections are unbolted.

Situated in Maryland, a southern state, as it is below the Mason Dickson Line, the house has been designed to minimise the need for mechanical air-conditioning despite peak summer time

Fig. 1.59   Loblolly House, architect KieranTimberlake, Taylors Island, Maryland

Fig. 1.60   Loblolly House, architect KieranTimberlake, site plan [bottom]

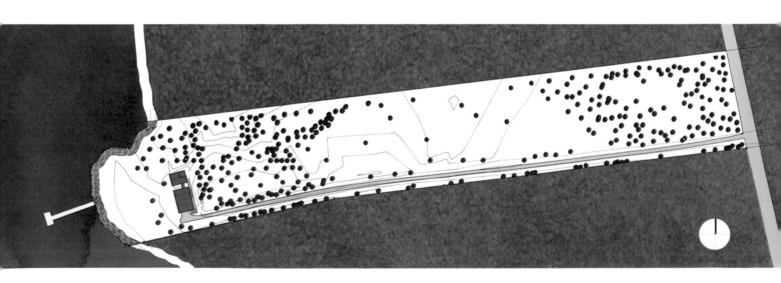

Fig. 1.61 Sitting in the Loblolly House looking out on Chesapeake Bay

Fig. 1.62 The layered dynamic façade of the Loblolly House revealed by twilight

temperature reaching in excess of 38°C with a relative humidity of about 75%. Willis Carrier, the inventor of air conditioning filled his key patent in 1906 having been inspired by a foggy day in Pittsburgh.[38] Air conditioning enabled the expansion of the inhabitation of the southern states of America. This energy hungry invention is one of the reasons that America's carbon footprint is four times the world average. In essence we need to un-invent this technology, to provide comfort without recourse to mechanical systems. Loblolly House is a bold step on this journey and KieranTimberlake is monitoring this layered façade, which can preheat the air in cold weather and provides shade and ventilation in summertime. The budget of many modern buildings is dominated by the cost of services, creating comfort via the building fabric returns the investment into the visible architecture as well as reducing the demand for energy.[39]

'Loblolly House is not only a statement in favour of a more ecological approach, it is an essay in prefabrication demonstrating KieranTimberlake's engagement, with craft, industry and manufacturing. The new techniques they utilise, including, scaffolding, blocks and cartridges'[40] Loblolly House gains its authenticity from the integration of space, structure and layered environmental systems. Loblolly House also preserves

embodied energy with the easy disassembly and reassembly of its essential elements. The disassembly and redeployment potential is evident in the detailing and quality craftsmanship of the energy intensive scaffold, blocks, cartridges, and service spines. This ensures a design-for-disassembly strategy where the components with the highest embodied energy can be disassembled and redeployed with a minimal loss of energy.

The Cellophane House designed and by KieranTimberlake for the *Home Delivery Exhibition* at MOMA, New York, was disassembled and recycled after this exhibition, with an overall materials recovery rate of 98.95% recovery rate. The details of this process are recorded in *Cellophane House*, a book by KieranTimberlake.[41] 99.99% of the extruded aluminium frame was recycled. For many elements including the envelope and bathroom pods 100% recovery was achieved. Only the concrete footings were left behind in central New York. James Timberlake reflecting on humankind's need for resourcefulness in the twenty-first century considers the route to achieving this and suggesting this is *the age of the prototype.*

Prototyping Architecture

Michael Stacey curated three exhibitions in conjunction with the Building Centre Trust. The venues for the exhibition were the Wolfson Prototyping Hall at The University of Nottingham, The Building Centre, London and Cambridge Galleries with Waterloo Architecture, in Cambridge, Ontario. The exhibition was designed and constructed in Nottingham by his Sixth Year students from the Making Architecture Research Studio [MARS], with the Protocell Mesh largely constructed by Fifth Year Architecture students led by Chantelle Niblock.

Fig. 1.63 Cellophane House, architect KieranTimberlake, being assembled in prefabricated chunks at MOMA, New York

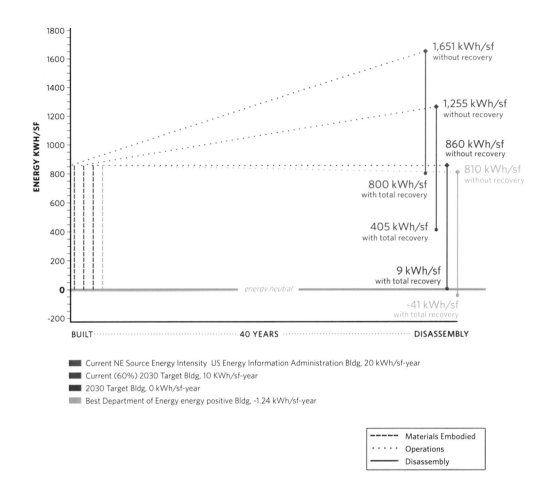

Fig. 1.64 KieranTimberlake's comparison of operational and the embodied energy highlighting the importance of recovering the embodied energy

Wolfson Prototyping Hall

Located in the new Energy Technologies Building at The University of Nottingham, the Wolfson Prototyping Hall is a unique facility for the prototyping and testing of assemblies and components. Architecture and Urbanism Research Division is engaging in collaborative partnerships with industry, practice and manufacturers to develop and test new components and construction assemblies.

The 400m² facility has a clear height of 9 metres. It has been designed to allow full scale testing of façades and other building elements, with a further 200m² of external hard standing for real time weather and daylight tests. Other testing facilities include a Climate Chamber. Built on a brownfield former industrial site, the Energy Technologies Building has been designed, by Maber Architects and Price & Myers Engineers, to achieve BREEAM Outstanding.[42] The Wolfson Prototyping Hall was in part funded by the Wolfson Foundation and European Union Regional Development Fund. Research within the Prototyping Hall is focused on performative architecture, prefabrication and prototyping for live projects. A key aim is to help reduce the demand of energy consumption of architecture and the built environment. This unique facility became operational in September 2012.

The Building Centre: London

The Building Centre Trust provides support for educational, research and cultural activities connected with the built environment. It is based at the Building Centre in London and produces a programme of exhibitions and events that complement its commercial information services a permanent product gallery and an online product selector, can be found at Specifinder.com. The Building Centre brings together all sectors of the construction industry to share information about how to create better environments with a particular emphasis on materials, energy and innovation. The Trust provides a neutral place where crafts and planning, architecture and manufacture, surveying and engineering, construction and government can meet and exchange ideas and develop policy.

Major initiatives include a celebration of engineering in architecture through a series of events and hosting the Engineering Club; Lower Carbon Drive, which promotes sensitive low carbon retrofit in existing buildings; Materials of Invention looks at the development of materials and technologies - both learning from the past and predicting the future.[43] As well as its programme of events in London, The Building Centre reaches out both nationally and internationally through major international conferences, publications and video broadcasts of the events. The Trust is also making a contribution to the local environment through the creation of a new public space in Store Street itself.

Fig. 1.65 Prototyping Architecture in the Wolfson Prototyping Hall at The University of Nottingham, Autumn 2012

The Trust is a principle sponsor of New London Architecture whose model of London and educational programme are based at The Building Centre. Many major industry organisations are based at The Centre including the Construction Products Association, the Construction Industry Council and the UK Green Building Council. The Building Centre is an independent not for profit organisation, which began in the 1930's as a resource to provide information to architects and builders about modern materials of construction. It is run by a board of Trustees drawn from various sectors of the industry and a board of Directors who oversee its commercial activities.

Cambridge Galleries and Waterloo Architecture, Cambridge Ontario

In 2004 the Department of Architecture at The University of Waterloo, left the main Waterloo Campus for a refurbished Silk Mill in the Centre of Cambridge on the Grand River. The mill was given to the university by the City of Cambridge on the basis that the arrival of Architecture in the centre of the city would stimulate

Fig. 1.66   Prototyping Architecture at The Building Centre, winter 2012

post-industrial regeneration.[44] The School of Architecture is now simple known as Waterloo Architecture. In 2012, Waterloo Architecture was selected by Azure Magazine as one of the top five architecture schools in North America.

Cambridge Galleries presents contemporary art, architecture and design from three locations in the City of Cambridge: Design at Riverside, Preston and Queen's Square. Design at Riverside, Canada's only municipal public gallery dedicated to architecture and design, became part of the mix-use redevelopment of the old mill, opening its doors in November 2004. The first exhibition was *Digital Fabricators*, curated by Michael Stacey, which was designed to coincide with the Fabricators Conference hosted by Waterloo Architecture. Riverside has since mounted over 60 exhibitions including the 2008 Canadian entry to the 11th International Architecture Exhibition – the Venice Biennale and launched an extensive program of lectures, events and publications.

Prototyping Architecture curated by Michael Stacey, will be presented at both Design at Riverside and the Atrium Gallery of Waterloo Architecture (allowing for the presentation of large scale assemblies such as the Loblolly House Prototype and the products of the Fabric Formwork Workshop) and will be on display prior to and during the ACADIA 2013 Adaptive Architecture Conference.

When casting with in situ concrete using conventional rigid formwork, up to 40% of the cost of the element is the rigid shuttering. For much of the Twentieth Century this was predominately timber shuttering and false work. Typically this virtual architecture, the precursor of the cast form was simply burnt after a single use. One environmental response to this has been the development of reusable formwork and false work, as exemplified by the flexible formwork of exhibitor PERI. However, standardised formwork responds best to rectilinear geometry combined with well-considered modularity.

Fabric formwork is a new construction method for concrete structures that utilises sheets of fabric as flexible, lightweight moulds. This offers geometric freedom and facilitates curvature and double curvature in the cast concrete. Yet it is much more cost effective and lower carbon formwork, compared to rigid formwork. The prototype cast using fabric formwork by Anne-Mette Manelius and MARS is a tripartite concrete column, it is form-optimised for stability and constructed with minimal means. It is fair to suggest this column would have delighted Augustus Welby Northmore Pugin as it evokes the columns in the naïve of many great English Gothic Cathedrals.

Based on her recently completed PhD thesis at CINARK, which focused on the architectural potential of fabric formwork for

Fig. 1.67 Digital Fabricate - the first exhibition in Cambridge Galleries when it opened in 2004, curated by Michael Stacey

concrete, *Fabric Formwork - Concrete as Material and Process*, Anne-Mette began an investigation and material prototype of a lightweight, prefabricated fabric moulds, which unfold to be cast on site. The principles of tensioning the fabric, of restraining it, and placing concrete have a direct formal consequence, like a material dialogue between relaxation and control; thus the technique encourages an architectural understanding of concrete as material and as process. In an eloquent demonstration of the economy of means of fabric formwork, Anne-Mette brought the fabric formwork and timber stiffeners form Copenhagen in her budget airline flight bag.[45] This formwork was subsequently set out using laser cut templates, fabricated in Nottingham using Anne-Mette's design files. The concrete was mixed and poured by MARS students. The concrete mix used was 3 (ballast coarse aggregate) 2 (fine sharp sand) 1 (cement) with a super plasticiser and sufficient clean water to form a porridgy consistency - plastic enough to work with but not too runny. Simply mixed with a shovel and cement mixer. To further reduce the CO_2 footprint of concrete cast in fabric formwork, industrial by-products could be

Fig. 1.68 Laura Gaskell of MARS mixing concrete for Anne-Mette's fabric formwork column at Prototyping Architecture, Nottingham

Fig. 1.69 Anne-Mette Manelius removing the fabric formwork from her tripartite column [right]

used such as ground granular blast slag.[46] Although based on the body of work of her PhD Thesis, the tripartite clustered column was a truly experimental prototype moving beyond an existing body of knowledge. It will be honoured as the first prototype fabricated in the Wolfson Prototyping Hall at The University of Nottingham, which had only been completed two weeks earlier.

Another approach to an economy of means to produce sustainable low cost low carbon enclosures is exemplified by the work of the Swiss Engineer Heinz Isler (1926-2009), who throughout his career researched shell structures, predominantly formed with in situ concrete. In this approach the structural form leads the architecture, a minimum amount of materials is required to achieve long span enclosures. The exhibit case study, however, illustrates a glass fibre reinforced polymer dome produced by Isler in the early 1960's using a sand / earth mould, simply casting in the open air.[47]

Additive Manufacturing (AM) is the direct fabrication of end-use products and components employing technologies that deposit material layer-by-layer from a single 3D digital file. It enables the manufacture of geometrically complex, low to medium volume production components, in a range of materials, with little (if any) fixed tooling or manual intervention beyond the initial product design. Over the past twenty-five years this technology has evolved from a support tool for product development into an independent production method. The SLT 3D fill format was introduced in 1988, only six years after the launch of AutoCAD in 1982. In 1999 engineers Elliott Wood with the University of Nottingham produced individual geometry rapid prototypes

Fig. 1.70 The construction of Anne-Mette Manelius' fabric formwork concrete column at Prototyping Architecture, Nottingham

Fig. 1.71 Anthony Gormley's Quantum Cloud, outside the Millennium Dome, London, completed for New Year's Day 2000

for the diverse nodes of the fractal construction of Anthony Gormley's Quantum Cloud, which is located outside the Millennium Dome, London. 364 rapid prototypes, fabricated in wax and paper LOM, were used to form the ceramic shells for lost wax cast steel nodes, produced by BSA in Birmingham.[48]

This technology has now developed to enable the direct printing of fully functional components. Additive Manufacturing has been deployed to print a Violin. It's every violinmaker's dream to produce an instrument to rival the sound of a Stradivarius, The University of Nottingham are trying to do just that... using additive manufacturing technology. Dr Joel Segal teamed up with EOS GmbH to produce a laser-sintered violin. EOS produced the violin body made from Alumide® (aluminium filled polyamide) using one of their advanced laser-sintering systems, the EOSINT P390. A typical applications for Alumide® is the manufacture of stiff parts of metallic appearance for applications in automotive manufacture, wind tunnel tests or parts that are not safety critical, for tool inserts for injecting and moulding small production runs. Mark Bury however questions whether EOS can print a violin 'that will pay as perfectly as a Stradivarius original?'[49] He questions the cultural impact of additive manufacturing 'when we talk of 'digital fabrication' what exactly are we 'making' here – if we machine-print a design as a working object, do we redefine the role of 'model', 'prototype' and 'archetype'?'[50]

Fig. 1.72 Printed Wax and LOM paper based rapid prototypes - the void formers the 364 nodes investment cast steel nodes of Quantum Cloud

Fig. 1.73 A galvanised investment cast steel node for Quantum Cloud, produced by BSA

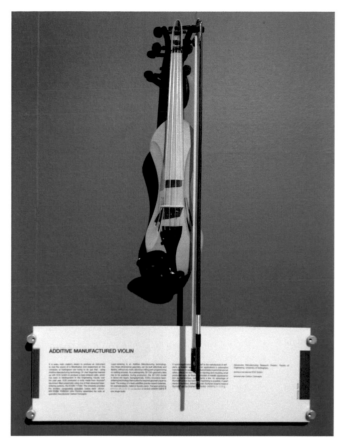

Fig. 1.74 Additive Manufactured Violin by Dr Joel Segal and EOS GmbH, as displayed at Prototyping Architecture, London

Using selective laser melting it is now possible to print components directly in metals, such as stainless steel or titanium. This enables components to be optimised using finite element analysis and algorithmic parametric software, to establish the minimum material required and directly printed layer by layer - just 30 microns in each pass. This generates significant weight savings and economy of means. One barrier to mass adoption is the build speed of current selective laser melting machinery. It is also possible to combine materials in Additive Manufacturing, for example, including printed electronic circuitry. The EPSRC Centre for Innovative Manufacturing in Additive Manufacturing at the Universities of Nottingham and Loughborough is a new nucleus of research activity focused on next generation multifunctional AM technology and how this will impact manufacturing and society.

Some argue that Additive Manufacturing eliminates the need for prototyping. It clearly compresses the development stages for the research and design of components. However, prototyping complex holistic assemblies of components, as used in the construction of architecture, will remain necessary.

Additive Manufacturing may appear to be in the realm of potential technology transfer. However, Holger Strauss and Ulrich Knaack from the ConstructionLab in Detmold, Germany, have already developed an Additive Manufactured Aluminium node, Nemotox II, for geometrically complex curtain walling. Nematox II seeks to address the geometric complexity of many contemporary façades by the development of an integrated node. By digitally merging the mullion and transom, all deformations and joints of the members within the façade-system are virtually planned, checked and prepared for AM-production. Digital planning and digital fabrication ease the difficult details in the workshop and on-site, enabling simple 90° cutting of extrusions to pre-planned

Fig. 1.75 An additive manufactured component incorporating electronic circuitry, produced at the EPSRC Centre for Innovative Manufacturing in Additive Manufacturing

Fig. 1.76 Topology optimised structural component in Titanium 6AI-4V, 3D printed by selective laser melting, an Additive Manufacturing process.

geometric precision. The geometrical complexity is all situated within the digitally printed node, embraced in the simplicity of a 3D digital file. The product of extensive research commissioned by Kawneer-Alcoa, *Influence of Additive Processes on the development of façade constructions*.

Digital fabrication, a world wide web of things and additive manufacturing potentially heralds the beginning of a second industrial revolution. Chris Anderson observes 'midsized manufacturing companies in the United States and Europe are increasingly able to compete with low cost labour in China by using digital manufacturing techniques to automate what used to require either lots of human labour or ruinously expensive equipment.'[51] Pertinently he recognises the importance of people and collaboration in this process, 'behind all of them are the same thing: people working together with extraordinary new tools to create a manufacturing revolution.'[52]

Chris Anderson in *Makers, The New Industrial Revolution*, 2012 observes that it is the World Wide Web that will enable this second industrial revolution, providing the community of makers

Fig. 1.77 Nematox II an additive manufactured aluminium node for geometrically complex curtain walling

low cost access to market. Chris Anderson, although former editor of Wired magazine, is a late adopter, six years ago Emily Campbell wrote in Craft Magazine that makers could be industries of one, 'many designers are 'industries of one'- engaged in production and sales of their own products. These practitioners invent new and entrepreneurial forms of distribution, especially through the internet, eliminating agents and middle men. Maintaining the integrity of product, source and consumer continuity in a new craft which deliberately thwarts the conventional channels and media of commercial production'.[53]

Protocell Mesh

Prototyping Architecture includes the current *Living Architecture* research programme, a collaboration between the Universities of Waterloo, Nottingham, and Universitet Syddansk, funded by The Social Science & Humanities Research Council of Canada. A manifestation of this research is *Protocell Mesh*, which was designed in Toronto by Philip Beesley Architect Inc., and digitally fabricated in Nottingham, both at the university and using the local manufacturing base of this region. This was an example of file to 'factory', whereas Philip's normal practice is as a designer maker with all the machinery under his direct control. The components of the mesh were then assembled by The University of Nottingham Architecture students under the guidance of Philip Beesley and Jonathan Tyrrell, of Waterloo Architecture and PBA Inc.

Region and Country Profiles Economy 30 May 2012
Chart Title Manufacturing contribution to regional GVA, 2009
Chart Subtitle

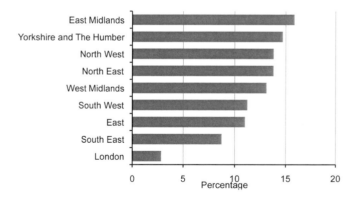

Alt text for image Manufacturing GVA as a percentage of region's total GVA: by region, 2009
Notes 1 Workplace based gross value added (GVA) headline estimates at current basic prices
Source Office for National Statistics
Survey name

Fig. 1.78 Graph of comparative employment in Manufacturing in the United Kingdom in 2009, Office of National Statistics

Industrious not Post Industrial

The United Kingdom has been too quick to brand itself post-industrial and there are very significant regional variations in employment within Britain. The latest data form the Office of National Statistics on Gross Value Added [GVA] generated by manufacturing shows that the East Midlands has the highest contribution to its economy from manufacturing in the UK, over 15.8% which compares to only 2.8% in London.[54] However, this is still a situation of relative decline since the 1950's. At the time of the Festival of Britain, in 1951, Britain was described as 'the workshop of the world' with 50% of people in employment working in manufacturing.[55] This also represents the peak of production at the Raleigh Bicycle Factory, Nottingham, once the largest bicycle factory in the world, at this point in time Raleigh employed 8000 people and manufactured 2 million bicycles a year. Raleigh's advertisements in the 1950's boasted agents throughout the world.

'Piled-up passions were exploded on Saturday night, and the effect of a week's monotonous graft in the factory was swilled out of our system in a burst of goodwill.'[56] The monotonous graft that Alan Sillitoe was describing in *Saturday Night & Sunday Morning* (1958) took place in the Raleigh Bicycle Factory, Nottingham. Sillitoe's protagonist Arthur observes 'the treadmill. Monday was always the worst; by Wednesday he was broken-in, like a greyhound.'[57]

The Raleigh Bicycle Factory on Triumph Road was demolished in 1996 and is now the University of Nottingham's Jubilee Campus. Arthur lived in a Nottingham red brick terraced house with his parents.

'Once out of doors they were more aware of the factory rumbling hundred yards way over the high wall, generators whined all night, and during the day giant milling-machines working away on cranks and pedals in the turnery gave to the terrace a sensation of living within breathing distance of some monstrous being that suffered from a disease of the stomach. Disinfectant-suds, grease, and newly-cut steel permeated the air over the suburb of four–roomed houses built around the factory, streets and terraces hanging on to its belly and flanks like calves sucking the udders of some great mother. The factory sent crated bicycles each year from Despatch Department to waiting railway trucks over Eddison Road, boosting post-war (or perhaps pre-war, Arthur thought, because these days a war could start tomorrow) export trade and trying to sling pontoons over a turbulent unbridgeable river called the Sterling Balance.'[58]

The new Energy Technologies Building has been constructed on this aforementioned former industrial site on Triumph Road. To construct the Protocell Mesh, this new research building once

Fig. 1.79   Wheel assembly within the Raleigh Bicycle Factory, Nottingham

Fig. 1.80   The Raleigh Bicycle Factory, Nottingham, used to span the Triumph Road and the railway lines

again became a factory, with volunteer piecework by Nottingham Architecture students led by Philip Beesley and Jonathan Tyrell from his office. Although this work was repetitive, to assemble relatively small-scale laser cut parts into a meshwork that is immersive and of a spatial architectural scale. This was not the monotony experienced by wage slaves in the mid-twentieth century, when mechanisation had taken command. The meshwork was assembled on time for the opening of *Prototyping Architecture*. In time for all to return to the School of Architecture to listen to Philip Beesley explain his approach to architecture. He started this discourse by questioning whether it is now possible to generate a living architecture.

"Might an architecture come alive? Might it know, and care? I am speaking about a tradition of organicism, an evocation of life-like qualities that have perhaps been with architecture since its genus in western culture for 2,500 years or so ago. We can think of the myth of Pygmalion, and the idea that as makers we try to breathe life into form, generating an intense relationship with it and attempting to evoke all that we are. Speaking of 'organicism' might suggest that we are working only with symbolism, but I think we are now speaking of something more than that. I think things have shifted over the past 20 years, with the progress that has been made with the genome project, the comprehensive information set that increasingly records the systems and form of living organisms. This kind of research gives an absolutely remarkable library of information, offering radical potency to our ability to act and fabricate. This kind of information is helped by new crafts such as digital fabrication, self-generating and embedded computation, and by synthetic biology...it is

Fig. 1.81 Philip Beesley reintroduces piece work to the Triumph Road, Nottingham, autumn 2012, temporary converting the Energy Technologies Building into a component based factory

increasingly possible to speak about an architectural design space that that is working directly with life, and with functional living qualities."[59]

Here we also learn that collaborating on and exhibiting the *Protocell* textile meshwork in Nottingham was a form of homecoming for him. As Philip Beesley is a 5th generation direct relative of Richard Arkwright, a key textile pioneer of the Industrial Revolution, whose major contribution was the development of a spinning machine called a water frame in 1768. This could not be operated by hand and needed the power of a water wheel, this led directly to the develop factory based manufacturing. He moved to Nottingham in the same year 'in search of capital; and formed a partnership with Need & Strutt. A house in Hockley, then on the northeastern edge of the town, was acquired to accommodate his roller-spinning machines, and a horse-powered capstan. The installation was small, and was probably regarded by the partners from the outset as a pilot project for their more ambitious factory system of production. Arkwright left for Cromford [Derbyshire] in 1771 to develop his water-powered system, subsequently building a chain of mills in Derbyshire and Lancashire. Meanwhile James Hargreaves, inventor of the spinning jenny, followed him to Nottingham in 1769, with the support of another merchant hosier partnership, Rawson, Heath & Watson. They built a factory to accommodate manually-operated spinning jennies. This was across the street from Arkwright's first factory in Hockley.'[60]

Manufacturing is a vital component of sustainability and it is essential to all creative industries, whether these are based on pens and paper or tablets and laptops. Manufacturing needs to be reinvented as a liberating force, where humankind commands the mechanisation. Industry and manufacturing are key components of sustainability, these are not the dark satanic mills that William Morris feared in the nineteenth century, but places of decent employment, which are environmentally responsible and safely managed. As a nation we should invest in industry. In my career I have needed industries such as aluminium extruders, with whom I could develop the components of a new architecture. Part of the role of the Prototyping Hall is to bring industry to campus to collaborate on one to one test assemblies, breaking new ground, whilst educating the engineers and architects of the

Fig. 1.82   Philip Beesley Architect Inc's Workshop and Offices in Toronto

future. It is vital that the United Kingdom retains sufficient of its industry to maintain its inventiveness and knowledge base, good manufacturers not only make added value products, they help fuel the knowledge economy of our nation.

Research should also be undertaken to establish whether manufacturing is recorded in national statistics. Philip Beesley Architect Inc's own premises in Toronto, Canada, is a redundant industrial building, although they are adding value by design they also fabricate and assemble their installations in this workshop. Does the Canadian Government return this practice in its official GDP statistics as part of its creative industries or manufacturing? Nor should we under rate the economic contribution of creative industries in Britain. Christopher Frayling, former Chairman of the UK Arts Council, observes that "Financial Services contribute to GPD only about 1% more than the Creative Industries [in the UK economy], which employs 2 million people and Financial Services only 1 million people…yet receives but few column inches"[61]

Prototyping Architecture demonstrates that inventiveness has not been lost within architecture. Both architecture and technology are malleable in the hands of a well-informed architect.

Fig. 1.83 A prototype from Digital Intimacy, a thesis project at The University of Nottingham by Stephen Townsend

Notes

1   Italo Calvino, Invisible Cities,1972, English translation William Weaver, 1974, Vintage Edition, 1997, p. 115

2   David Leatherbarrow Uncommon Ground, 2000, MIT Press, p. 122

3   This can be contrasted with the design of the Royal Festival Hall by Leslie Martin and Peter Moro, which was completed for 1951. John McKean records "in the post-war period of tightly controlled austerity, 'prestige' buildings were not being built, and there simply was no range of quality product which could be specified form a catalogue. So they designed everything: the equipment, the light fittings, the door handles. The necessity to design from first principles – exemplified in the music stand, designed by Moro – was, however, a particularly attractive constraint; inventing rather than specifying and assembling "Many of the mock-ups were built by the LCC supplies division. John McKean, Royal Festival Hall, London County Council, Leslie Martin and Peter Moro, Architecture in Detail, Phaidon, 1992.

4   This set of ideas is explored further by the author in the book chapter Digital Craft in the Making of Architecture, in: Bob Sheil ed., Manufacturing the Bespoke - The Making and Prototyping of Architecture (an AD Reader), Wiley, 2012, pp. 58 – 77.

5   Oxford English Dictionary, 1996 Edition

6   Ibid

7   In too many contemporary architectural texts innovation is used when invention is a more appropriate description.

8   Primo Levi, The Wench, first published in Italian, 1978, English translation, 1986, Abacus 1992 edition, p. 53

9   Robert McCarter, Frank Lloyd Wright Architect, Phaidon, 1997, pp. 284 - 285

10   Jan Knippers, Biometric Strategies for an Elastic Architecture, in Kristina Schinegger, Stefan Rutzinger, Martin Oberascher and Guther Weber, SOMA, Theme Pavilion Expo Yeosu, One Ocean, Residenz Verlag, 2012, pp. 81-83

11   Ibid

12   Ibid

13   Dirk Krolikowski, Digital design and fabrication of carbon fibre beam prototypes, in Michael Stacey ed., Prototyping Architecture – the conference papers, Building Centre Trust, 2013.

14   For more information on the work of sixteen* (makers) see Michael Stacey, Digital Craft in the Making of Architecture, in Bob Sheil ed., Manufacturing the Bespoke - The Making and Prototyping of Architecture (an AD Reader), Wiley,2012, pp. 58 – 77, Michael Stacey Tectonics: Steel Folding into the landscape, Building Design Magazine, 14.10.10 pp. 19-20 and 55/02, sixteen* (makers) Project Monograph, Riverside Architectural Press, 2011

15   Bob Sheil, De-Fabricating Protoarchitecture in Michael Stacey ed., Prototyping Architecture – the conference papers, Building Centre Trust, 2013 pp. 404 - 422

16   Philip Beesley by email with author, June 2012

17   Barkow Leibinger, Atlas of Fabrication, Architectural Association, London, 2011, fig. 336

18   Stephen Groák, Idea of Building, Spon, 1992 p.180. This book was commissioned on the occasion of the Building Centre 60th Anniversary.

19   Ibid

20   Stephan Kieran and James Timberlake, refabricating architecture, McGraw-Hill, 2003

21   Michael Stacey, ed., Digital Fabricators, Waterloo University Press, 2004

22   Michael Stacey, Fast Forward: The New York Five – review of Home Delivery at MOMA including Cellophane House, Building Design Magazine, 22 July 2008

23   Sir Richard MacCormac and Rogier van-der-Hiede, Immaterial – Light, in the Making Architecture: Tectonics Lecture Series, at ABE, The University of Nottingham, 26 February 2009

24   For more information on this inventive and environmentally responsible cooling method see Brian Ford et al eds., The Architecture & Engineering of Downdraft Cooling: A Design Sourcebook, PHDC Press, 2010

25   Piero della Francesca, born in Borgo Santo Sepolco, Tuscany c. 1415 and died 12 October 1492.

26   Current Locations in the Uffizi, August 2013, Hall 7 and Hall 35 respectively

27   Phyllis Richardson and Lucas Dietrich XS, Big Idea, Small Projects, Thames & Hudson, 2001

28   Michael Stacey, Tectonics – Bricks, Building Design Magazine 18 September 2009, pp. 14 - 15

29   Michael Stacey, Concrete: a studio design guide, RIBA Publishing, 2011, pp. 54, 56 84 - 85

30   Michael Stacey, Tectonics – Bricks, Building Design Magazine 18 September 2009, pp. 14 -15

31   see catalogue page 4.01 High Pressure Turbine Blade in Prototyping Architecture for production sequence images

32   Transcribed by Michael Stacey, Summer 2012.

33   For an more detailed history of the development of glass in architecture see Michael Stacey, Component Design, Butterworth, 2001, Glass, pp.113-167

34   Jaguar Land Rover Directors' Report and Financial Statements, Year Ended 31 March 2012, Jaguar Land Rover PLC, p. 66

35   JLR Third Generation of lightweight vechiels please see Mark White's Keynote in Prototyping Architecture: The Conference Papers, Michael Stacey Ed., Riverside Architectural Press, 2013 pp. 376 - 393

36   Mark White, Why does the European Car Industry need Light Metals to survive in a Sustainable World, in 11th INALCO Conference 2010, New Frontiers in Light Metals, Katgerman L. and Soetens F., eds., IOS Press, 2010 , p. 23

37   Bill Bryson, The Life and Times of the Thunderbolt Kid, Double Day, 2006 p.145, see also p.5 –Bryson observes that in the 1950s 'No country had ever known such prosperity. When the war ended [World War Two] the United Stares had $26 billion worth of factories that hadn't existed before the war, $140 billion in savings and war bonds just waiting to be spent, no bomb damages and practically no competition.' He continues 'By 1951 … almost 90% of American families had refrigerators and nearly three quarters had washing machines, telephones, vacuum cleaners and gas or electric stoves… Americans' owned 80 per cent of the world's electrical goods, controlled two-thirds of the world's productive capacity, produced 40 per cent of its electricity, 60 per cent of its oil and 66 per cent of its steel. The 5 per cent of people on Earth who were Americans had more wealth than the other 95 per cent combined.'

38   See Reyner Banham's Architecture of the Well Tempered Environment, University of Chicago Press; 2nd Revised edition, 1984, for a short history of the development of air-conditioning.

39   Michael Stacey, Introduction, in Kieran, S., Timberlake, J., eds. Loblolly House: Elements of a New Architecture, Princeton Architectural Press (New York), 2008, sets out further the research, design, development, construction and experience of visiting and living in the house.

40   Ibid pp. 10-11

41   KieranTimberlake et al, Cellophane House, KieranTimberlake, 2011, pp. 102-121

42   Subject to the ETB successfully passing of its Post Occupancy Evaluation

43   Andrew Scoones & Michael Stacey 'Materials of Invention Catalogue: 100 Years of Technological Change', Building Centre, London, 2006

44   For evocative portrait of the industrial heyday of the Grand River please see Margaret Atwood's Blind Assassin, Virago, 2000 To be added to the Introduction of Prototyping Architecture by Michael Stacey

45   This process took inspiration form Mark West, see Anne-Mette Manelius, Fabric formwork – Prototyping Concrete as Material and Process, in Michael Stacey, ed., Prototyping Architecture – the conference papers, 2013, pp. 9 - 26

46   For further information on how to specify low carbon concrete see Michael Stacey, Concrete: a studio design guide, RIBA Publishing, 2011

47   For more information on Heinz Isler body of work see John Chilton, Heinz Isler (Engineer's Contribution to Architecture), Thomas Telford, 2000

48   Michael Stacey, Component Design, Butterworth, 2001

49   Mark Burry, Models, Prototypes and Archetypes: Fresh Dilemmas emerging from File to Factory in Bob Sheil ed., Manufacturing the Bespoke - The Making and Prototyping of Architecture (an AD Reader), Wiley, 2012, p. 43

50   Ibid

51   Chris Anderson, Makers, The New Industrial Revolution, Random House, 2012, p. 31

52   Ibid

53   Emily Campbell, E., Personal Touch, (Crafts Magazine, Issue no. 200, Crafts Council, May/June 2006) pp. 54-55. Cited in Michael Stacey, Searching For Excellence: Ballingdon Bridge, ARQ, Vol.11, No.3/4, Cambridge University Press, 2007 pp. 210-222

54   http://www.ons.gov.uk/ons/rel/regional-trends/region-and-country-profiles/economy---may-2012/economy---east-midlands--may-2012.html, accessed January 2013

55   The nineteen fifties represent the peak level for employment in manufacturing in Britain the percentage employed in manufacturing was approximately 42%, see Nicholas Crafts, Britain's Relative Economic Decline 1870-95, London: Social Market Foundation, 1997. He also observes that employment in manufacturing peaked in West Germany in the mid- nineteen seventies.

56   Alan Sillitoe, Saturday Night & Sunday Morning, W.H Allen, 1958, p. 9 [note page numbering from Harper Perennial 50th Anniversary Edition, 2008]

57   Ibid, pp. 25-25

58   Ibid, p. 27

59   Philip Beesley's lecture Living Architecture at Architecture & Built Environment, The University of Nottingham, 16 October 2012, in celebration of the opening of Prototyping Architecture, transcribed by Michael Stacey form the video file

60   John Beckett ed., A Centenary History of Nottingham, Phillimore, 2006 p. 321

61   Christopher Frayling, Start the Week, Radio 4, Monday 19 November 2012, transcribed by Michael Stacey from audio file

PROTOTYPES

2.1 Protocell Mesh

Philip Beesley and Waterloo Architecture

Fig. 2.1.2 The completed Protocell Mesh at Prototyping Architecture, Nottingham, Philip Beesley Architect. Inc.

Architect:	Philip Beesley Architect Inc.
Researchers:	Universitiy of Waterloo, School of Architecture[1]
Materials:	Bespoke aluminum hyperbolic grid-shell with aluminum and stainless steel details, glass and polymer filter assemblies, protocell chemical inclusions, essential oils.
Location:	Wolfson Prototyping Hall, the University of Nottingham.
Exhibit:	Protocell Mesh

Philip Beesley's 'work is a very humane response the contemporary condition of ecology. He seeks to progress beyond an abstract Modernism to something richer and more productive.'[2]

The Protocell Mesh project integrates first-generation prototypes that include aluminium meshwork canopy scaffolding and a suspended protocell carbon-capture filter array. The scaffold that supports the Protocell Mesh installation is a resilient, self-bracing meshwork waffle. Curving and expanding, the mesh creates a flexible hyperbolic grid-shell. The meshwork is composed of flexible, lightweight chevron-shaped linking components. The chevrons interconnect to create a pleated diagonal grid surface. Bifurcations in mesh units create tapering and swelling forms that extend out from the diagrid membrane, reaching upward and downward to create suspension and mounting points. Floating radial compression frames provide local stiffening and gather forces for anchorage. Arrayed protocells are arranged within a suspended filter that lines this scaffold. The array acts as a diffuse filter that incrementally processes carbon dioxide from the occupied atmosphere and converts it into inert calcium carbonate. The process operates in much

Fig. 2.1.1 The completed Protocell Mesh at Prototyping Architecture,
Nottingham, Philip Beesley Architect. Inc.

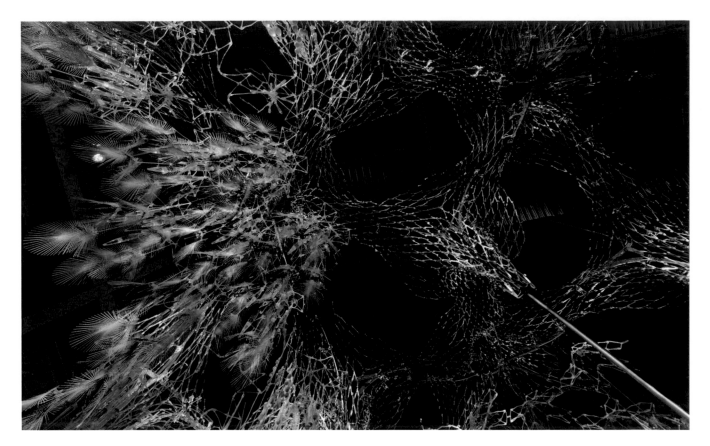

Fig. 2.1.3 Protocell Mesh at Prototyping Architecture, Nottingham

the same way that limestone is deposited by living marine environments. Within each cell of the filter array, laser-cut Mylar valves draw humid air into a first chamber of concentrated sodium hydroxide. The solution enters a second chamber containing waterborne vesicles suspended between upper and lower oil layers. Chalk-like precipitate forming within these vesicles offers an incremental process of carbon fixing.

Surrounding the active flask arrays is a grotto-like accretion of suspended vials containing salts and sugar solutions that alternately accumulate and exude moisture, contributing to a diffusive, humid skin. Scent glands act as lures to encourage occupation of this synthetic aerial soil.

The Protocell Mesh project builds upon component systems that have been developed within the Hylozoic Series, a collaborative project that is pursuing near-living architectural systems combining lightweight flexible structures, interactive distributed computation and protocell metabolisms. The meshwork integrates research from the Universities of Waterloo, Nottingham, and Southern Denmark.

"This architecture is sitting on the frontier of new possibilities; some might say is this art or architecture? In a sense that is not what is important about this piece, it is really in the thoughts and provocations it produces, where its importance lies. It is more like literature than conventional architecture. It is how the imagination of the viewer is stimulated, where the cultural importance of the work of Philip Beesley lies." Michael Stacey at Prototyping Architecture.[3]

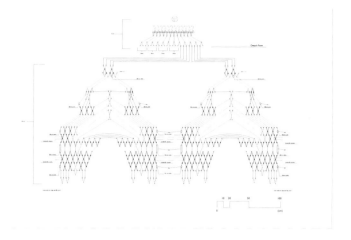

Notes

1   Primary researsh for this project are as follows: Nottingham, Architecture & Tectonics Research Group; and Southern Denmark, Center for Fundamental Living Technology Social Sciences and Humanities Research Council, Canada.

2   Michael Stacey, From Flat Stock to Three-Dimensional Immersion in Philip Beesley, ed., Kinetic Architecture & Geotextile Installations, Riverside Press, 2010 p.59

3   To see this video follow the links from - http://www.buildingcentre. co.uk/galleries/galleries_main.asp, posted January 2013

Fig. 2.1.4   PBA Inc.'s drawing of the lilies and how they are assembled

Fig. 2.1.5   Assembling the laser cut aluminium components of a lily

Fig. 2.1.6   RIBA President Angela Brady in the Protocell Mesh at the opening of Prototyping Architecture, London

2.2 Tripartite Fabric Formwork Column

Anne-Mette Manelius[1] with MARS[2]

Fig. 2.2.2 Anne-Mette Manelius revealing the trabeated concrete column by removing the fabric formwork

Architect:	Anne-Mette Manelius
Materials:	In situ concrete cast in a geotextile formwork, with softwood battens and birch ply laser cut templates. Concrete Mix; 3parts Aggregates, 2parts Sharp Sand, 1part Cement with superplasticier and water to a porridgey consistency. Mixed by hand with a Cement Mixer and placed in the fabric formwork with mild steel reinforcement.
Fabricators:	Anne-Mette Manelius with MARS
Location:	Nottingham and London
Exhibit:	Tripartite Fabric Formwork Column and Hanging Fabric Formwork[3]

Fabric formwork is a new construction method for concrete structures that utilises sheets of fabric as flexible, lightweight moulds. Based on a recently completed PhD project about the architectural potentials of fabric formwork for concrete, the fabric-formed column is the investigation and material prototype of a lightweight, prefabricated fabric mould, which unfolds to be cast on site. The tripartite concrete column is form-optimised for stability and constructed with minimal means. The principles of tensioning the fabric, of restraining it, and placing concrete have a direct formal consequence as a material dialogue between relaxation and control; thus the technique encourages an architectural understanding of concrete as material and as process.

Fig. 2.2.1 Anne- Mette Manelius' trabeated fabric formwork concrete column
and formwork exhibited at Prototoyping Architecture, Nottingham

Fig. 2.2.3   Anne- Mette Manelius' with MARS pouring the concrete into the fabric formwork at Wolfson Prototoyping Hall, Nottingham

The formwork was assembled and the column cast by the students of MARS, under Anne-Mette Manelius guidance. The column was allowed to cure and the formwork removed by the students as Anne-Mette had leave for Canada to write a book on the technique with Mark West. The fabric formwork is exhibited, in Nottingham only, hung next to the concrete object and details of the sculptural concrete object can be compared with its two-dimensional textile origin.[4]

Fabric Formwork: Prototyping Concrete as Material and Process
Anne-Mette Manelius

Fig 2.2.4 Concrete detail from International fabric-formwork workshop with the International Society of Fabric Forming (ISOFF), photograph Anne-Mette Manelius

Essentially the tripartite column prototype can be understood as the formwork, the process, and the concrete object – the contribution discusses the future of industrialised concrete architecture by emphasising the prefabrication of intelligent, lightweight moulds as an alternative to heavy and dumb concrete elements. Fabric formwork has recently been defined by Veenendaal, West, and Block as 'formwork that uses a flexible membrane for the structural support of fresh concrete or rammed earth.'[5] This definition includes soil, air or fluid pressure-supported formwork as well as the use of different types of fabrics such as non-woven membranes. It excludes the simple use of fabric as a form liner. The construction method is characterised by the development of catenary curves, a filter effect during casting, as well as an intense material dialogue during construction. The shape of a hanging chain is described as a catenary curve. Membranes deflect into catenary curves

in all directions across the surface when exposed to an evenly distributed load such as hydrostatic pressure from poured concrete. This material negotiation between the concrete and the flexible membrane allows the latter to structurally organise itself to a form that achieves equilibrium in relation to the load. The allowed deflection of the surface under pressure makes the membrane an efficient formwork material.

Textile Filter Effect

The porous structure of woven fabrics acts as a filter that leads excess water and air through the formwork membrane. This happens immediately after fresh concrete has been placed, and the hydrostatic pressure is still high. The release of excess mix water from the fresh concrete mix lowers the ratio of water to cement in the concrete surface, reduces the amount of air bubbles and blowholes, and increases the surface strength

Fig. 2.2.5 Concrete detail from fabric-formed concrete chair - Ambiguous Chair, photograph Anne-Mette Manelius

Fig. 2.2.6 Detail of the fabric and timber formwork, photograph Michael Stacey

of the cured concrete, Lamberton, 1980.[6] Special, often non-woven, fabric liners are placed inside rigid formwork systems to improve the water-cement ratio for concrete in harsh conditions such as salt water. With fabric formwork, the formwork itself has this effect.

Expressive construction

Besides formal geometry, concrete takes on the characteristics and details of any formwork surface. For fabric formwork, the pattern of the weave, the fibre used in the fabric, the direction or tailoring of the fabric, and the shape and method of restraining and tensioning fabrics become evident in the form and surface of the concrete. These formal consequences are very distinct in concrete cast in fabrics and demand a renewed understanding of concrete construction as well as the role of formwork. Where as the role of formwork technologies traditionally is to control a predetermined sculptural form, the roles of the formwork elements in fabric formwork deals with releasing fabric/concrete or restraining it. The technical task of the restraining form ties in fabric formwork offering the architect the role of *tying form,* linking the designing with the processes of construction.

Stereogeneity – concrete as material and process

The material prototype is crucial in understanding and developing new methods of construction through making. For fabric formwork the details of construction are expressed directly as a formal consequence of construction. This enables the formwork tectonics to be closely related and readable in the finished fabric formed concrete, leading to a poetic concrete. The relation between materiality and process for concrete is described in the concept of stereogeneity, coined by the author.[7] Based on the ancient Greek words stereos, hard or solid, and geneity derived from Gr. ginomai, to begin to be. Stereogeneity is the expressed manifestation into solid material form of a series of conditions from the construing and construction of structural formwork principles and concrete. In more general terms, stereogeneous construction is concrete as material and process and is linked to a way of thinking concrete in architectural constructions.

Background

Pioneers in the field consist of three parallel practices in the 1980s and 90s. The built practice by the Japanese architect Kenzo Unno, the sculptural practice by the American architect and builder Mark West, and the construction products patented by the Richard Fearn.[8] Centre for Architectural Structures and Technology (CAST) at the University of Manitoba is the pioneering research centre founded in 2002 by Mark West.[9] Here concrete columns, beams, walls, wall elements, shells, and rigid moulds have been cast and sprayed in fabrics. The exhibited prototype continues a practice at CAST of travelling with lightweight, prefabricated fabric moulds,[10] when Mark literally brought fabric formwork to Denmark in a duffle bag.[11] Today, leading research also includes work in Britain undertaken at the University of Edinburgh, East London University and the University of Bath. Architectural research and teaching is categorised by a material practice; research projects in engineering are categorised by a combination of digital simulations and empirical testing and iterative development of construction techniques.

Future

The question is not whether fabric formwork can be used in construction. The future of fabric formwork in industrialised architectural constructions is however, yet to be determined, but prototyping may be part of it. An examination of the development and roles of the formwork in a form-optimised fabric-formed concrete beam, produced in a PhD project (Sang-Hoon Lee 2010)[12], suggests that fabric formwork has a future for simple adaptations of mock-ups with complicated geometric shapes. The potential is that it is simple and cheap to adjust and develop complex concrete elements in a number of prototypes for empirical testing. The production of large numbers of identical concrete elements may, however, be cheaper if a rigid formwork is made and is discussed by comparing Lee's work with similarly shaped beams in projects by Harry Seidler.[13] On the other hand, a newly patented building technology combines ordinary and lightweight concrete in a sequenced mode of construction.[14] With both technologies still in their infancy, an increase in the possible scale of constructing fabric formed concrete is a benefit from the use of lightweight concrete because the lower density concrete has a lower formwork pressure during the concrete pour.

Fabric moulds and textile construction

Candela, a Spanish-born Mexican engineer, built his first concrete shells in 1956, inspired by the development in low-tech fabric-formed construction of thin concrete shells by the engineers, Irishman James Waller and German Kurt Billig[15]; but Candela moved on to other methods of construction when he adopted mathematical methods of design. A double-curved brick vault by the Uruguayan engineer Eladio Dieste displays a similar structural shape.[16] Dieste did not apply fabric as formwork; instead the innovative use of reinforced brick can be categorised as a form of weaving and in this regard, the further developments of Dieste's corrugated brick structures are indeed very textile. Like any fabric formed concrete, Dieste's Gaussian vaults display a series of catenary curved sections.[17] One can then speculate if a branch of the fabric-formed prototypes produced at the present time will also leave the fabric moulds behind and develop into textile-based construction?

Notes

1 Exhibitor: Dr Anne-Mette Manelius, is an architect and a board member of the International Society of Fabric Forming (ISOFF). Her PhD project was undertaken at the RDAFA, School of Architecture, Centre of Industrialised Architecture (CINARK) and sponsored by E. Pihl & Son and Schmidt Hammer Lassen Architects as part of the Danish Industrial PhD Programme.

2 Making Architecture Research Studio [MARS] is a sixth year RIBA Part 2 design research studio led by Michael Stacey. For more information on MARS please see: Graham Farmer and Michael Stacey In the Making: pedagogies form MARS, ARQ Vol 16-No4, 2012, pp 301-312.

3 Exhibited at Prototyping Architecture, Nottingham and London

4 In Cambridge, Ontario, new fabric formwork castings are exhibited, that are the product of a Fabric Formwork Workshop at Adaptive Architecture: ACADIA 2013 Conference led by Michael Stacey Architects.

5 Veenendaal, Diederik, Mark West, and Philippe Block. 2011. History and Overview of Fabric Formwork: Using Fabrics for Concrete Casting, Structural Concrete 12 (3) (September 1): pp. 164–177. doi:10.1002/suco.201100014

6 Bruce Lamberton, Fabric Forms for Erosion Control, Concrete Construction, The Aberdeen Group, 1980

7 Anne-Mette Manelius, Fabric Formwork for Concrete - Investigations into Formwork Tectonics and Stereogeneity in Architectural Constructions. PhD-Dissertation / Industrial, Copenhagen, Denmark: RDAFASA, CINARK, 2012.

8 See more of this history see ISOFF website: www.fabricforming.org or in the article by Veenendaal et al. 2011

9 http://www.umanitoba.ca/faculties/architecture/cast/ accessed September 2012

10 Mark West, Fabric-Formed Concrete Columns for Casa Dent in Puerto Rico. CAST, University of Manitoba, 2002. http://www.umanitoba.ca/cast_building/resources.html.

11 Anne-Mette Manelius and Anne Beim, Creative Systems – Arkitektur i En Nyindustriel Kontekst, Arkitekten (14), 2007, pp. 48–52.

12 Daniel Sang-Hoon Lee, Study of Construction Methodology and Structural Behaviour of Fabric-formed Form-efficient Reinforced Concrete Beam. PhD-Dissertation, Edinburgh, Great Britain: Department of Architecture, University of Edinburgh, 2010.

13 Anne-Mette Manelius, Fabric Formwork for Concrete - Investigations into Formwork Tectonics and Stereogeneity in Architectural Constructions. PhD-Dissertation / Industrial, Copenhagen, Denmark: RDAFASA, CINARK, 2012.

14 Kristian Hertz, Light-Weight Load-Bearing Structures Reinforced By Core Elements Made Of Segment And A Method Of Casting Such Structures - Patent Application.

http://www.faqs.org/patents/app/20110146170.

15 Colin Faber, Candela, the Shell Builder, Reinhold Pub. Corp.,1963.

16 Remo Pedreschi and D. Theodossopoulos, The Double-Curvature Masonry Vaults of Eladio Dieste. Proceedings of the ICE - Structures and Buildings 160 (1), 2 January 2007: pp. 3–11. doi:10.1680/stbu.2007.160.1.3.

17 Ibid

Fig. 2.2.7 Detail of the fabric fornwork [opposite]

Prototyping Architecture

2.3 GFRP Shell Prototype

Heinz Isler

Fig. 2.3.2 GFRP shell being carried away for the formed sand/earth mould by Isler's assistants

Engineer:	Heinz Isler
Materials:	Glass Fibre Polyester on an Earth Mould
Fabricators:	The model is understood to have been made by Heinz Isler
Location:	The grounds of Heinz Isler's office at Lyssachschachen near Burgdorf in Switzerland
Exhibit:	1:10 scale GFRP shell model[1]

Better known for his bubble and inspiring free-form thin reinforced concrete shells, the Swiss engineer Heinz Isler (1926-2009) also pioneered the use of Glass Fibre Reinforced Polymer [GFRP] for building components.[2] The model itself made from GFRP, reputedly by Isler himself, the prototype is for a 6 metre span GFRP roof module destined to be used to line military vapour and moisture proof storage facilities in long tunnels in the Swiss mountains. The GFRP shell clearly fulfilled the requirement that system components should be light enough to be carried by four people manoeuvring through the restricted tunnel entrances.

The mould for the full-scale shell, a synclastic double curved surface, was formed on a mound of sand, in the open air, in the grounds surrounding Isler's office at Lyssachschachen. This demonstrated the application of one of three innovative shell forming techniques described in Isler's historic paper *New Shapes for Shells*, which he presented at the first Congress of the International Association for Shell Structures, in Madrid, in September 1959.

Notes

1   Exhibited at Prototyping Architecture, Nottingham

2   For more information on Heinz Isler body of work see John Chilton, *Heinz Isler (Engineer's Contribution to Architecture)*, Thomas Telford, 2000

Fig. 2.3.1 1:10 scale GFRP shell model made by Heinz Isler

2.4 GFRP Kinetic Façade of Yeosu Expo Theme Pavilion

soma

Fig. 2.4.2 The kinetic façade in context, soma

Architects:	soma
Engineer:	Knippers Helbig Advanced Engineering
Materials:	Glass Fibre Reinforced Polymer [GFRP] Prepeg, hand consolidated on curved steel moulds, supported by CHS Steelwork and driven by electrical screw drives.
Fabricators:	Ojoo
Location:	Yeosu, South Korea
Exhibit:	13 metre GRP Lamella Responsive Solar Shading System [screens only due to size].

The gill like solar shading to the harbour side elevation of Ocean One, the Yeosu Expo Theme Pavilion, designed by Austrian architects soma. This shading system is a beautiful example of constructional simplicity. Exploiting biomimetic principles, the Glass Fibre Reinforced Polyester [GFRP] solar shading blades are deflected into opening in a gently curved form by electrical screw drives. The movement principle was initially demonstrated with simple paper models.

The energy stored in the deflected form of the GFRP solar shading is used to take the shading back to the flat position. This simple yet sophisticate assembly needed to be proven via the testing of a full-scale prototype. Due to the scale of this prototype at 13 meter high, it is only possible to exhibit this exemplar in the digital screens, which include this adaptive architecture in action and the fabrication of the GFRP lamellas. These were fabricated by hand on steel moulds using Prepreg, sheets of woven glass fibre pre-impregnated with polyester resin, with consolidation of the resin fibre mix by hand only.

Fig. 2.4.1 The kinetic façade in opened state, soma

Adaptive Formations: Two Pavilions, One Adaptation and One Tower

Kristina Schinegger and Stefan Rutzinger[1]

Adaptability lies at the very core of every architectural project, since a concept or design idea is constantly adapted to fit its medium of expression: thoughts, words, sometimes sketches, models, computer drawings, prototypes and finally built space. For soma the concept leads through this process and every design decision can either be deduced from or has to be negotiated with it. Thus we do not understand the initial idea as the irreducible essence; instead it is constantly improved and altered as well.

In the following we would like to show how such design concepts are evolved on multiple levels and in interdisciplinary design processes. All projects were developed in collaboration with structural and kinematic engineers and each of them shows a strong research agenda. These processes do not follow a conventional logic of pre-conceived form and its subsequent post-evaluation. Instead architectural design, functional concepts, and structural evaluation are co-evolved with the help of digital tools and parametric models. Yet besides these parametric tools that facilitate adaptive designs, the main focus when it comes to adaptability for soma lies still in the multi-directional interaction of user, space and context and its atmospheric and bodily effects.

Expo Theme Pavilion – combining the sensational with the sensation

The synergy of spatial vision and technological innovation has always been an important aspect of world expositions. The Theme Pavilion, with its complex geometrical system and kinetic façade, renews this tradition. Its movable lamellae expand the notion of a shading device and perform when individually actuated an elegant and smooth choreography reliant on geometry, light and material bending performance. As a showcase for applied biomimetic research they more than fulfil the client's wish for a future-orientated architecture that is inspired by nature. The up to 13m long lamellae almost weightlessly move and create stunning spatial effects. As an emotional experience, they combine sensations with the sensational, while communicating the Expo theme in an innovative manner.

The kinetic façade is an integral part of the Thematic Pavilion, a major and permanent building for the Expo 2012 in Yeosu, South Korea. The design proposal by soma was selected as the first prize winner in an open international architecture competition and the office was commissioned to plan the entire building. The biomimetic research and expertise in kinematics of Knippers Helbig Advanced Engineering, who joined the planning team right after the competition, enabled a technical solution to be found that could fulfil the architectural intentions as well as responding to the constraints of the site. The development of the biomimetic principle was further enriched by scientific research carried out at the ITKE Institute at the University Stuttgart.[2] Further consultants involved were Transsolar (sustainability concept and daylight simulation) and pod-pod (lighting design). The overall building design was not aimed at a visual representation of the

Fig. 2.4.3 View from expo axis

Expo's theme, but at an embodiment of its agenda, which is the responsible use of natural resources, through its sustainable climate design or the biomimetic approach underlying the kinetic façade. Furthermore it intends to transform the theme of the world exhibition into a multi-layered architectural experience. The pavilion's architecture is conceived as a series of spatial sequences that evoke different kinds of atmosphere and moods. As Kari Jormakka observes: 'wandering through the building, one experiences moods ranging from the trivial to the sacral, from intimidating to intimate, from rational to poetic.'[3]

Fig. 2.4.4 Detail of exposed concrete shell façade

Entering the pavilion is an experience of gradual immersion. After gathering in the cool shade underneath the exhibition area, visitors walk into the open foyer that stretches across to the exterior promenade. They move into the vertical cavities of the massive concrete cones. From the open lobby, escalators take them to the day-lit upper exhibition floor via the smooth, twisting surfaces. The roof landscape is conceived as a third exhibition area and as a freely accessible architectural promenade. Meandering paths between the leaning cone walls guide visitors to the roof garden and enable them to enjoy the constantly changing views of the surrounding seashore framed by the architecture. Contrary to the general understanding of a theme building the pavilion should not propose any fixed and symbolic meaning, but is meant to give rise to a multitude of individual readings. Consequently, its design has to be evocative, yet abstract enough to leave room for interpretations. The varied forms of the building's appearance are also due to the conditions of the site: Its exposure in relation to the Expo's area designates the Theme Pavilion as a landmark building and demands an expressive, yet embedded architectural design. Visible from all directions, its exterior is multi-layered and shows many faces blending continuously into each other. Towards the sea, the aggregation of solid cones protects the pavilion from the impact of large waves. On the opposite side, facing the calm water basin of the Expo's Big O, the building develops out of the ground as an artificial landscape with plateaus and scenic paths. The topographic lines of the roof merge into the lamellae of the kinetic façade that faces the Expo's entrance and draws attention to the pavilion by its moving patterns.

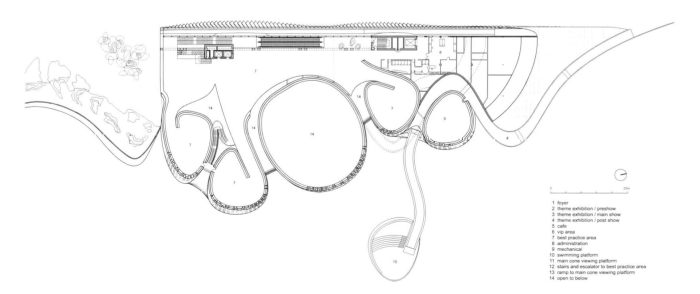

1 foyer
2 theme exhibition / preshow
3 theme exhibition / main show
4 theme exhibition / post show
5 cafe
6 vip area
7 best practice area
8 administration
9 mechanical
10 swimming platform
11 main cone viewing platform
12 stairs and escalator to best practice area
13 ramp to main cone viewing platform
14 open to below

Fig. 2.4.5 Ground floor plan best practice area

The building's geometry is inspired by our two-fold experience of the Ocean as an endless surface and as depth in which to immerse ourselves. In order to achieve an indivisible coherence of interior and exterior freeform surfaces twist from the vertical to the horizontal, defining all significant areas without losing their spatial continuity. The multimedia exhibition inside the vertical concrete cones, which invites the visitor to immerse himself in the Expo's theme, gives way to horizontal levels that become the ceiling of the foyer and a flexible stage for the individual exhibitors in the Best Practice Area. The final geometry is the result of the examination of a series of variations that were assessed for their performative and expressive qualities, until the optimal version was obtained. This process could also be understood as gradual adaption of the initial design idea to organisational and spatial requirements. Kari Jormakka states that this method produces a new form of organic architecture: 'The parametric method by which the forms of the Theme Pavilion were generated can also be understood as a further development of organicism almost in the sense of Renaissance Neoplatonism. Much like the ontogenesis of natural organisms, the shapes of the building grow out of simple algorithms that can produce extensive variation if the values of the parameters are changed. The forms are mechanically drawn and organically transgressed, in order to avoid finite determination.' Yet different to the usual parametric approach, the outcome is not governed by one algorithm: 'In relating to its site, soma's pavilion does not treat the ocean as one but rather as a multiplicity: in formal-geometrical terms, for example, the architects see it both as an endless plane and as a bottomless pit.' Correspondingly in such a space as the Ocean 'there is no over-arching law that would govern all elements and no suggestion of a totality, not even one derived parametrically from one algorithm. This space is defined only through the action of a body moving within it.'[4]

Fig. 2.4.7 Image of mock-up showing actuators

While the building's geometry is informed by the concept of continuity of spaces and flows of people, the media façade actually moves. Although movement is intrinsic to any media façade, architecture usually just provides the stable, immobile screen for digital motion. The kinetic façade exemplifies architecture as a medium in itself and emphasises the experiential potentials of analogue architectural effects. The façade covers a total length of about 140m, and is between 3m and 13m high. It consists of 108 kinetic louvers supported at the top and the bottom edge of the façade. The lamellae are made of glass fibre reinforced polymers (GFRP), which combine high tensile strength with low bending stiffness, allowing for large reversible elastic

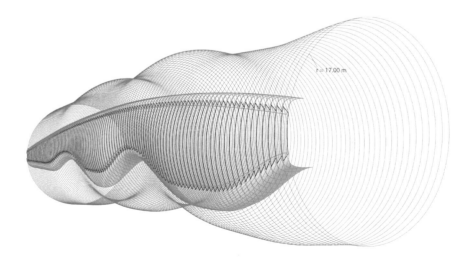

r = 17.00 m

Fig. 2.4.6 All louvers follow a consistant radius of 17 metre

Fig. 2.4.8 Image of mock up louvers in opened state

filtering solar gains according to the building's needs. In the basic mode of operation they allow light conditions to be controlled in the interior spaces. In the second operation mode the lamellae are individually actuated and create animated patterns along the façade. The choreography ranges from subtle local movements to waves spreading over the whole length of the building. After sunset, the analogue visual effect of the moving lamellae is intensified by linear light bars located at the inner side of the front edge of the lamella. When in open position, they illuminate the neighbouring lamella, depending on the opening angle. Thereby the material performance of the biomimetic louvers produces an interrelated effect of geometry, movement and light: the longer the individual lamella—the wider the opening angle— the larger the illuminated area.

The moving façade that is seamlessly integrated into the building's skin was already proposed during the competition and developed together with Knippers Helbig Advanced Engineering during the planning phases. To achieve the architectural intention of a smoothly swaying façade, a mechanical solution that applies hinges and joints seemed inappropriate; therefore a biomimetic approach was pursued. Furthermore the target of increased adaptability and energy efficiency, as well as reduced weight and maintenance costs led to the investigation by Knippers Helbig Engineering how the morphological form and functional principles of nature could be used.[5] While in architecture movable parts mostly rely on hinges and the combination of stiff elements or textiles, natural role models like plants show a range of movements that rely on elastic deformations, such as the opening and closing or flowers or leaf orientation. 'Botany provides the most radical insights. Many plant organs move without any specific mechanical elements, through the locally adapted and adaptive flexibility of their components'[6] According to Jan Knippers nature prolongs a material strategy that is opposed to that of architecture. While the latter usually separates components and layers 'natural systems are multi-layered, finely tuned combinations of a few basic components that make up structures featuring multiple interrelated functions.'[7]

The selection and use of material is crucial; fibre-reinforced polymers provided suitable material characteristics since they allow reversible elastic deformations. Although the application is novel, the technology itself does not fall under the category high-tech: 'The Theme Pavilion constitutes a completely new approach to kinetic structures in architecture, even though the materials and fabrication methods used are relatively simple and have been well known for many years. In this case, the innovation does not lie in the latest high-end technologies, but in a change of perspective inspired by and derived from the observation and analysis of natural role models.'[8]

deformations. Actuators move the louvers on both the upper and lower edge of the GFRP blade and induce compression forces to create the complex elastic deformation. They reduce the distance between the two bearings and in this way induce a bending which results in a side rotation of the lamella. The actuator of the louvers is a screw spindle driven by a servomotor. A computer-controlled bus-system allows the synchronisation of the actuators. Each lamella can be addressed individually within a specific logic of movement to show different choreographies and operation modes. The realisation of the kinetic façade required intensive prototyping and testing. The 13m high prototype of the GFRP lamellae and its screw drive actuator proved both robust and reliable, proving the effectiveness of the elastic deformation of these gill like blades of GRFP.

Upper and lower motors often work with opposing power requirements (driving-braking). Any energy generated can thus be fed back into the local system to save energy. As an integral part of the sustainability concept the lamellae save energy by

Fig. 2.4.9 Extension of Building Academy, Salzburg

Fig. 2.4.10 Pouring in place of concrete, Construction site Building Academy

Viscous Affiliation – adapting to an existing space

The extension of the building academy adapts to an existing building yet creates a distinct character and atmosphere. In a digital simulation a viscous mass was manipulated until the aimed for geometrical adaption was achieved and multiple purposes could be fulfilled: Structural performance, lighting and functional zoning, as well as the creation of an intuitively understandable guidance system had to correlate in one continuous structure. The initial task was to design a new foyer and an entrance to the Building Academy, a training centre of the local building sector, as well as to transform an existing technical training hall into a cultural venue. After the conversion, the foyer now serves multiple purposes - as a lobby for the school and as a public space for various cultural events in the adjacent halls, such as presentations, movie screenings, concerts or rehearsals.

The new foyer creates a consistent and smooth transition between the exterior and the interior of the building. It connects the different functional areas in one continuous fluid space and creates an open and evocative atmosphere. The widening of the pattern from a framed into a freely spreading geometry can be read as a contingent affiliation of the existing spatial characteristics. The three-dimensional pattern was generated in a simulation of fluids based on particle flows. Liquids have three essential parameters: viscosity, density and surface tension. The interactions between these three physical properties have been tested on the computer in a series of variations to generate a pattern with a big amount of holes and a high level of coherence. Realising the complex structure in exposed concrete posed major challenges in the area of formwork construction,

which was tested and optimised in 1:1 prototypes. The finely triangulated surface of the concrete structure allows a subtle play of light and shadow, which was achieved by testing different milling techniques. The choice of material and the innovative construction process reflect the competencies and teaching focus of the Building Academy in the field of concrete application.

Fig. 2.4.11 Detail of concrete stairs Building Academy

The design proposes a new tower typology: conventional observation towers have one massive and enclosed core for vertical circulation and services. In the case of the Fibrous Tower this massive core is dissolved into eight tower legs. The structure emerges out of the interplay of the individual members, forming a synergetic whole. It is dissolved at the bottom allowing the park landscape to flow freely between the tower legs and creating a cell pattern, which defines the layout of the building volumes, squares, green areas, and networks of paths. Each tower leg fulfils a particular function: the four inner legs contain all circulation like panoramic elevators, fire elevator or emergency stairs. The outer legs create spaces for intermediate platforms, the restaurant and the observatories. With the help of digital modelling tools the tower's geometry was simultaneously designed by the architects and evaluated by the structural engineers of Bollinger Grohmann Schneider. Thereby the natural role model of fibres became a guiding concept for all participants from which design solutions and structural principles could be deduced.

Fig. 2.4.12 Fibrous tower proposal for Taichung City

Taiwan Tower – multiple natures

Adaptability of the Taiwan Tower is not only understood as mutability of the design during a generative process but also in terms of conformity to local climate conditions and availability of materials and construction methods. The idea of a bundled fibrous tower is able to react to these constraints and turn them into productive drivers for the design. The fibrous tower was a proposal for the two-staged open international Taiwan Tower Complex competition and was awarded the second prize. The given task was to create a novel kind of landmark building for the urban renewal of the former area of Taichung Shuinan Airport. The new tower should become the main attraction of Taichung Gateway Park and reflect the ecological agenda of the newly planned low-carbon city quarter. The client asked for at least a 330 metre high structure with restaurant and observation facilities on top and a museum and tower lobby at ground level, integrated in a landscape design of over 4.4 hectares.

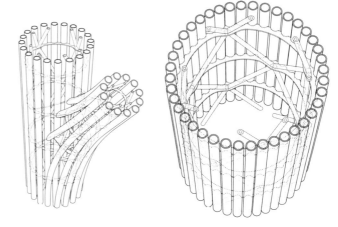

Fig. 2.4.13 Detail of tower section by Bollinger Grohmann Schneider ZT GmbH

The design was evolved in a bottom up approach, using swarm intelligence systems. Algorithms underlying natural processes are applied in digital models to organise multiple members into one performative fibrous structure. The geometry of the tower emerges as one possible scenario from a solution space created by interactions among and between individual agents. The results were overlaid with functional requirements and further developed by using evolutionary methods combined with comprehensive structural evaluation.[9] The idea of dissolving the tower legs into bundled tubes instead of producing eight mega-tubes provided advantages for manufacturing as well as the overall performance of the tower: 'The towers legs with a diameter of 5.1m cannot be easily manufactured as single profiles, as these would have to be composed of bended steel plates with a thickness of around 100mm. Such plates can hardly be bent and the necessity to

Fig. 2.4.14 Mobile pavilion at the historic City centre of Salzburg

compound these results in extra weld seam lengths. Bundled tubes allow the usage of standard profiles with a diameter of about 350mm with a thickness of 12 to 30mm, types in large amount available everywhere. Dissolving the legs into smaller single tubes has two impacts on the occurring wind loads. First, if no function is placed inside the tube, wind can pass through gaps between the profiles, reducing the contact surface. Second, and this applies on all legs, the waved hull surface causes a turbulent boundary layer resulting in a reduced pressure drag, analogue to dimples on a golf ball.'[10] Furthermore the dissolution reduced the welding effort and increased the adaptability to the specific loading of the tubes, since the standard profile can vary easily in wall thickness.

The bundled tubes are clad with flexible PV modules that follow the organic shape of the exterior surfaces. That way, a total area of around 25.000m² of exterior surface of the tower is available for electricity production. This strategy, which was developed with the engineers of Transsolar turns the tower into the world's largest vertical absorber that functions as a self-sufficient system.

Vague Formation – a mobile music pavilion

The proposal for a mobile art pavilion by soma was chosen as the first prize winner in an open, two-stage competition in October 2010. It was erected for the first time in the historic centre of Salzburg in March 2011 for a period of 3 months and housed the contemporary music festival Salzburg Biennale. Since then it has been assembled in the rural valley Krakautal, in Styria, Austria

and in the inner centre of Maribor, Slovenia. At each location a different cultural activity inhabited the pavilion, the events showed a range from concerts, to exhibition, lectures, readings, installations or performances.

The structure can be divided into individual segments. By combining these in different ways or by reducing their number, it can adapt to its location. The removable interior membrane and the adjustable floor increase the flexibility of use. The pavilion's appearance is intended to provoke curiosity and invite visitors to encounter the unknown and unusual. It emphasises the understanding of art as a cultural process involving many participants within a discourse. This process does not reveal itself at first sight, but unfolds through engagement. The pavilion refers to a theme that is inherent to architecture as well as music – rule and variation. Its design process is based on a simple repetitive element, a set of rules for aggregation, and the definition of the architectural effects aimed at. The single aluminium profiles with a uniform length produce an irregular, mass-like conglomerate that changes its appearance during the day, according to the different light conditions. The structure allows an ambivalent reading as single members and as a merging whole, depending on the distance it is viewed from. The speculative intention behind this obliteration of the pavilion's structure is to prevent any conventional notion or cliché of construction. Instead the ambiguous mass should invite visitors to come up with their own associations and interpretations.

Thanks to computation complex structures employing disorder and randomness can be created and controlled. Although these irregular patterns are often applied to special building parts like façades, applications for load bearing structures are still an exception. Furthermore irregular complex structures are often based on highly individual components.[11] The bottom-up strategy of the music pavilion is based on a repetitive linear base element that does not change shape. Furthermore the aluminium profile is cut from stock ware (6m length) to avoid leftover material. The overall structural system of the pavilion is divided into 5 individual sections to increase flexibility of use. Each section consists of 20 vertical construction layers with a spacing of 200mm, the start and end sections have fewer layers. On each layer intersection curves with the reference surface will host starting points for the structural members. The distribution of points and positioning of the structural members takes place within a range of randomised distances and angles but at the same time prevents intersections. The first layer of structure was successfully prototyped at the fabricators, Unterfurtner, as shown in Fig. 2.4.7.

Due to individual positioning of members along each section curve, projection intersections with neighbouring layers are generated. This process produces an interconnected structure.

The structural optimisation by Bollinger Grohmann Schneider engineers takes the design rules above into account but also considers working loads, amount of connection elements and the maximum deflection of each segment. To evolve a structure Karamba[12] was applied within Grasshopper. Combined with a genetic algorithm the optimised solution was filtered out of the multiplicity of solutions through combination, selection and mutation over many generations. The elements are aligned iteratively and interact in a parallel way. By repetition of the same calculation step and with the feedback of the results, the system

Fig. 2.4.16 Mock up of mobile pavilion at Unterfurtner GmbH

Fig. 2.4.15 Mobile pavilion competition proposal

Fig. 2.4.17 Pavilion under construction, welding of joints at Unterfurtner GmbH

is incrementally evaluated until a certain target value is reached or the system converges to a threshold value. Multiplicity denotes the simultaneous and parallel observation and adjustment of the individual elements in a single step. The coactions of multiplicity and iteration result in the system's ability to adapt to a given task.

Optimisation is here understood by Bollinger Grohmann Schneider Engineers as enhancing structural performance within architectural parameters and aesthetic intents given by the architect. In addition to structural aspects the amount of members is minimised without losing the mass-like appearance. The parametric model, based on Grasshopper and Karamba, enabled the architects and the engineers to simultaneously design and evaluate the structure. This collaboration cannot be considered as a strictly parametric straightforward generation process, but is rather a back and forth negotiation between architectural aspiration, structural behaviour, buildability, logistics of assembly, and cost control. In the case of the music pavilion the design process is actuated by the set-up of rules and framing conditions that could be understood as the inherent logic of the emerging structure. 'On this modest project, costing 300,000 Euros' Michael Stacey's opinion is that 'parametric tools and specifically the Grasshopper plug in to Rhino has been used wisely.'[13]

Nevertheless, the experiential qualities of the design and its external expression remain a principal focus. The mass-like appearance aims at underlining the creative character of our perception, since our brains are constantly trying to distinguish figures and patterns within disorder. Rather than to produce forms

Fig. 2.4.19 Mobile art pavilion at Mozartplatz, Salzburg

Fig. 2.4.20 First assembly in Salzburg

Fig. 2.4.18 Mobile art pavilion at Mozartplatz, Salzburg

or meanings, the ambiguous mass of the pavilion triggers visitors to come up with their own interpretations and associations. In this way the pavilion could be called performative, since it wants to engage visitors, not by being complicated or difficult, but by displaying the playfulness of complexity and creating a changing appearance that triggers visitors' curiosity. Michael Stacey's review observed 'the exoskeleton of aluminium sections provides a dynamic pattern of shadows in the interior of the pavilion, which is revealed by the translucent membrane. The aggregated aluminium structure formed from standard aluminium extrusion generates a striking and delightful architecture both inside and outside, appropriately this is a new example of architecture as frozen music.'[14]

This tendency towards the design of rules and display of inherent principles is also a shift from an interest in external form towards the inner logic or, as Stan Allen puts it, from object to field.[15] Form or figures do not disappear altogether, they rather appear in the eye of the beholder, and step out of a heterogeneous field as a local effect. 'What is intended here is a close attention to the production of difference at the local scale, even while maintaining a relative indifference to the form of the whole.'[16] Allen calls these fields 'systems of organisation capable of producing vortexes, peaks, and protuberances out of individual elements that are themselves regular or repetitive.' He highlights the 'suggestive formal possibilities' and the questioning of conventional top-down form controls. In his opinion fields also have the potential to provoke a re-addressing of use: 'More than a formal configuration, the field condition implies an architecture that admits change, accident, and improvisation.'[17] Following Stan Allen adaptability could be understood as a certain openness and experiential ambiguity in architecture that allows multiple readings and therefore multiple uses, that might be unplanned und unforeseen. At soma we advocate that this openness is not composed by the neutral and flexible, but the distinct and complex, the evocative and sensational, the multi-layered and fuzzy.

Notes

1   Kristina Schinegger and Stefan Rutzinger are directors of Soma please see http://www.soma-architecture.com
2   Julian Linhard et al., "Flectofin: a hingeless flapping mechanism inspired by nature," in Bioinspiration and Biomimetics, Vol.6 (2011)
3   Kari Jormakka, "Architecture that does not stand still," in One Ocean.Theme Pavilion Expo Yeosu, ed. Kristina Schinegger et al., (St.Pölten: Residenz Verlag, 2012), p. 24
4   Jormakka, Architecture that does not stand still, p. 19
5   Jan Knippers, "Biomimetic strategies for an elastic architecture," in One Ocean.Theme Pavilion Expo Yeosu, ed. Kristina Schinegger et al., (St.Pölten: Residenz Verlag, 2012), p. 80-87
6   Jan Knipper, Biomimetic strategies for an elastic architecture, p. 82
7   Jan Knipper, Biomimetic strategies for an elastic architecture, p. 80
8   Jan Knipper, Biomimetic strategies for an elastic architecture, p. 84
9   Kristina Schinegger, Stefan Rutzinger, Arne Hofmann, Dieter Hauer, "Multiple Natures – Taiwan Tower" in AAG2012 Proceedings Volume
10   Kristina Schinegger, Stefan Rutzinger, Arne Hofmann, Dieter Hauer, "Multiple Natures – Taiwan Tower" in AAG2012 Proceedings Volume
11   Fabian Scheurer, "Turning the design process downside-up – self-oranization in real-world architecture, " in Computer Aided Architectural Design Future 2005, ed. B.Martens, A. Brown, (Wien: Springer, 2005) pp. 269-78
12   http://twl.uni-ak.ac.at/karamba/
13   Michael Stacey, "Frozen music" AT219, June 2011, pp. 12-14
14   Ibid
15   Stan Allen, "From Objects to Field, " in Architectural Design Vol 67, 1997, pp. 24-31
16   Stan Allen, From Objects to Field
17   Stan Allen, From Objects to Field

2.5 Centre for Sustainable Energy Technologies
The Koo Lee Institute of University of Nottingham
Mario Cucinella Architects with Brian Ford

Fig. 2.5.2 Night view of CSET, revealing that this architecture is based on the concept of a Chinese lantern

Architect: Mario Cucinella Architects

Engineer: Luca Turrini

Environmental Consultant: Professor Brian Ford, A&URD

Location: Ningbo, China

Exhibit: CSET model[1]

The Centre for Sustainable Energy Technologies (CSET) building on the University of Nottingham's Ningbo campus in China, was designed by Mario Cucinella Architects with environmental design by Professor Brain Ford, completed in November 2008. An exemplar of low energy architecture the Centre for Sustainable Energy Technologies is located in Ningbo, one of China's oldest cities, in the heart of Zhejiang province, and hosts the Centre for Sustainable Energy Technologies, University of Nottingham. It stands on a broad meadow skirting a watercourse, which crosses the campus. The design draws inspiration from traditional Chinese paper lamps and fans. The building is entirely clad with a double glass skin with serigraphic motifs that evoke local historic buildings, and change from day to night. Its façade recedes dramatically, creating a dynamic form. It houses a visitors' centre, research labs and lecture halls. A generously proportioned opening on the roof conveys daylight to all floors of the building while creating a chimney-effect that ensures natural ventilation both in summer and winter.

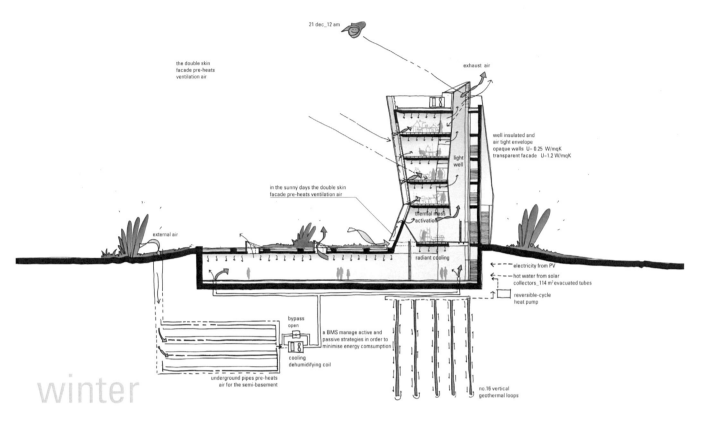

Inside the figure:

21 dec_12 am

the double skin
facade pre-heats
ventilation air

exhaust air

well insulated and
air tight envelope
opaque walls U= 0.25 W/mqK
transparent facade   U=1.2 W/mqK

light
well

in the sunny days the double skin
facade pre-heats ventilation air

thermal mass
activation

external air

radiant cooling

electricity from PV

hot water from solar
collectors_114 m² evacuated tubes

reversible-cycle
heat pump

bypass
open

a BMS manage active and
passive strategies in order to
minimise energy comsumption

cooling
dehumidifying coil

underground pipes pre-heats
air for the semi-basement

no.16 vertical
geothermal loops

winter

Fig. 2.4.3 CSET – section in wintertime

The Sustainable Research Building uses internally exposed GGBS-based concrete for thermal mass, which is over clad with insulation that is protected from weathering by translucent glass cladding. The CSET building provides laboratory, office and seminar accommodation, and has been designed to serve as an exemplar building, demonstrating the state-of-the-art techniques for environmentally responsible, sustainable construction and energy efficient internal environmental control. It has been designed to minimise its environmental impact by promoting energy efficiency, generating its own energy from renewable sources, and using locally available materials with low-embodied energy wherever possible. It responds to diurnal and seasonal variations in ambient conditions by means of a five-point environmental design strategy:

- high performance envelope;

- exposed thermal mass;

- daylight and solar control;

- natural ventilation to tower; and

- piped ventilation to laboratory and workshop.

Floor-fitted radiant-panels exploit geothermal energy for heating and cooling. In winter, primary air introduced into the tower is pre-heated by the double-skin exposed to the south or by finned piping along the perimeter of the front (during cloud cover). In summer, primary air in the tower is pre-cooled by a refrigerator within the roofing. Air is distributed to the offices by free fall, via

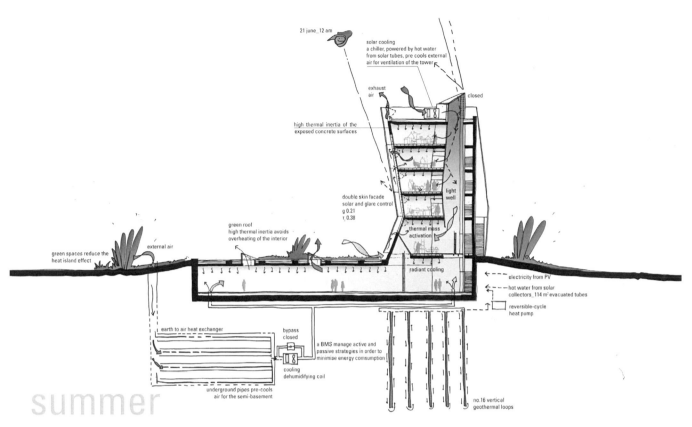

21 june_12 am

solar cooling
a chiller, powered by hot water
from solar tubes, pre cools external
air for ventilation of the tower

exhaust
air

closed

high thermal inertia of the
exposed concrete surfaces

light
well

double skin facade
solar and glare control
g 0.21
τ, 0.38

thermal mass
activation

green roof
high thermal inertia avoids
overheating of the interior

green spaces reduce the
heat island effect

external air

radiant cooling

electricity from PV

hot water from solar
collectors_114 m² evacuated tubes

reversible-cycle
heat pump

earth to air heat exchanger

bypass
closed

a BMS manage active and
passive strategies in order to
minimise energy comsumption

cooling
dehumidifying coil

underground pipes pre-cools
air for the semi-basement

no.16 vertical
geothermal loops

summer

Fig. 2.4.4 CSET – section in summertime

the light well. It is extracted though chimney-effect by means of the double-skin exposed to the south. In the basement, primary air is pre-heated in winter and pre-cooled in summer by heat exchange with the ground. Low thermal transmittance values of the opaque walls (U = 0.25 W/m²K) and of the transparent walls and light well (U = 1.2W/m²K) curb dispersion and determine greater winter heating energy savings while the thermal inertia of the structural mass lowers climate control energy requirements due to thermal phase lag. Through thermal activation of the mass, ceiling-installed radiant panels ensure high levels of comfort both in summer and in winter. The panels are fed by reversible-cycle heat pumps with 16 vertical geothermal probes, enabling further energy savings. Evacuated-tube solar collectors fitted into the roofing produce hot water but also power the absorption refrigerators.

Mario Cucinella designed the building 'to minimise the need for additional energy for heating, cooling and ventilation. In fact, the residual heating, cooling and ventilation load is estimated to be so low that this residual load, plus demand for electrical power for computing, lighting will be met from renewable energy sources.'[2]

Notes

1   Exhibited at Prototyping Architecture, Nottingham
2   Mario Cucinella in Michael Stacey, Concrete a studio design guide, RIBA Publishing, 2011, p.198

2.6 Optical Fibre Concrete

Johannes Rauff Greisen[1]

Fig. 2.6.2 Optic fibres being very carefully placed in the mould

Designers:	Johannes Rauff Greisen, Lars Nyholm Thrane, Claus Pade and Christoffer Dupont
Materials:	Self Compacting Concrete cast on epoxy resin coated expanded polystyrene moulds incorporating optic fibres
Fabricators:	DuPont Lightstone, Danish Technological in collaboration with CINARK Institute
Exhibit:	1:1 Optic fibre concrete prototype[2]

Optical fibres transmitting light through concrete can be used to show live images on concrete surfaces, which is advantageous compared with well known image projecting. The display technology used has been developed for planar concrete screens by DuPont Lightstone. The display technology requires that the optical fibres are embedded precisely into the concrete, therefore the formwork must provide a high level of spatial control of the fibres during casting. Applying this display technology on double curved surfaces involves major challenges in achieving accurate fibre position and angle: Formwork rigidity is critical in order to maintain fibres orthogonal to the surface during casting and yet allow reasonable deforming. The research conducted at Danish Technological Institute solves these challenges by utilising a new composite concrete formwork material and three and five axes robotic milling and drilling operations. The experimental work consists of five phases. The first three phases are Pixel-Pattern, Formwork-System and Concrete. Covering the technology research and development for each stage. The subsequent two phases Demoulding & Surface Finish and Interface & Projection Device are of more practical ad-hoc nature.

Fig. 2.6.1 Optical Fibres transmitting light through concrete

Pixel-Pattern

The interface divides the input image into interface-pixels and each pixel is passed through its respective optical fibre becoming a surface-pixels. Pixels must therefore be placed in a pattern able to transfer the two-dimensional interface input correctly to the three-dimensional image output on the concrete surface. Various patterns were tested, and it is concluded that a triangular pattern offers a non-distorting concrete screen with a high degree of formal freedom.

Formwork-System

The metal sheet originally used for planar concrete screens must be replaced by a material allowing three-dimensional shaping and still is stiff enough, so the large amount of optical fibres could be fitted effectively with a tolerance of less than 1mm (position) and 2° (angle), and kept in position and angle during concrete casting. Various formwork materials were tested, and the conclusion is a formwork system based on epoxy resin coated expanded polystyrene. This formwork system can easily be fabricated by three axes milling and five axes drilling, and it proves to be rigid enough to control concrete and optical fibres during casting and yet relatively easy to remove after curing without damaging fibres and concrete.

Concrete

Low viscosity and small aggregates are necessary to ensure complete enclosure of fibres and to avoid blocking in between them. The concrete must be self-compacting (SCC) because experiments with vibration showed that air bubbles formed around the fibres. The final requirement was a concrete surface of high quality without blowholes, with uniform colour and no traces of the expected variations in casting pressure resulting from the variation in geometry. Various mixtures were tested, and a ready mix mortar proves to be useful in regards to form filling, enveloping optical fibres, the even colour and final surface quality being suitable for subsequent grinding and polishing.

Demoulding and Surface Finish

A critical aspect of demoulding is the interlocking between formwork and cast concrete, caused by the different orientations of the cast in place optical fibres. The formwork must therefore be cut away. Surface finish is effected by manually, dry grinding followed by wet grinding and wet finishing using pneumatic tools with rotating diamond based abrasive discs.

Interface and projecting device

A light-projecting device is used in the display technology of the concrete screen. This projector has obsolescence and may be regarded as interchangeable, according to needs and technology development. The presented prototype uses an off the shelf low emission, long life LED projector with a light intensity of 2000 lumens. The three first phases used iterative methods, which are commonly known within product development, design, and artistic development. The aims of using them were problem solving and value creation. In the two final practical phases just plain skill and craftsmanship were deployed. Evaluations of cast concrete screens, were done by qualitative methods to assess the appearance of concrete surfaces and quantitative methods to evaluate the efficiency and accuracy in fabrication. These evaluations were made continuously informing the iterative development process.

The presented prototype is a final cast result of this research and development of the next generation of formwork technology for optical fibres. The research is an example of new digital tools being used to obtain durable, functional and beautiful architectural surfaces, by innovative use of traditional and inexpensive materials. The optical fibre concrete tends to have a highlight on the areas facing towards the observer. This highlight compromises the relevance as a traditional screen, but shows new spatial, aesthetic and formal potentials. The conclusion is that utilising robots within the process of fabrication of concrete buildings, opens new perspectives:

Fig. 2.6.3 Optical fibre concrete

Controlling and embedding hitherto unseen amounts of delicate inserts is now technically possible, and when the efficiency of computer aided manufacturing is combined with the flexibility of craftsmanship the embedding can be customised and executed within a reasonable economy. Concrete as building material is a composite, but has sometimes nevertheless been conceived as a homogeneous grey mass. Optical fibre concrete is to be conceived as a true composite material with translucent and opaque components controlled by computer tools to a degree resulting in a new breed of transparency.

Notes

1   Johannes Rauff Greisen, is a Consultant Architect, MAA, and Industrial PhD-Student at CINARK.
2   Exhibited at Prototyping Architecture, Nottingham

2.7 Aquatic Centre Formwork

Zaha Hadid Architects and PERI

2.7.2 PERI formwork units supported on a falsework constructed from the PERI UP Flex system scaffold

Architect:	Zaha Hadid Architects
Engineer:	Ove Arup & Partners
Materials:	MDF Fins – generating the form, Softwood Substructure and Phenolic Faced Plywood Shutter Linings
Contractors:	AJ Morrisroe & Sons
Formwork Fabricators:	PERI
Location:	Queen Elizabeth Olympic Park, London
Exhibit:	76% digital prototype of the formwork for the Aquatic Centre, London[1]

Teamwork is required to achieve engineering and architectural excellence. This is exemplified by Aquatics Centre, which has become one of the most iconic structures at the 2012 London Olympic Park. PERI was the major supplier of formwork for this extraordinary project. For the Olympic Games in London Zaha Hadid, one of the best known and influential figures in contemporary architecture has created an arena resembling the shape of a large wave. The design of her buildings often cross the boundaries set by forms previously considered as non-realisable in modern architecture. The highly visible curved shape of the roof construction is consistently transferred to the inside of the building leading to a complexity of design that was met by the PERI design engineers.

Fig. 2.7.1 The exposed in situ concrete of the Aquatic Centre, London, designed by Zaha Hadid Architects for 2012 Olympics

Prototyping Architecture   93

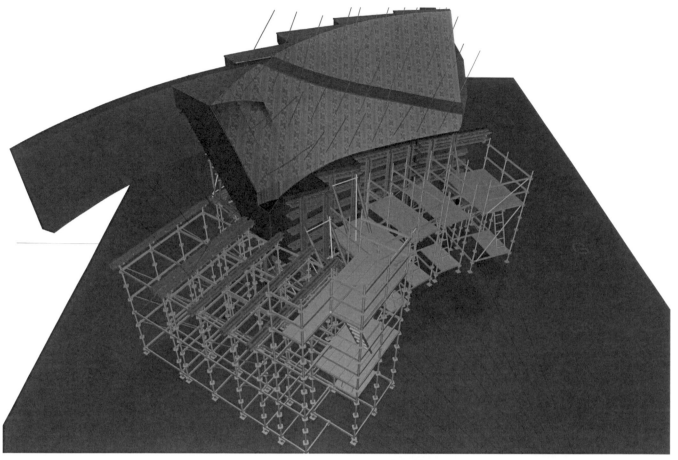

Fig. 2.7.3 Digital model of PERI formwork

One particular challenge was the concrete construction of the Scoreboard Wall and Welcome Zone. Their complex geometries and doubled-curved surfaces required more than 200 PERI 3D formwork units to be designed, planned, precision manufactured and delivered to the construction site. On site the customised elements were accurately positioned and connected while being supported on a falsework constructed from the PERI UP Flex system scaffold. The extremely high tolerances demanded by the Architect required precise dimensional accuracy and was of utmost importance especially at the interfaces with existing structural elements and the subsequent glazing system. To ensure a uniform concrete finish, PERI engineers created each structural element including all the joints and anchor points in a 3D virtual model and coordinated all details with the architectural team. The architects demands for a totally blemish free concrete surface with no rivet or screw impressions, this required the PERI assembly teams to secure a final layer of plywood to the sub structure with glue and 'double-sided' tape in order to achieve the highest possible architectural concrete.

Notes

1   Exhibited at Prototyping Architecture, Nottingham

Fig. 2.7.4 Assembley of the digitally cut landscape of MDF fins

Fig. 2.7.5 The MDF fins are covered in softwood, then finished with phenolic resin coated plywood

Fig. 2.7.6 The layered construction of the PERI doubly curved formwork [opposite]

2.8 Green School Gaza
Architecture as a Sign of Peace
Mario Cucinella Architects

Fig. 2.8.2 Mario Cucinella's sketch outlining the environmental strategy for the Green School Gaza

Architect: Mario Cucinella Architects

Engineer: Luca Turrini

Environmental Consultant: Professor Brian Ford, A&URD

Location: Gaza, Palestine

Exhibit: Green School Gaza model[1]

Designed to respond to the water and electricity scarcity of the region, this pilot school is an off-grid building, which relies only on locally available and renewable resources. The concept has been designed pro-bono by Mario Cucinella Architects, and donated to UNRWA (The UN Agency for Palestine Refugees). The construction work was funded by the Kuwait Fund for Arab Economic Development, through the Islamic Development Bank. The school will provide an education for 1500 children in the Gaza Strip. The project is expected to break ground at the beginning of 2013.

Fig. 2.8.1 Images of the Gaza Green School model, designed for UXX, by Mario Cucinella Architects

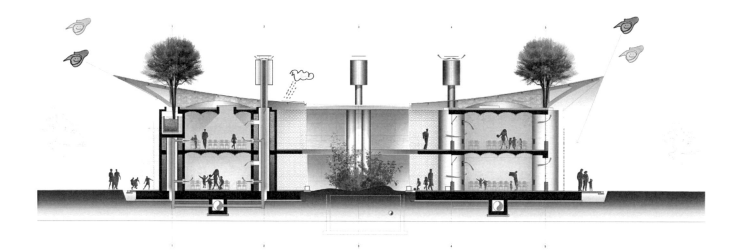

Fig. 2.8.3 Outline of the environmental design of the Green School Gaza

The construction system is composed by four distinctive elements:

- Concrete slab as foundation: acts as climatic moderator thanks to its thermal mass;

- Pillars with 2.2 meters in diameter: made of concrete-earth blocks precast on site with the inner cavity filled with excavation ground in order to reduce costs and increase inertia;

- Vaulted slabs: compressed earth block floor made of jack arches acts like lost formwork;

- Overhanging roof composed of steel beams and a reflecting metal sheet on earth bricks wall enables natural ventilation and shades the facades.

The building is equipped with:

- An underground tank that collects rainwater from the roof to be used for cleaning and personal hygiene. The wetland enables the recovery of wastewater for non-potable purposes such as toilets flushing (grey water) and irrigation (black water).

- 272 square meters of amorphous photovoltaic cells will provide green energy for all electrical devices. 100 square meters of evacuated solar heaters provide hot water for the heating coil located in the plant room.

The design of this school is not only environmentally resourceful and responsible it is an act of great politic optimism. This is architecture as a sign of peace, an act of civilization and common humanity.

Notes

1   Exhibited at Prototyping Architecture, Nottingham

Fig. 2.8.4 Internal views from the model of the Green School Gaza

Fig. 2.8.5 Internal views from the model of the Green School Gaza

Fig. 2.8.6 Internal views from the model of the Green School Gaza

2.9 Reversible Construction with Wooden Panels

Søren Nielsen[1]

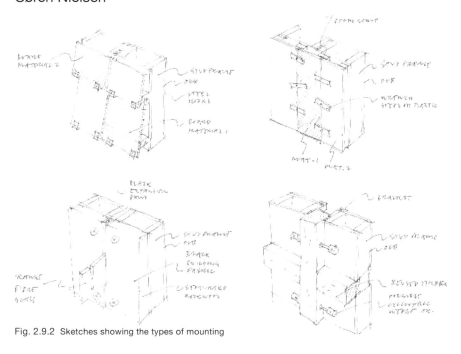

Fig. 2.9.2 Sketches showing the types of mounting

Architect and Fabricators:	Søren Nielsen and Katrine West[2]
Materials:	See text for each prototype
Location:	Copenhagen
Exhibit:	Four full size prototypes[3]

Providing affordable homes for an increasing urban population is an important topical task for Scandinavian architects as people with ordinary incomes are challenged by the high market prices for homes in the growing cities. One of the most efficient tools for lowering production costs is low-tech industrial prefabrication and the demand has resulted in a growing number of manufacturers of wooden panel elements. Experiences from the last decade's Scandinavian low-cost residential projects have shown that it is possible to build in high technical and architectural quality with wooden panel elements. Furthermore, from a resource preserving perspective timber based construction represents a significant improvement in building practice due to a carbon footprint that is low or even negative, as wood absorbs CO_2. At the same time, the focus of resource saving is about to shift from energy for building operation to energy consumed in building lifetime processes. This implies the need for introducing constructive principles, which enable reuse of components. On the one hand, wooden panel construction systems seem to be able to meet both the demand for low carbon and to constitute a suitable platform for reversible construction methods. On the other hand, it provides an atectonic structure as the load bearing members are usually disguised, all wrapped in skin components such as gypsum and chipboard. As when constructing with steel, the architectural expression is left to be performed in the more volatile layers of the building, and thus the detailing of the cladding comes to play the leading role in the exterior side of all four prototypes. The result can be described as architecture of deep surfaces.

Fig. 2.9.1 Four full size prototypes exhibited at Prototyping Architecture Exhibition, Nottingham

Prototype for rapid on site mounting

The tectonic principle explored in this prototype is pitching. The pitched boards reflect the on-site mounting process where boards are placed in position from a scissor lift. By using untrimmed, stock-measured board modules and frictional fixation screws, instead of drilled penetrations, the cladding construction is designed for disassembly and salvaging for reuse. Rhythmically placed steel hooks generate a characteristic motif imparting an atmosphere of constructive openness by rendering visible traces of the assembly process as well as anticipating future dismantling. The bent forks of stainless steel are not meant as a gimmick! Customised production of stainless hooks is costly and more functional specific than forks, which are apparently more versatile despite their strong identity. The principle has been proposed for a major residential project in 2009 but was eventually rejected by the contractor as part of a budget revision. The boards ended up being mounted in the traditional destructive way by penetrating fixations, for example screws. Interior detailing: to enable easy access to joints between elements a groove has been made between the interior cladding boards. The groove is covered by a removable lid element held in place by mouldings. A separate, demountable panel covers a zone for power installations, giving easy access for changes and replacements. The products used are: Rockpanel Natural, OSB, reused timber, recycled stainless forks, plywood boards, EPDM P-profiles and tarmac felt.

Fig. 2.9.3 Prototype for rapid on site mounting – principle explored: pitching

Prototype for an adaptable façade

In order to separate the more volatile skin layer from the permanent structural layer non thermal-conducting intermediary consoles of recycled fibreglass are deployed, resulting in a gargoyle-like motif. The tectonic principle explored in this prototype is consoling. Additional applications can be attached to the consoles such as balcony elements, sunscreens or windshields. The building becomes a paper-doll that can easily be dressed up in new ways. As background for the free configurable façade a cladding of fabric mounted on hard insulation boards are suggested. The coconut washers are not meant as a gimmick but as an example of a strong and durable organic alternative to synthetics. The principle has been proposed in the competition for adaptable building typologies held by the Adaptable Futures research team at The University of Loughborough in 2011. Interior detailing: the cladding boards are separated by grooves in order to enable access to joints between structural elements. A heavy quality fabric mounted with velcro-strips covers the grooves generating a modular pattern in the interior. Products used are: Barsmark PD-1700 fibreglass board, Barsmark Glapor insulation board (foamed recycled glass), acryl-coated cotton fabric, OSB-boards, reused timber, Rigidur fibre-gypsum board, EPDM P-profiles (for air-tight mechanical assembly), tarmac felt, velcro, leather.

Fig. 2.9.4 Prototype for rapid on site mounting – principle explored: consoling

Fig. 2.9.7 Prototype for rapid on site mounting – principle explored: renovation

Fig. 2.9.8 Prototype for rapid on site mounting – principle explored: renovation

Fig. 2.9.9 Prototype for rapid on site mounting – principle explored: frame and filling

Prototype for façade renovation

Façade cladding boards are mounted on battens. Instead of penetrating the boards by screws, small pins are penetrated and used as clamps to wrench the board in place. The mounting system allows easy dismantling and undamaged components suitable for reuse. The tectonic principle explored in this prototype is wrenching. The principle has been proposed for a major renovation project and is currently being designed for realisation. Interior detailing: the structural members are rendered visible and the cladding boards are mounted as a filling. To enable easy dismantling and to avoid penetration by screws or nails the cladding is fixed with dowels of bamboo. The products used are: Barsmark PD 1700 (recycled fibreglass), OSB-boards, reused timber, rubber P-profiles, pins of bamboo, tarmac felt.

Prototype for plug-in panels

The tectonic principle explored in this prototype is frame and filling. The structural grid is constructed in advance and the prefabricated panels are additions, which fill out the framework of rough timber. The exterior gaps between the sides of the panel elements can be respected or ignored by demountable claddings, which can respectively reveal or hide the structural system. The principle is well known from many projects, for instance KieranTimberlake's Loblolly house, but is here shown in a version with reused timber. Interior detailing: the structural grid appears as pillars at the inside of the façade wall. At the floor a board covers the gap between the floor elements indirectly revealing the structural system. The products used are: OSB-boards, recycled timber, Rigidur fibre-gypsum board, EPDM P-profiles, tarmac felt, hemp rope.

Notes

1   Søren Nielsen, architect and partner in the architectural office
        Vandkunsten, Copenhagen, Industrial PhD Student at CINARK.
2   Katrine West, architect and partner in the architectural office
        Vandkunsten.
3   Exhibited at Prototyping Architecture, Nottingham

2.10 Autarki 1:1 Pavilion

CINARK

Fig. 2.10.2 Autarki exhibited at Prototyping Architecture Exhibition, Nottingham

Architects/ Design Team:	Jesper Nielsen, Nikolaj Callisen Friis, Tenna Beck and Jan Schipull Kaschen, CINARK[1]
Materials:	Cross Laminated Softwood, Wool Fibre Insulation and a Painted Timber Triple Glazed (Argon Filled) Opening Window
Fabricators:	Grontmij Carl Bro, KTS (Copenhagen Technical College)
Location:	Royal Danish Academy of Fine Arts, Copenhagen
Exhibit:	1:1 Prototype of a corner detail (1 x 1 x 1m)[2], with 1:10 wooden model (400 x 400 x 500mm)[3]

Autarki is the Ancient Greek for Self-sufficient. This pavilion, Autarki 1:1, has a cross-laminated timber (CLT) structure and, Autarki 1.1, Autarki is the Ancient Greek for Self-sufficient, has beenwas erected at the Royal Danish Academy of Fine Arts, School of Architecture in Copenhagen in the autumn of 2011 and is the subject of on going performance monitoring. The aim of the project is to investigate constructions that will improve recyclability and reduce the energy consumption of the building by optimisatingon both the process and the technical aspects of CLT. Autarki 1:1 is constructed as a Passivhaus with the sun as the main source heating source and natural ventilation as a focal point. By building with a double shell principle the thermal bridges have been reduced significantly, and the homogeneity of the building allows for a more simple and sustainable building process. During 2012-13 we will conduct measurements of the building's thermal performance will be conducted, this can be followed in real time at www.AUTARKI.dk.

A Self Sufficient Pavilion

Emanuele Naboni, Alessandro Maccarini and
Jesper Nielsen[4]

The research focuses on the investigation of Cross Laminated Timber (CLT) technical configurations that optimise construction processes, whilst reducing buildings' life cycle impact, operational energy and maximising thermal comfort. To explore such scenarios, a building prototype, named Autarki 1:1, was built on the campus of the Royal Danish Academy of Fine Arts, Copenhagen. There are various aims of the present research. One of the main aims is to test newly designed details of CLT according to the EU targets for 2020, which prescribe that all new buildings consume very little energy, nearly Zero-Energy Building (nZEB). The sub-focus is the investigation of potential for energy saving, driven by solely constructive and passive means; therefore, no mechanical or active systems were added to the prototype. To guarantee air changes, an air-to-air recuperative heat exchanger, inspired by studies carried out in the early '90s at the Technical University of Denmark (DTU), was integrated. A second aim is to investigate how, when coupling the use of a prototype and parametric energy simulations, it is possible to obtain the best possible performative design.

Concept

The project is not meant to be directly industry-related or demonstrating a proposed route for the CLT industry. It is a tectonic experiment, meant to generate, through an idealised statement, a discussion on wood, manufacturing, comfort and sustainability. The main criteria for the experiment is:

- Full visibility of the material;
- Mono-strategy;
- Structural logic;
- Low-tech climate strategy;
- Design for disassembly

Full visibility of the material, like masonry and concrete, CLT is capable of being surface as well as structure, allowing use as a homogeneous building material. Mono-strategy, by allowing the panels to act both as façade and structure, the building process is simplified and a number of part deliveries are eliminated. This makes it easier to go directly from design to production. The structural logic optimises the structural principle using the entire cross-section of the exterior envelope for carrying load and creating stability. Low-tech climate strategy proves a healthy and well-insulated building, and by implementing a natural convection driven heat exchanger the aim is to fulfil the Passivhaus Standard[5]. Design for disassembly is an added benefit from the mono-strategy, to create a house that can be taken apart into its individual components and either recycled or re-erected elsewhere.

Fig. 2.10.3   Autarki 1:1 Pavilion at the Royal Danish Academy of Fine Arts - School of Architecture, Copenhagen

Process

The house was built with the help of carpenter apprentices from the Copenhagen Technical College. The CLT components were delivered pre-cut on site and were assembled using a crane. It was built from the inside out, with the panel layout planned, so that temporary bracing wasn't necessary, and due to the bonded connections, the next panel could always be fixed directly to the former. The two shells are constructed so that, in principle, they are independent of each other. After the inner shell was erected the wood fibre insulation battens were mounted. The building was capped off with the roof plates, which were then covered with a building paper. Finally the glazing was delivered and mounted.

Materials

CLT panels have been used as a construction material during the last twenty years, but recently it's popularity has increased due to it's inherent sustainable properties, one could argue CLT to be a legitimate alternative to concrete as a first choice industrial material. In the Autarki 1:1 Pavilion, CLT is used both as the inner and the outer wall. This is more material consuming than a similar construction of frames and boards, such as Gypsum and OSB, but it opens up for some tectonic advantages that are tempting to explore: by using only CLT panels you can build with fewer parts which again allows for a simple construction with less studs, fasteners, boards, screws, gaskets, foils, etc. What you see is what you get and there are no endless layers of glue, fibreglass, filler and paint. Also by digitally crafting the CNC manufactured laminated timber, the components are pre-fabricated to the architects/engineers specifications. This means that the designer has a much more direct influence on the components, in which the form is pre-determined. Additionally the whole process is much more material saving, as nothing is cut on site. The building is insulated with wooden fibre battens from the German company Homatherm. Their product has the ability to distribute moisture more evenly than mineral wool, allowing us to build without a vapour barrier. In addition, wooden fibres allegedly have a higher thermal capacity than mineral wool, which gives a more stable indoor climate with less temperature fluctuations.

Tectonics

The pavilion is constructed with a principle similar to masonry diaphragm walls. In masonry, a block work diaphragm wall is a wide cavity wall, with two leaves of block work bonded together with cross ribs. But in our case the cross-laminated wooden leaves can withstand a considerable amount of bending out of the plane and we can restrict the ribs to areas around the corners. This double-skin principle leaves us with a house that is effectively a thermos bottle. Two only partially interconnected layers create a continuous void for insulation between them. The cold bridging between inner and outer layer is only a fraction of what they are in conventional construction. Apart from the ribs in the corners, the two layers are only connected at the windows.

Performance

The pavilion is placed on a site right in the middle of the campus of the School of Architecture. The openings in the box have been optimised in relation to sunlight, with the main opening towards the south, but twisted slightly to the east, as the heat gain in the mornings is important. On the outside, the southern window is shaded in the summer by a projecting sheet, cantilevered from the inside balcony. The windows are newly developed (and sponsored) by Rationel Windows. They are 3-layer, argon-filled with an U-value of 0.79 W/m²K. To achieve the Passivhaus standard it is necessary to keep heat loss by infiltration of air at a very low level. The low natural infiltration means, that it is impossible to sustain a reasonable air quality in the space without some kind of ventilation going through a heat exchanger. For this we have built a heat exchanger driven solely by natural convection. It is based on an earlier research project at The Danish Technical University from the early Nineties.[6]

Cool air from the outside is drawn from the top part of the south façade, where the pressure is often higher due to the prevailing wind, into the exchanger, where it is lead through a series of thin-walled aluminium tubes. Leaving the tubes again, the air continues to the bottom of the room, where it leaves the device at floor level. This airflow is countered by a similar movement of warm interior air from just below the balcony into the exchanger, where it flows along the aluminium tubes in the opposite direction, delivering its energy to the incoming air through the tube walls. The whole system takes its energy from the differences in height and pressure of the two airflows. During 2012-13 measurements will be conducted, revealing how well the building performs throughout the year. The pavilion is equipped with loggers measuring temperature, luminosity and relative humidity, and by comparing simulations and models with our measurements we will be able to see how the building performs.

Fig. 2.10.4   The self finished timber interior of Autarki 1:1 Pavilion

Future Potential

The research team is optimistic that the project will demonstrate the tectonic potential of CLT panels as more than a technical option, and that it will inspire architects to challenge the boundaries presently set by the manufacturers. This pavilion also promotes the idea of homogeneous construction, for the benefit of sustainable construction and for architecture in general. This experiment is not an attempt to present a buildable construction - it is meant to help promote a debate on how to build with CLT and what potentials lie therein. Some aspects of this investigation might not be feasible in the real world, but our hope is that by producing this architectural prototype we can attempt to push the boundaries and hopefully pave the way for new ,otherwise not considered tectonic possibilities.[7]

Notes

1   Supported by Daniel Reinert, Finn Ørstrup, Svend Jacobsen, Rikke-Julie Schaumburg-Müller, Emanuele Naboni and Nina Belokonskaia.

2   Exhibited at *Prototyping Architecture*, Nottingham and London

3   Exhibited at *Prototyping Architecture*, Nottingham

4   Emanuele Naboni[1], Associate Professor, Alessandro Maccarini, Assistant Researcher, Jesper Nielsen Associate Professor, at the Institute of Architectural Technology Royal Danish Academy of Fine Arts, School of Architecture, Copenhagen, Denmark.

5   For information on the Passivhaus Standard see – http://passiv.de/en/ or http://www.passivhaus.org.uk/standard.jsp?id=122 (accessed February 2013)

6   Jørgen M. Schultz, Naturlig Ventilation med Varmegenvinding, Laboratoriet for Varmeisolering, Meddelelse nr. 249, Technical University of Denmark, 1993

7   Further explanation the research basis for Autarki 1:1 Pavilion can be seen in in Michael Stacey, ed., *Prototyping Architecture: The Conference Papers*, Riverside Press, 2013, pp. 268-285

2.11 Timber Wave

AL_A with Arup

Fig. 2.11.2 American red oak laminated timber cords, manufactured for the Timber Wave by Cowley Timberworks

Architect:	AL_A
Engineer:	Arup
Materials:	Curved and Laminated American Red Oak
Fabricators:	Cowley Timberworks
Location:	Entrance of Victoria and Albert Museum, London
Exhibit:	American Red Oak Prototype Sections[1]

Designed by AL_A with engineers Arup, Timber Wave was installed at the entrance of the Victoria and Albert Museum in London, for the London Design Festival 2011. The most ambitious commission of the festival to date, this 12 metre-high installation showcased the interest in design and making that is at the heart of the V&A's collections and London's creative industries. Timber Wave was about taking the V&A out onto the street, celebrating the London Design Festival residency at the museum and the use of American red oak as a material. The V&A's Cromwell Road entrance is vast, multilayered and very ornamental. The form responded to this with a single dynamic gesture in timber; the use of wood as a structural material is well documented at the V&A. Repetition of motif is very much part of the decorative and didactic tradition of the V&A, and this structure was born from that. Three-dimensional and asymmetric in form, it created its own balance and was visible from long views as you approached the museum from along Cromwell Road. Cowley Timberworks used lamination techniques typically used in furniture-making applied at a vast scale to create a structure that echoed the grand proportions of the museum's magnificent arched entrance. The chords were manufactured from thin slices

Fig. 2.11.3 Timber Wave components exhibited at *Prototyping Architecture Exhibition*, London

of timber (lamellae), curved and glued together to create a pattern and geometry expressing the structural forces inherent within the form. Curving the elements created significant engineering challenges. In a truss all the members are either in compression or tension; curve the members and those in tension will try and straighten while those in compression will try and fold up. The more curved they are, the larger they will need to be to stop them straightening or folding.

Amanda Levette and her colleagues in practice used digital parametric tools facilitated the fine-tuning of the pieces and their connections to enable repetition whilst maintaining the dynamism of the wave. With software called Grasshopper, architect and engineer were able to rapidly explore the effect of varying both member size and degree of waviness on the overall appearance and behaviour of the structure. This means that visitors could instantly see which members were working harder adding to the dynamism of the piece; the elements towards ground level are obviously working hardest, particularly the outer chords, which attract the largest forces as the prevailing wind tries to blow the structure against the museum. The curved nature of all the members also enabled the design team to explore different ways of forming the wood into curved shapes. These digital techniques maximised the complex varying geometry whilst maintaining the structural integrity. American red oak's inherent structural strength enabled Timber Wave to be self-supporting so as not to touch the Grade 1-listed building, be able to withstand a once-every-100-years gale force wind and allow for an entire rugby team climbing the structure.

Fig. 2.11.4 Timber Wave, designed by Al_A, at the Victoria and Albert Museum

2.12 TRADA Leg Prototype and Pavilion

Ramboll Computational Design

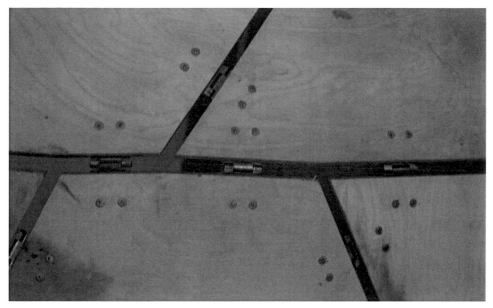

Fig. 2.12.2 Hinged joints of the TRADA leg pavilion

Engineers / Fabricators:	Ramboll Computational Design
Materials:	Birch Ply, Stainless Steel Nuts and Bolts securing domestic Steel Hinges
Location:	Coventry, England
Exhibit:	1:1 TRADA Pavilion Timber Leg and 1:10 TRADA Pavilion Model[1]

The form of the structure of the TRADA Pavilion was designed using an in-house form-finding application to develop structures optimised to resist their self-weight efficiently via in-plane forces. The complex surface created would have been difficult and expensive to replicate exactly so it was discretised into planar faces. The plywood structure is locked together by simple hinges, connecting adjacent panels. The geometry of the panels and the overall form restrains the panels – which allowed the same connection detail to be used throughout the structure - drastically reducing costs and manufacturing complexity. The development of the connection detail and production of a parametric model to automate the positioning of hinges, numbering and nesting are described. Prototyped in three stages: an early paper model, an accurate 1:10 scale model and a full scale leg. The prototypes addressed many of the design team's concerns, including but not limited to overall stability, aesthetic, ease of construction and fabrication processes. Details of the manufacture and implications of the prototypes are included, recommendations for future projects and the value of such prototyping is discussed. Despite the innovative and irregular form, unnecessary complexity was avoided by considering all phases of development at the earliest stage.

Fig. 2.12.1 The TRADA Pavilion by Ramboll Computational Design

TRADA Pavilion, Design, Research and Development

Stephen Melville, John Harding and Harri Lewis[2]

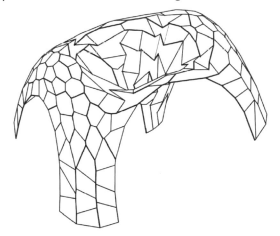

Fig. 2.12.3 Digital model of the TRADA Pavilion, designed by Ramboll

Fig. 2.12.4 The completed pavilion at the Timber Expo 2012

In late 2011, the Timber Research and Development Association (TRADA) commissioned Ramboll Computational Design (RCD) to design, analyse, fabricate and construct a pavilion to be a showcase for inventive use of timber and a working trade fair stand for the Timber EXPO 2012. A re-useable thin-shell structure optimised for the often conflicting drivers of structural efficiency, cost of fabrication and ease of erection was created. A single design team rarely have the opportunity to manage and take responsibility for a project from concept to construction so it was seen as an opportunity to apply and demonstrate the advantages of digital design tools. This essay describes the processes and methodologies utilised by the Ramboll Computational Design team including the important role physical prototyping made towards the success of the project.

Introduction and Brief

The history of the pavilion in architecture is that of innovation and the expression of creative freedom and many have incorporated a high level of technical research and design exploration that belie their small size. In late 2011, having seen Ramboll Computational Design's (RCD) experimental foyer structure, TRADA commissioned the team to design, structurally analyse, help fabricate and build an enclosure for their stand at the Timber Expo 2012. The brief was to create a practical demonstration of how simple timber elements can produce innovative and elegant structural forms. TRADA hoped to fire the imagination of the public and encourage new ideas about what could be achieved with timber. The RCD team resolved to extend that brief to show how digital design techniques could be used to simplify the construction of complex forms by automating menial tasks and allowing the use of simple timber elements, with inexpensive fabrication techniques and without complex joints.

The brief also stipulated that the pavilion must be simple and quick to construct and to be demountable once the show was complete. Only two days were available on-site prior to the show opening and only one day after to demount. A tight budget was imposed by TRADA and minimal material wastage was highlighted as a priority. The plan dimensions and height were dictated by the size of the plot within the conference hall, six metres by eight metres and a maximum height of four metres. Although the plan dimensions and height were set, it was also important to ensure that there was sufficient room inside the pavilion for an information desk, a literature stand plus ample space for staff and public to move around freely. It was seen as a very open brief, especially for a team of engineers. The response was a funicular shell structure with a central funnel and four legs in birch plywood, drawing on previous work with digital form finding by the RCD team. The shape was not explicitly determined but allowed to form an optimal surface from imposed boundary conditions in response to the self-weight of the structure. By adopting this approach the shell was extremely efficient and could be constructed from thin timber elements. The form finding process is described in Form Development.

The surface itself was discretised into a mesh where three flat faces meet at every vertex (known as a three-valent planar mesh), an arrangement rarely seen in the construction industry but prevalent within nature. The technique used to achieve this is described in Surface Discretisation. This reduced the number of connections required, performed better structurally in comparison with a triangulated mesh and lent a unique visual quality to the shell.

Physical prototyping supported the innovations and was an indivisible part of the design process, starting with a paper 1:10

scale model of an approximate form, then a thin ply scale model of the final design then finally a full scale test leg. Without the assurance provided by the prototypes, delivery of the structure may not have been possible.

Form Development

The complex, curvaceous and highly structurally efficient forms of Frei Otto and Heinz Isler have often inspired the RCD team. These structures were designed using intricate scale models where a range of materials such as chains or fabric were hung with varying boundary conditions, see Fig. 2.12.5. With little or no bending resistance the material hangs in pure tension and the form they find in equilibrium can be 'flipped' to produce a structure, which works in pure compression. These methods produced slender structures capable of spanning long distances.

As with previous RCD projects these form-finding methods have been transferred into digital 3D environments by creating a network of springs and nodes to simulate flexible materials. There are a number of advantages to this – it is quicker and easier to adapt the form for a range of boundary conditions,

Fig. 2.12.5 Form finding model for Frei Otto's Mannheim gridshell

Fig. 2.12.6 Experiment combining form-finding with equal length members

material properties can be changed during the simulation and complex forces can be applied with ease. Once the form has been calculated there are further advantages – rather than having to painstakingly measure the complex shape physically, the exact vector positions can be exported directly to CAD or structural analysis packages.

The design team created the software using the Processing[3] libraries for creating Java applications. For this project the method was evolved to include 'dynamic mass'[4]. This involves updating the mass of each node at each iteration of the simulation, in response to the extension of the connected springs, therefore improving the validity of the resultant form. The software is fully interactive and the design team experimented with various boundary conditions to find a form that fitted within the site constraints and could work as an interesting focal point to the exhibition. An early experiment was to further adapt the software by setting the natural length of spring edge member equal to the average length of all the edge members. With a high enough spring stiffness this produced a mesh with members of approximately identical length, see Fig. 2.12.6. Whilst this was an interesting experiment, it was felt that with the ease of fabrication of timber of varying lengths this method did not actually offer any considerable benefits. It has been suggested that for other materials this may not be the case and the system was shelved for future reference.

In contrast to the grid-shell structural typology of the foyer sculpture, the team decided at this stage they would widen their experience and aim to produce a shell structure. This decision meant that the previously used connection details and rationalisation techniques would not be suitable - in effect forcing them to innovate and develop new methods. The challenges and solutions that arose as a result of this decision are discussed later.

The brief defined a maximum height of 4m. This and a desire for a maximised useable floor area led to the four legged and central funnel form that is seen. As form found shapes cannot be directly manipulated (without affecting the structural efficiency)

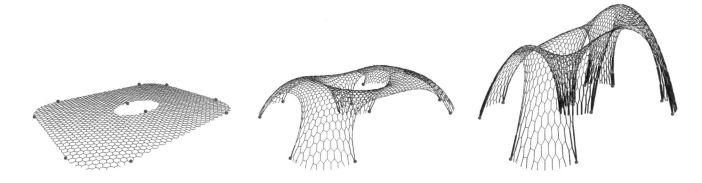

the designer must play a role similar to a puppeteer – tweaking and adding boundary constraints as they see fit. An initial design made up of four legs on the perimeter highlighted one of the challenges this method can generate - the lower the angle of the legs the more inhibited the space becomes, however if this angle is increased by increasing the "mass" of the digital fabric the maximum height is quickly exceeded. The solution was a central funnel form, which pulled this maximum height down whilst maintaining a high angle for the legs. The output of the form finding process was a high-resolution mesh of triangles to be used as a base surface from which to develop a buildable structure.

Surface Discretisation

Having decided upon the form and shell typology the next stage was to investigate how to discretise the surface into panels. Sheets of timber can be bent or milled to create curved surfaces however this would have been prohibitively expensive, as each panel would have required a unique jig or be highly wasteful of material. The challenge was therefore to divide the surface into completely flat or planar panels. The initial solution was to work with triangular panels. A plane can be defined by three points therefore a triangle must always be planar. Fig 2.12.7 shows a preliminary design using this method.

Although the result was an interesting form, there were a number of concerns about this solution. Firstly, it was felt that triangulated surfaces were too common and would not offer a significantly new aesthetic for the structure. Triangulated meshes also have lines of edge continuity throughout the surface and it was predicted that these would allow the shell to fold as it deforms and therefore require stiff connections to resist this action. Finally, as one move beyond triangles to many-sided shapes there is no guarantee that the shape will be planar – in fact, for a freeform shape, it is highly unlikely they will be. The challenge to solve this was one relished within the team and they saw the opportunity to implement a new algorithm to extend their suite of custom tools for future projects.

In their research of various methods for producing a planar mesh the team came across the work of Cutler and Whiting, whose paper Constrained Planar Re-meshing for Architecture[5] adapted a technique called Variational Shape Approximation[6] for use in the building industry. The technique had not been previously applied to a structure larger than a desk, which appealed to the team. The algorithm takes a high-resolution mesh as an input and from this a user-defined number of seed triangles are chosen on the mesh at random. The remaining triangles are then grouped into clusters around each of these seeds in relation to metrics such as distance or difference in triangle face direction. Once all of the triangles in the mesh have been assigned to a cluster, the triangle closest to the centre of the cluster is defined as the

Fig. 2.12.7 Design using triangulated surface rationalisation

new seed and the process repeats. This process is repeated iteratively; until the clusters are evenly spaced over the mesh.

At this stage a plane is created at the centre of each cluster. These planes are then intersected with all neighbouring planes and each intersection line becomes an edge of the planar face. Corrections are then made if the neighbouring topology of the clusters is not the same as the planar mesh. This system creates what is known as a three-valent mesh. This means exactly three faces and edges are attached to each vertex. This is advantageous both structurally and geometrically – continuous fold lines are broken and fewer panels have to fit together at a single point.

The appearance of the mesh is irregular but ultimately related to the curvature of the surface. In areas of positive Gaussian curvature such as the dome-like areas at the top of the structure the panels are convex. In areas that are close to cylindrical or have approximated zero Gaussian curvature, such as the legs, the panels are generally rectangular. Finally, in areas of negative curvature such as the funnel we see the interesting concave bow-tie shapes, see Fig. 2.12.8.

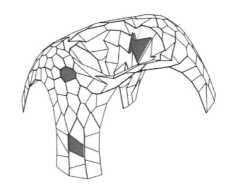

Fig. 2.12.8 Panel shapes reflecting the underlying curvature of the surface

To implement the algorithm the team chose to use Rhino[7] a 3D surface-modelling program which, with the addition of parametric plug-in Grasshopper[8] has become ubiquitous within the computational design community. Grasshopper allows users to create visual networks of components to create a parametric model. Whilst this basic functionality is appropriate for the majority of users the complexity of the algorithm meant the RCD team had to move beyond this and develop their own custom components.

Previously, (and for the form-finding software) the RCD team have created lightweight standalone programs rather than plug-ins to existing software; however they found there are a number of advantages of working within the Rhino environment. Firstly, they can utilise all of the functions and data structures available in the software. A good example of this was when they needed to check whether a curve was self-intersecting - rather than having to write and test a series of geometrical algorithms they could simply call an existing robust function, which returned a detailed output of the existence, position and nature of all the intersections. This saved a huge amount of time and it is recommended to be utilised wherever possible. In addition to this, once a component has been created, it is easy for other users to implement it without any detailed knowledge of how it works – they can simple drag and drop it into their existing parametric model.

Despite these timesaving advantages there are a number of limitations and negative aspects to working within Rhino. Meshes (linked collections of vertices and faces) in Rhino are strictly limited to only three or four sided faces. The team knew the output of the re-meshing would be made up of faces with a wide range of edge numbers and so they had to write and implement their own mesh data structure. This was a time consuming process but it was written to be re-usable for future projects.

The algorithm was successfully implemented however it was not completely robust. Problems arose when the adjacency of the clusters did not match the adjacency of the planar faces. This can be fixed by switching which clusters should be intersected to create the edges of the planar faces. However, it was found that to program a robust algorithm that worked for every possible self intersecting situation would have been inefficient for the project timescale. A more practical solution was to automate corrections for the most common situations and then manually fix any errors. The form chosen for the structure turned out to be a particularly challenging one to discretise – free edges, holes and a range of Gaussian curvatures all added to the complexity for the algorithm.

Connections

As with all timber structure, the connection design was an integral part of the debate on how the funicular surface could be constructed. The joints between panels of the timber shell must transfer in-plane loads resulting from the self-weight and restrain the panels against the rotation of adjacent panels. They are also needed to transfer out-of-plane shear at the interface between panels. The triangular and three-valent panel configurations were evaluated and each required the joints to provide different levels of restraint. The triangulated configuration required partial moment continuity whereas three-valent arrangement provides geometric constraint to rotation of adjacent panels and hence a simple pinned mechanism could suffice. In Figure 9 it can be seen that unless there is a rigid connection along the edge the triangular node can be progressively collapsed. With the three-valent node - the opposite face of any edge of will resist any rotation and therefore resist collapse. This appealed to the structural engineering background of much of the design team, as it was understood that this would lead to lighter and less obtrusive details. This structural behaviour was confirmed globally with scale and full-size models, see Physical Prototyping.

In addition to technical considerations the client's brief called for an easily demountable structure this meant neither glued joints nor screwed connections were possible solutions. Another significant challenge was that the angles between panels throughout the structure are irregular and every angle is unique. Creating a unique connection detail for each angle would have been time consuming and undoubtedly expensive throughout design, fabrication and erection. Also, unless copies were made of each (which would have been potentially very wasteful), there would have been no recourse in the event of a missing or broken detail during the short build time.

After sketching and mind-mapping came the realisation that the combination of different angles being required but no rotational resistance were complimentary – a system allowed to rotate could fit any angle. In order to express this concept as clearly and as 'honestly' as possible it was ultimately decided to use common steel hinges and flush Allen head bolts within a rebate

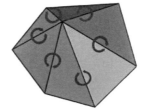

Fig. 2.12.9 Comparison to show how the three-valent node locks the surface even without rotational restraint on edges

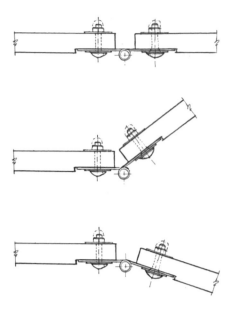

Fig. 2.12.10 Hinge connection detail

into the timber face. These satisfied all of the technical and practical constraints extremely well and the design team were attracted to the concept that they were creating a complex structure with only the ingredients for a simple door – flat sheets of timber, bolts and hinges.

Parametric detailing

Once the form, discretisation and connection design was complete, the next stage was to detail and prepare for fabrication. As the team wanted to showcase the use of digital design techniques throughout the delivery of a project this was seen as a perfect opportunity to automate what would otherwise have been a laborious process. As can be seen in Fig. 2.12.10, there is a small gap between adjacent panels; this was created for a number of reasons. Firstly, as many pieces must fit together in a highly constrained system a tolerance between panels provides room for error during fabrication and construction. In addition to this, a shadow gap was seen as aesthetically preferable to highlight the interesting shapes of the panels. Finally, as the team only had access to 3-axis CNC machining, the edges of each panel could not be cut at an angle – therefore as the angle between two panels varies a gap must be included stop intersection between adjacent panels

The calculation and modelling of this offset, a hinge rebate, a panel reference number and bolt positions were automated by creating a parametric model using the Grasshopper platform and the edge curves of the three-valent mesh as an input. Once the detailed 3d model had been created, each individual panel was translated onto a horizontal plane and, using a 3rd party plug-in called RhinoNest[9] arranged in an optimal position onto standard

plywood sheet sizes to minimise material wastage. Finally, this information was exported in the .dxf file format and sent to the fabricators. This method of parametric detailing is highly recommended for the delivery of such projects.

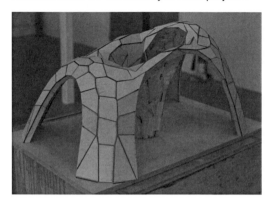

Fig. 2.12.11 1:10 thin ply scale model

Physical Prototyping

Three prototypes were created at different junctures in the design development. Firstly, an early paper model to test the overall massing and look of the form and give an early indication of the critical modes of failure. This is a common approach for structural engineers and gives the designer an opportunity to physically push the structure and observe its deflected form. Following the paper model, and after the decision had been made to use a three-valent mesh, a 1:10 scale thin ply model was built. This was necessary in order to test the theory that the double curved nature of the form and the three-valent mesh gave the pinned jointed panels adequate mutual restraint against rotation. The model was very successful in this respect and also gave a valuable morale boost for the team - it was the first time the team could see how the pavilion would appear in real life and gain a sense of the internal space. It also served to help visually plan the construction sequence and formed a focal point in meetings and internal technical reviews.

The last, and possibly most important, prototype was a full-scale leg constructed at Ramboll UK's head office, see Fig. 2.12.12. The driving force behind this model was to finally confirm the structural performance of the full system and connections, with material inconsistencies, joint slip, and other problems, rather than the idealised scale or finite element models that had been used up to this point. Also it was understood that although the mesh should lock itself into a rigid structure, it was not expected that this behaviour would be exhibited at the free edges. To support these areas, a line of edge stiffeners fixed at 90 degrees to any edge panels were installed. Once fully connected, the structure was observed to be extremely robust.

In addition to the structural feedback, the team were conscious that when it came to erect the structure no heavy lifting equipment and a limited amount of scaffolding would be available. The structure was also to be built by the design team who were relatively inexperienced in actual construction. The prototype leg therefore gave a valuable understanding of the weight of the elements, how difficult they were to handle (especially once several had been hinged together) and how the predicted tolerances translated into the real world. This information meant the team could effectively plan and predict their time on-site. The same fabricators and machines were used which meant that any issues in the fabrication and transfer of information could be ironed out before full production.

One of TRADA's guiding principles was that the pavilion should embody the natural beauty of timber and hence the team were determined that it should be fabricated as cleanly and neatly as possible and that any finish applied to the plywood enhanced rather than detract from its appearance. The panels also had to be fire protected with which could leave some staining. After viewing the whole test leg it was felt that the natural pale appearance of the plywood was the most attractive and that a darker wood stain would give a sense of oppression within the space. The staining from the applied fire protection was felt to be minimal and could be left without further treatment. The full-scale leg prototype proved extremely valuable in alleviating any concerns and it gave the team confidence to proceed. It also gave the Ramboll UK staff that were not intimately involved in the project an early insight into the project and instilled a sense of support throughout the company.[10]

Fig. 2.12.12 Full-scale prototype of a single leg of the structure

Notes

1   Due to spatial constraints the 1:10 model was exhibited at Nottingham only.

2   Stephen Melville, John Harding and Harri Lewis helped set up Ramboll Computational Design in 2010 after a number of years researching and developing digital design tools for the built environment. Stephen Melville BEng MSc DIC MIStructE FRSA, leads the Ramboll Computational Design Team which is dedicated to the research and application of digital tools for building and masterplan design. Stephen writes a weekly blog for Building Design and is a member of the Bristol Urban Design Forum and RIBA education panel. He is also a part time tutor at the Oxford Brookes School of Architecture and has also tutored or lectured at TU Delft, Texas, Copenhagen, Bristol and Cardiff Universities.

John Harding is a current doctoral candidate in computational design at The University of Bath. His research is in parametric modelling, multi-objective optimisation and the application of complex systems theory in the design process. Recent advances in computing modelling and analysis have involved rethinking the relationship between architect and engineer, particularly at the concept design stage. His practical application of computational design theory to real world projects has led John to collaborate with various architectural practices during his research.

Harri Lewis MEng MPhil, enjoys collaborating with architects and artists to help them develop innovative structures. He completed his MPhil degree at the University of Bath as part of their Digital Architectonics program where he developed a number of interactive software applications to help designers create elegant forms with embedded structural logic. Since returning to Ramboll he has combined this with his structural engineering background to help deliver a number of intricate projects.

3   Processing Software (http://www.processing.org), accessed January 2013

4   J. Harding and P. Shepherd, Structural form finding using zero-length springs with dynamic mass. In: 2011 IASS Annual Symposium: IABSE-IASS 2011: Taller, Longer, Lighter, 2011-09-20 - 2011-09-23, London

5   B. Cutler and E. Whiting, Constrained Planar Remeshing for Architecture, Proceedings of Graphics Interface,2007, available from - http://www.cs.rpi.edu/~cutler/publications/planar_remeshing_gi07.pdf

6   Variational Shape Approximation (http://hal.inria.fr/docs/00/07/06/32/PDF/RR-5371.pdf)

7   Rhino 3D software

8   Grasshopper software

9   Rhinonest software

10   For the authors conclusions on the process please see their paper Searching for innovation and elegance in complex forms supported by physical and software prototyping in in Michael Stacey, ed., *Prototyping Architecture: The Conference Papers*, Riverside Press, 2013, pp. 302-315

2.13 One Main

Mark Goulthorpe[1]

Fig. 2.13.2 Refectory of One Main in offices for C Change / Zero+, 2009

Architect:	dECOi Mark Goulthorpe, Raphael Crespin (Project Architect), Gabe Cira, Matt Trimble (Scripting), Priyanka Shah, MIT: Kaustuv de Biswas,
Mathematics:	Professor Alex Scott, Oxford University Consultants: Helen Heitman, Gensler Associate
Materials:	CNC Machined Spruce based Plywood
Fabricators:	CW Keller with General Contractor Tricore
Location:	Cambridge, Massachusetts
Exhibit:	Screens Only

This refurbishment of penthouse offices is for an investment group in green building and clean energy technologies, C Change Investments / Zero+. The design drew from dECOi's prior sculpture, *In the Shadow of Ledoux,* 1993, and the *Galerie Miran,* 2003, proposing the milling of all elements of the interior from sustainably-forested spruce plywood using numeric command machines: information carves renewable carbon-absorbing resource.

The project essentially comprises two planes - the floor and ceiling, both of which are articulated as continuous surfaces inflected by function. The curvilinearity expresses both the digital genesis and the seamless fabrication logic, with the architect providing actual machining files to the fabricator. As far as possible, the ethos was to replace typical industrial components (such as vents, door handles, etc) with articulate milled timber, offering a radically streamlined protocol for delivery of a highly crafted interior. The intention was to offer a reduced carbon footprint whilst celebrating both a new formal virtuosity and a radical level of detail finesse. Effectively this allows the architect to fully customise all elements of the building, placing material in space with full authorial control (for the first time since industrial components became standard). Other than sprinklers, lights, glass and hinges, the substance of the interior architecture was realised via this unitary material/fabrication logic, with a high degree of prefabrication.

The early sketch design grasped the potential for plastic control of the spatial and detail definition allowable within a fully CAD-CAM environment. The client asked that the work chairs be purchased for liability reasons, but all shelves, desks, benches, storage units, and other necessary details were accepted for direct fabrication in plylam via the same method. Ultimately we devised automated algorithms for generating actual milling files, passing from design to fabrication seamlessly and with high tolerances and extremely low percentages of error.

The developed design was nuanced parametrically in celebration of the indifference of the CNC machine to formal complexity. The entire project was nested onto 1200 4ft x 12ft (1,220 x 3,658mm) plywood sheets, and milled using a small 3-axis CNC router, which effortlessly carved the ply sections according to our prescribed weeping tool paths. Well over a million linear feet of cut were issued, yet the mechanic process was essentially error-free and highly accurate. Assembly proved relatively straightforward given the accuracy of the milling, and we enjoyed the elegance of the emerging forms.

The project was nuanced down to the smallest detail, such as the ventilation grille for the computer boxes being inflected to provide a handle to open the door; or the milling of custom mathematical surfaces for each office; even the door handles were carved as customised elements, proving cheaper than stainless steel handles. The architects aimed for formal coherence at macro and micro scales.

Functional needs such as ventilation grilles and shrouds for the bright LED lights gave a detail finesse to the ceiling; whilst focal elements such as the conference table or directors' desks were plastically formed to permit electrical data outlets in the spine, and were embellished mathematically according to parameters of 'tension' and 'irony'. Quite literally, the material substance of each space was nuanced according to the character and mood of each client during the fabrication period!

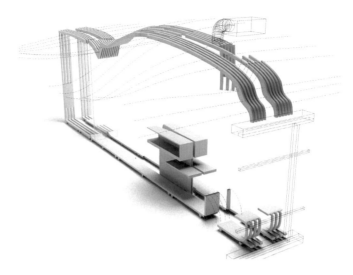

Fig. 2.13.3 Prototype Office Section - infected with desks

Fig. 2.13.4 CNC fabrication of a bespoke desk

Fig. 2.13.5 CNC milled plywood sheets being assembled into prefabricated chunks

Summary

One Main uses sustainably forested Finnish spruce ply with non-toxic water-based glue. The 10,000sq ft (1000m2) project nested onto 1200 sheets of 1.5" thick 4ft x 12ft ply, (38mm by 1220mm by 3658mm), milled locally by a single 3-axis milling machine. The use of a renewable plywood means this interior results in the sequestration of 100,000kg of CO_2. dECOi provided the actual tooling paths (over 1 million linear feet of cut), with no plans or sections, just 3D instructional files. Wastage was about 10%, pulped and recycled.[2]

Notes

1   Mark Goulthorpe is an Associate Professor at MIT Department of Architecture and Director of dECOi Architects. He studied architecture at Liverpool School of Architecture.

2   http://www.decoi-architects.org/2011/10/onemain/ [Accessed August 2013]

Fig. 2.13.7 Other than sprinklers, lights, glass and hinges, the substance of the interior architecture was realised via this unitary material/fabrication logic, with a high degree of prefabrication

Fig. 2.13.6 One Main - Conference Room Table and Bench

Fig. 2.13.8 The space nuanced parametrically by dECOi in celebration of the indifference of the CNC machine to formal complexity – integrating surface furniture and ventilation

2.14 Passive Downdraft Evaporative Cooling

Brian Ford and Ingeniatrics-Frialia

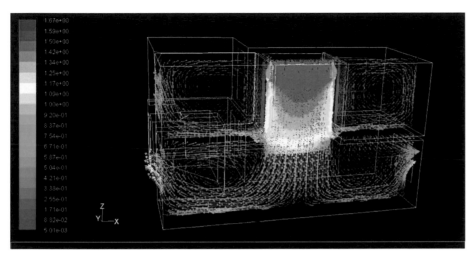

Fig. 2.14.2 Nottingham House velocity vectors coloured by velocity magnitude

Researchers: Brian Ford and Ingeniatrics-Frialia with the Nottingham House
Team

Materials: For a full description of the materials and techniques used provided
                      in the Nottingham House chapter, which follows

Fabricators: Ingeniatrics-Frialia with the Students and Staff of the Department
                      of Architecture and Built environment at The University of
                      Nottingham

Location: Ecobuild, London and Rio Parque, Madrid

Exhibit: 1:1 Demonstration prototype of PEDC and Gull Wing Roof Light
                      from the Atrium of the Nottingham House[1]

Cooling System for the Nottingham Solar Decathlon Europe House. The integration of PDEC (Passive Downdraught Evaporative Cooling) in the Nottingham House for the Solar Decathlon Europe 2010, Madrid, was the first application of this technique in southern European housing. Cooling is induced through the evaporation of water droplets from misting nozzles suspended below a roof light. The cooled air falls and flows towards the perimeter of the house, where it is exhausted. During the competition in June 2010 the house's thermal performance was tested and the results are set out in the chapter that follows. Performance data indicates that the combination of a high-performance building envelope and the PDEC system can create comfortable internal conditions, even when the outdoor temperature is above 35° Celsius. Estimates of the cooling achieved, based on the measured results, were compared with the energy required by the system to derive an indicative range of coefficient of performance (CoP) values under varying ambient conditions. The results suggest that PDEC can deliver significant energy savings and achieve comfortable thermal conditions without the need for additional mechanical cooling. This technique may therefore have wider relevance to housing in central and southern Spain, and other hot, dry regions of the world.[2]

Fig. 2.14.1 PEDC prototype below the roof light of the Nottingham House on test at Solar Decathlon 2010, Madrid.

The Nottingham House: Responsive Adaptation and Domestic Ecology

Brian Ford and Michael Stacey[3]

Fig. 2.14.3 The Nottingham House at Rio Parque, Madrid

The University of Nottingham's entry into the 2010 Solar Decathlon Europe competition - the Nottingham House, is a prototype of a zero carbon affordable starter home that can be constructed throughout Europe.[4] The research aims included the realisation of a fully prefabricated house providing a comfortable and domestic environment that would have little or no running costs. Thus, simultaneously tackling fuel poverty, eliminating the need for winter fuel payments whilst protecting against over heating in summer, which can be equally injurious to human health and well-being. Underscoring this was a wider societal goal of tackling global warming and reducing our dependence on fossil fuels, seeking to contribute to achieving the carbon reduction of the Stern Review, 2006.[5] However, the design aim of the Nottingham House was firmly focused on domesticity, with technology as a servant of this homely environment. The plan form can be used to create two storey terrace housing and courtyard housing depending on the climatic situation, local traditions and culture. This is based on the placement of the L-shaped plan. The Nottingham House is a prototype for a housing system that is adaptable both culturally and technically so that it can be used throughout Europe. In essence, this means that the Nottingham

House is pre-adapted to the risk of elevated temperature ranges in the summers of Northern Europe, as predicted by some climate models, later in the twenty first century.

The Nottingham House was Britain's only entry into 2010 Solar Decathlon Competition. This was the first time the competition was staged in Europe having been initiated in America in 2002. The design process started in the form of a competition within the Masters and Diploma [RIBA Part 2] design research studio ZCARS [Zero Carbon Architecture Research Studio], led by Michael Stacey with Swinal Samant and Lucelia Rodrigues, with input from Brian Ford and Mark Gillott. The strict spatial requirements of the competition were included in the ZCAR studio brief, as shown in Figure 2.14.8, alongside wider issues related to zero carbon housing. The ten tasks of the Solar Decathlon Competition are: Architecture, Engineering, Market Viability, Communications, Comfort, Appliances, Hot Water, Lighting, Energy Balance, Getting Around, thus, the title a Solar Decathlon. The students researched the issues influencing the proposed houses collectively from the demographics of European households through to how to achieve super insulation and comfort in all seasons. In particular, they studied and modelled the climate of middle England and the significantly hotter and generally dryer climate of Madrid, in central Spain. Environmental and tectonic strategies were provided to all students by the authors. It is at this stage that the use of passive downdraught evaporative cooling (PDEC), was proposed to cool the house in Madrid, based on previous collaborative EU funded research into this innovative technique, coordinated at the University of Nottingham. In essence, nesting a prototype cooling systems within a prototypical house. The ZCARS competition brief also specified prefabrication to minimise waste and to deliver quality in a short construction timescale. The energy targets were set as both Code for Sustainable Homes Level Six and Passivhaus Accreditation.

The ZCARS students competed in teams, typically of three. This internal competition was won with a design authored by Rachel Lee, Chris Dalton and Ben Hopkins; they tested the design as a group of houses in the Meadows Nottingham, Figure 2.14.5. The spatial arrangement of the winning proposal spoke of homely starter housing. On arrival at the Nottingham House one notices that entry to the front door is sheltered by the first floor above.

Fig. 2.14.5 Testing the Nottingham House design on a site in the Meadows Nottingham

Passing through the draft lobby – essential to minimise unwanted air changes - there is daylight and views to the courtyard. Turning left, observing that the house has been designed to Lifetime Homes Standards for accessibility, one enters the house passing the downstairs toilet, which also accommodates hot water storage created by the rooftop solar thermal panel. Passing the stair to the first floor you can either directly enter the kitchen or proceed to the dining room and onto the living room. The corner of the living room is glazed, providing ample daylight and views to both the courtyard and landscape or streetscape beyond. On returning to the dinning room one becomes aware that this is a double height space. This is the heart of the house both socially and environmentally. In essence it is a mini-atrium providing spatial and communication opportunities to the house as well as

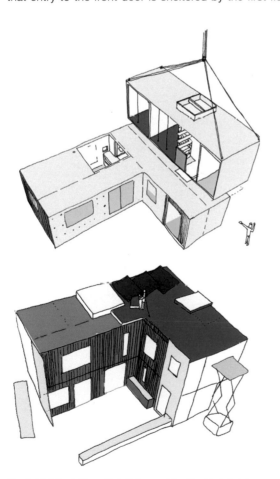

Fig. 2.14.4 Rachel Lee, Chris Dalton and Ben Hopkins' sketches of the Nottingham House

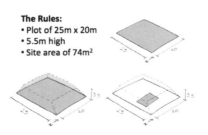

Fig. 2.14.6 The strict spatial requirements of the Solar Decathlon Competition

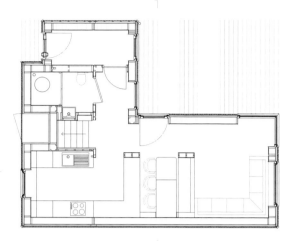

Fig. 2.14.7 Ground Floor Plan

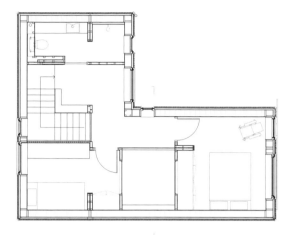

Fig. 2.14.8 First Floor Plan

stack ventilation. The kitchen is open to the dining room and is a modest and well appointed fitted kitchen, not unlike a twenty first century update of the fitted kitchens of AIROH post Second World War aluminium prefabs.[6] In the corner of the kitchen is a whole house heat recovery system, which remained exposed in the Solar Decathlon Competition for didactic reasons, Figure 2.14.9. The kitchen ceiling is a little lower to accommodate ducting primary in the kitchen, which is formed by bringing together Modules 1 and 4, see Figure 2.14.10. Fair face birch ply is used to delineate the spaces of the home. Ecophon, in a blood orange red, highlights the dining room wall and the staircase wall respectively, both vertical elements in the house design, whilst providing acoustic absorbency. As all other surfaces are hard including the bamboo floor. Bamboo was selected as it is fast growing and renewable. Stepping out to the courtyard here we find the homeowners are growing their own fruit and vegetables. The growing of edible plants was an important sub-theme of the Nottingham House, further contributing to reducing the carbon footprint of the family.

The walls of the stair to the first floor are fabricated from birch ply and one side has integrated bookshelves in the form of plywood niches. The top of the stair and the dinning space are guarded by clear toughened glass structural balustrades. To the left of the stair is the smaller bedroom for a child or guests; beyond the dining space, atrium, is the large bedroom, which can have a double bed, depending on the requirements of the homeowners. Back past the stairs the bathroom can be found, equipped with generous walk in shower rather than a bath. The floor area of the house is only 187m². A compact home in many ways reminiscent of a home designed by Sverre Fehn, except a hearth and a fireplace are missing.[7] The excellence of the students' design was recognised in a RIBA East Midlands Low Carbon Award, 2009, awarded before fabrication had commenced.

Fig. 2.14.9 The whole house heat recovery system is left exposed in the kitchen

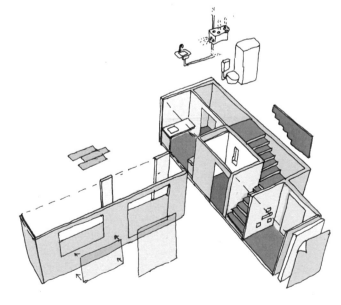

Fig. 2.14.10 The eight modules of the Nottingham House. The module that primarily contains the kitchen, No 1, is the most highly serviced module, incorporating the majority of services of the house

Nottingham House: Responsive Adaptation + Domestic Ecology

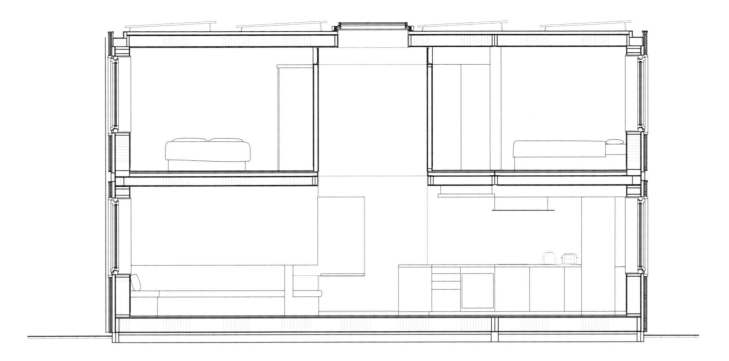

Fig. 2.14.11 Section A-A

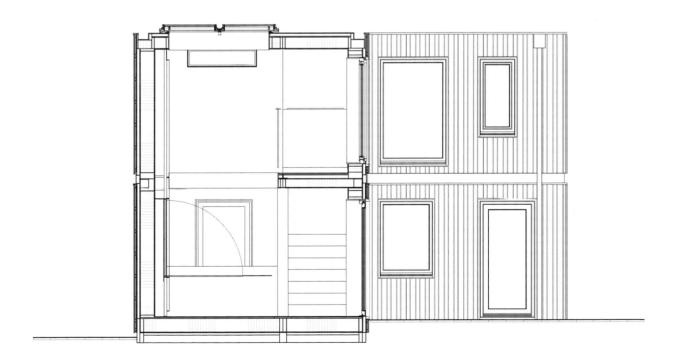

Fig. 2.14.12 Section B-B

Components of a Prototypical Home

The Nottingham House was designed from the outset as a fully prefabricated assembly. Thus the maximum transportable size was an important design constraint, however this was not allowed to dominate the internal domesticity. The house modules were fabricated and assembled by architecture students and staff at the University of Nottingham, coordinated by Mark Gillott. The primary sponsor of materials and components was Saint Gobain and its subsidiaries in the UK, without whom the project would not have been realised.[8] The final design comprised eight volumetric modules that were transported fully glazed with all services installed and fully finished internally, for final assembly on site in Madrid by a team of students and staff. The ground floor Module 1, which primarily forms the kitchen, is the most intensively serviced. The only services in most other modules are power and lighting, except where Module 5 and 6 come together to create the shower room. The modules are all open on one side and only form the enclosure of the house when all eight modules are in place.

In the original design cross-laminated timber [CLT] was selected as the primary structural material of these modules. However, at the time Saint Gobain did not have a company producing CLT panels within its organisation, therefore this was modified to prefabricated timber cassettes based on timber I-beams. This minimises the structure in the insulation zone. At very low U-values, say below 0.15 Wm^2/K, timber within the construction needs to be considered as cold bridge or a weakness in the thermal fabric. The module fabrication process was undertaken by the students in a former TV Studio (Carlton TV) on the Kings Meadow Campus, now owned by The University of Nottingham. The first process was setting out the geometry of each module and assembling the flat packed timber cassette panel system into volumetric units. In other site situations, the Nottingham House could be supplied flat packed and assembled on site. The wall cassettes comprise 245mm I-joists fully filled with glass wool insulation. Moisture protection and thermal continuity of the walls is provided by an outer layer of the 50mm glass wool [Isover RKL-Façade] which has a built in waterproof breather membrane. The house is insulated with glass wool, which has an 80% recycled glass content. To achieve air tightness the inner face of the wall structure is covered with a fully taped Vario KM duplex breather membrane that acts as a vapour check layer and can transpire into the interior. The taping up of the internal breather membrane was meticulously undertaken as this is key to achieving the low air infiltration rates necessary. The breather membrane is protected by a 12.5mm Rigidur lining. Rigidur is a dense gypsum fibreboard incorporating recycled paper. One advantage of Rigidur is that it comes in large format panels, up to 1200 by 3000mm, and in a factory set up for prefabrication rooms can be lined with no joints or the minimum of joints. The

Fig. 2.14.13 Sketch of the atrium at the heart of the Nottingham House

Fig. 2.14.14 The atrium at the heart of the Nottingham House

Fig. 2.14.15 Assembling the modules of the Nottingham House in the former Carlton Television Studio

Nottingham House: Responsive Adaptation + Domestic Ecology

floor cassettes have a similar construction, with 245mm I-joists and are finished with Bamboo Flooring, except in the shower room. The roof at Madrid achieved a U-value of 0.13 Wm^2/K based on 195mm I-joists, this was to fit within the competition height restriction, almost all of the entries to SDC are conceived as single storey pavilions. At Nottingham the roof construction has been up rated to a U-value below 0.1 Wm^2/K. The roof is weather proofed by a light grey single ply PVC membrane,[9] which is fully welded with PVC coated galvanised steel up stands to ensure continuity of sealing against the rain. This was well tested by the rain experienced in Madrid.

The walls of the Nottingham House are clad in 18mm thick ThermoWood® tongue and groove vertical weatherboarding. ThermoWood® is a process developed in Finland that enhances the properties of softwood by heating timber sections to 215°C and in particular improved durability against decay, better dimensional stability and reduced thermal conductivity, however the bending strength is slightly reduced with a lower splitting strength. This last quality was particularly apparent when cladding the Nottingham House modules and the holes for the stainless steel fixing screws had to be drilled in advance. The standard of workmanship for the timber cladding was established via an approved mock up, which was the first section of cladding on Module 2. Once all of the eight modules are assembled on site, the building fabric of the house is completed adding flush timber cladding to the vertical module interfaces and aluminium channels at first floor interface and copings at roof level. These are fabricated from 3mm aluminium and polyester powder coated dark grey. These sections were fabricated by Crown Aluminium and coated by Birmingham Powder Coatings: a division of Tomburn Limited. These sections and copings are secret fixed and articulate the prefabricated construction without emphasising the sense of the house as a stack of boxes. This is why the timber cladding runs through as a plane without articulation of the vertical module junction.

Fig. 2.14.17 Completing the timber cladding at the module joins in Madrid – note the aluminium channel has yet to be fitted

Fig. 2.14.18 The Nottingham House at Ecobuild

Fig. 2.14.16 Fixing the Solar Panels in the rain of Madrid

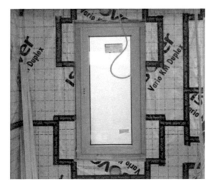

Fig. 2.14.19 The Vario KM duplex breather was very carefully taped to achieve the required airtightness

Module	Length (mm)	Width (mm)	Height (mm)	ULW
1	7672	2679	2743	6.12 tonnes
2	3621	1669	2743	2.04 tonnes
3	6848	1529	2743	2.55 tonnes
4	6848	2651	2743	4.59 tonnes
5	7710	2698	2551	5.10 tonnes
6*	3640	1688	2701	1.53 tonnes
7	6867	1548	2551	2.55 tonnes
8**	6867	2670	2701	4.08 tonnes

Note: Module equipped with: *Services inlet and **roof light
Table 2.14.1 module sizes and design weights

Fig. 2.14.20 Aluminium timber triple glazed windows manufactured by Hermann Gutmann Werke

The weights of the modules are shown in Table 2.14.1. Ranging from just over 2 tonnes to over 6 tonnes. Thus, once assembled the modules had to be very carefully handled by the use of a forklift truck, and on wheeled dollies. In order to crane the modules onto flat bed trucks for transportation and into position on site a bespoke steel lifting boom was designed by the consultant engineers Dewhurst Macfarlane. Before this could be used it had to be load test certified and approved. This steel-lifting boom could be adjusted to accommodate the diverse dimensions of the eight modules.

Aluminium plays a vital role in the assembly of the Nottingham House, in part, based on Michael Stacey's more than 30-year experience from research and practice in the use of aluminium in component based construction.[10] Stock aluminium angles have been used to create contemporary interpretations of skirting boards and architraves. Stock aluminium angles and channels also support structural glass balustrades. It is surprising that stock aluminium sections are still predominately sold in the UK in imperial sizes, suggesting that some of the dies are over 40 years old. Brackets made of three stock aluminium angles, expertly welded by Faculty of Engineering Technicians, support the corners of the ThermoWood timber cladding; the idea that aluminium is difficult to weld is 'history'. Although the aluminium is conductive it is only 3mm thick. The essence of this detail is to minimise the material in the insulation zone bridging between the structure and the cladding.

The windows of the house are triple glazed achieving a U-value of 0.5 Wm^2/K provided by 36mm thick units, comprising three layers of 4mm toughened glass with low emissivity coatings on surfaces 3 and 5, combined with 90% Krypton filled cavities. The window profiles are a combination of timber with insulated inserts, pultruded thermal breaks and polyester powder coated aluminium outer sections, manufactured in Germany by Hermann Gutmann Werke but fabricated in Derbyshire. On completion the windows, equipped with triple glazed low emissivity glazing units, proved to be very heavy. The largest window for the living room on the ground floor required three people to carry and install it. Apart from the fact that these window sections are bulky, they potentially represent the material future of architecture, with each material playing a distinct role; the timber safely in the warm dry interior capturing CO_2, the insulation ensuring that the low U-value is achieved, the pultrusion stops thermal loss through the frame and the aluminium retains the triple glazing and provides a guaranteed low maintenance finish via polyester powder coating.[11] All the external aluminium sections, including the window sections on the Nottingham House, are polyester powder coated a warm grey colour, Ral 7022. The house is completed by aluminium rainwater hoppers and downpipes, supplied by Marley Alutec and press braked 3mm aluminium copings and flashings, manufactured by Crown Aluminium and polyester powder coated by Birmingham Powder Coaters.

Fig. 2.14.21 Craning a prefabricated module onto a truck back at Nottingham with Director of Nottingham's Live Projects Office, architect and Lecturer in Tectonics, John Ramsay

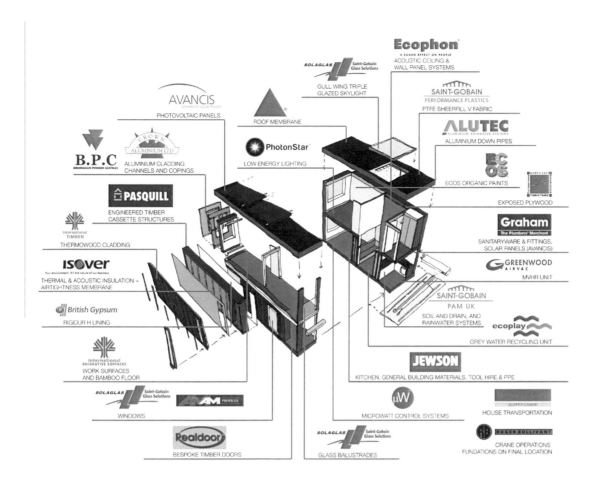

Fig. 2.14.22 Diagram of suppliers and sponsors of the Nottingham House

Reflecting on prefabricating and procurement of the Nottingham House

The prefabrication of the Nottingham House was demonstrated by assembling it at Ecobuild in March 2010. The house was fabricated in eight weeks, assembled at Ecobuild in 4 days and disassembled in 2 days, then returned to Nottingham. In June it was transported to Madrid and re-assembled for the Solar Decathlon Competition. It was then disassembled and returned to Nottingham, where it has now been re-assembled in its final location at the University Park, Nottingham. Once tested in use, for its first year of occupancy, it is anticipated to be the world's first fully prefabricated zero carbon house.[12] When the Nottingham House reaches the end of its useful life, it can be readily disassembled and recycled.

Jean Prouvé thought that 'when an architect has made his choice he must build immediately at college, which will have been transformed into a factory or a practice'.[13] This is a principle implemented at Nottingham School of Architecture,

as demonstrated by the Nottingham House and the design and construction of two schools in South Africa. A Prototyping Hall within the School has now been completed, September 2012, which will provide a permanent home for research and testing of full-scale prototypes and for our Live Projects Office.

The Nottingham House was designed and built more in the manner of Isambard Kingdom Brunel than a contemporary Design and Build Contactor working to an architect's initial design. Thus, the Nottingham House Team had all the advantages of making decisions swiftly and implementing them directly. However, we lacked a Main Contractor and its team who tend to act as a point of focus for the realisation of a project. The Nottingham House Team has a similar diversity to the Supply Chain; see the comparative diagrams in Figures 2.14.23 and 2.14.24. Contractually the procurement process was more like partnering than conventional design and build, avoiding the confrontational aspect of construction that bedevils many forms of constructional contact. Both the Thames Water Tower and Ballingdon Bridge, by Michael Stacey's practice, were successfully built using partnering. This encourages close cooperation and collaboration with the supply chain and specialists within industry.

In Madrid the Nottingham House was re-assembled and underwent the ten tests of the Solar Decathlon Completion ranging from cooking for ones neighbours using only solar power to the architectural merit of the project. The competition menu was written by Sat Bains, Nottingham's Two Michelin Star Chief, who also trained the student cooks.[14]

The ten contests of the Solar Decathlon 2010 were:

- Architecture (120);

- Engineering and Construction (80);

- Solar Systems and Hot Water (80);

- Energy Balance (120);

- Comfort Conditions (120);

- Appliances and Functionality (120)

- Communication and Social Awareness (80);

- Industrialisation and Market Viability (80);

- Innovation (80);

- Sustainability (120).

Potential maximum scope 1000 points, with some categories judged by the completion jury, for example *Architecture* and some simply by measurement, such as *Comfort Conditions*.

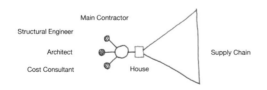

Fig. 2.14.23 A Conventional Architect Led House Building Construction Contract

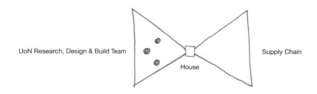

Fig. 2.14.24 The Nottingham House Partnering Contract

Fig. 2.14.25 Ballingdon Bridge designed by Michael Stacey Architects

Nottingham House Menu

Pre-Starter	English green gazpacho
Starter	Ham - egg - peas
Main course	Pork belly - peach - chorizo
Pre-Dessert	Raspberry - ricotta - granola
Dessert	Rhubarb - meringue - elderflower

Fig. 2.14.26 Solar Decathlon Dinner Party Menu written by Sat Bains

Starter   Ham - Egg - Peas

Primary Ingredients:

        10 duck eggs
        500g fresh peas blanched in salted water and
        refreshed
        10 slices of wafer thin toasted sourdough
        10 slices bellota ham
        200g pea shoots
        500g emulsion (250g butter - 250g - water - salt)

Ingredients for the sorbet:

        500g frozen Birds Eye peas
        500g 22% stock syrup
        Salt
        8 fresh mint leaves [from courtyard]

Preparation:

        Blitz all the ingredients of the sorbet together
        and pass, place in a Pacojet container and freeze,
        blitz twice just before serving.

Method:

        Poach the duck eggs in the shell at 62oc
        for 2 hours.
        Warm the peas up in the emulsion and
        spoon into the bowls.
        Crack open the eggs, season and place on
        top of the peas.
        Top with the ham, followed by the toast
        and the pea shoots.
        Place the sorbet next to the egg and
        serve.

Fig. 2.14.27 Sat Bains' recipe for the Starter: Ham - Egg - Peas

In Madrid, despite torrential rain that flooded our site, the Nottingham House was assembled in 11 days. What was billed as a new public park over a newly sunken urban highway, adjacent to the Palacia Real on the banks of the Rio Manzanares and designed by West 8, on arrival proved to be an un-landscaped building site, which soon became very muddy. After the competition the house was disassembled ready for transportation back to England in 2 days.

Pedagogical benefits of designing and assembling the house

The research, design and construction of the Nottingham House had a wide range of pedagogical benefits, at all stages of the process. From familiarisation with Codes and Standards, this included an understanding of the weakness inherent in Code for Sustainable Homes, in SAP and Passivhaus Standards. All Environmental Assessment Tools have the inherent weakness of encouraging the accumulation of points for specific acts of specification, for example within Code for Sustainable Homes, one point is available for specifying an external security light. The greatest weakness of Code for Sustainable Homes is its tendency to swap between performance and perception. Why does it state how big a bath should be? Code for Sustainable Homes is also very dependent of SAP and this software does not appear to truly reflect the overall performance and energy balance of windows. If architects and engineers are not very careful it can lead to houses with unnecessarily dark interiors that are dependent on artificial light and thus consuming more, not less, energy. The trap built into in Passivhaus Standards is the need to use Passivhaus accredited components; in essence it acts as a hub monopoly. Arguably Passivhaus is not well suited to the relatively temperate maritime climate of the United Kingdom. Both standards would be better if based on first principles and evidence based research providing architects and engineers with options to work with rather than restrictive prescriptions.

The Nottingham House combines pedagogical benefits for the student architects, at a range of levels from the design team of Rachel Lee, Chris Dalton and Ben Hopkins who saw the project through to completion during their sixth year of studying architecture, to the second year students who were the labour force. For a student of architecture it can often be very difficult to gain on-site experience, something that is key to the development of an architect. For those students involved in the Nottingham House however, they were able to not only get experience of observing site issues, but were able to understand and take part in the process of building.

This group gained extremely useful exposure to contemporary and cutting edge techniques in the realisation of low carbon architecture and the direct benefits of learning by doing. Exposure to state of the art products, most not made in Britain,

for example the Isover insulation and plastic spacers were imported from Finland. The second year students although mostly assemblers learnt a range of skills, from the realities, rather than the theory of Health and Safety, to the importance of teamwork and some quite sophisticated contemporary craft skills. The student designers spent three quarters of their RIBA Part 2 studies research, designing and realising a house design. Such reification is rare in Architectural Education, noting that globally there is now a nascent Live Projects movement in Schools of Architecture.

For Ben Hopkins 'the experience of building off a set of your own drawings was incredibly educational, both in terms of detailing and producing construction information. It also highlighted the strength of a collaborative and integrated team, and what was required of everyone to make that work. For some of the students involved, the experience has opened their eyes to new ways of applying their skills, with some moving into construction management and services design.'[15] He also observed 'it is very easy to forget the design behind the realised product. For the

Fig. 2.14.28 The sandy site of Solar Decathlon 2010 – the future Rio Parque, Madrid, before the rain started to pour.

easy to forget the design behind the realised product. For the designers involved in the project it was an intense educational experience, forcing each member to become experts in modular construction, transportation, sustainable design and all of the other factors that were required to develop the design for the Nottingham House. The design team also had access to world experts in their fields as consultants, as well as very close communication with the manufacturers and suppliers, which has further developed skills needed to work in the modern construction sector.'[16]

PDEC and The Nottingham House: Madrid Summer 2010

In hot dry climates, as found in southern Europe, the house is cooled by a Passive Downdraught Evaporative Cooling (PDEC) system, developed by Professor Brian Ford in collaboration with the Spanish company Ingeniatrics-Frialia. The core of this technique is adiabatic cooling from finely misted water linked to a gull wind roof light operated by electrical actuators. The tiny water jet nozzles were developed by Ingeniatrics-Frialia and the system was designed and tested by the University of Nottingham.

The specific research aim for the PDEC Prototype within the Nottingham House was to establish whether thermal comfort could be achieved and what the energy balance or coefficient of performance (CoP) would be, as part of a search for alternatives to conventional air-conditioning. The demand for air-conditioning for housing is increasing in Southern Europe, and is set to double by 2020.[17] This will impact on demands for electrical energy and the use of environmentally harmful refrigerants. There is, therefore, an urgent need to seek energy-efficient, environmentally benign and cost-competitive alternatives to conventional air-conditioning. PDEC is one such technique. Previous research has found down-draught cooling to be an energy-efficient and cost-effective alternative to conventional air-conditioning for new and existing non-domestic buildings.[18] Much of the evidence for this is based on post-occupancy performance evaluation of non-domestic buildings.[19] The evaluation of potential benefits in the residential sector has so far been limited by the lack of applications in practice. The research presented here seeks to address this gap.

In the context of rapidly rising demand for conventional air-conditioning in housing in Europe, downdraught cooling represents a potentially significant alternative to meet the cooling demand, while also reducing carbon emissions. Downdraught cooling relies on the effect of gravity on a body of (relatively) cold air, to create a downdraught, and thus circulate air from the source of cooling to the occupied zone within the building. The source of the cool air can be either passive or active. A passive downdraught can be achieved through the evaporation

Fig. 2.14.29 Rachel Lee, Chris Dalton and Ben Hopkins with second year Vicky 'the project manger' in the rain of Spain

of water within an air stream. PDEC is only appropriate in hot, dry conditions (wet bulb temperature < 24°C).[20] In Southern Europe previous research has demonstrated that PDEC can meet 25 – 85% of the cooling load of non-domestic buildings (equivalent to 15 – 60 kWh/m²/year).[21] In residential buildings PDEC can potentially provide thermal comfort without the need for additional mechanical assistance, although this will vary in relation to the external wet bulb temperature.[22]

In warm and humid conditions active downdraught cooling can be achieved by using chilled water cooling coils or panels. Although this relies on mechanical cooling, it avoids the need for fans, which can represent an energy saving of 25 – 35% of the electrical load in a non-domestic building. This approach also avoids the need for either bulky fan-coil units or air-handling units and related ductwork. While there is a risk of condensation on the coils, the on-coil water temperature can be set to be slightly above the dew-point. Also, any condensation can be collected in a drip tray.

A hybrid downdraught cooling system combines both passive and active downdraught cooling techniques.[23] Such a system can function in both hot and dry conditions, using PDEC, and warm and humid conditions, using chilled water-cooling coils. Conventional cooling systems use fans to drive the airflow to the occupied zones of a building. Downdraught cooling systems differ in that the primary mechanism for the distribution of cool air is either by buoyancy or by wind-assisted natural ventilation. This means that both energy costs and capital costs can be significantly reduced.[24] A wide range of building types are amenable to the integration of downdraught cooling systems, including commercial and industrial, residential, educational, health, and large-volume buildings such as transport interchanges. Downdraught cooling has been applied to buildings in many parts of the world and assessments have been made of its applicability to existing commercial and residential buildings in Europe, India and China.[25]

A study of the application of PDEC to existing commercial buildings in Southern Europe revealed that PDEC is applicable to potentially 70% of this stock, saving 3.7 – 5.7 million tonnes of carbon per year.[26] Analysis of applicability to the housing stock in Spain, Portugal, Italy and Greece has shown that the residential market for PDEC is even larger, with potential annual savings of 19 – 38 million tonnes of carbon per year.[27] However, prior to this project, residential applications had not been demonstrated in Europe. Typically the capital cost of a PDEC/hybrid cooling system for non-domestic buildings is comparable in cost with comfort cooling, whereas full air-conditioning is significantly more expensive. Expressed as a percentage of new-build costs, PDEC is in the order of 4 – 12% compared with 19 – 23% for centralised air-conditioning installations. Detailed life cycle cost analysis for Europe, China and India indicate that passive and hybrid downdraught cooling has significant life cycle cost benefits, typically providing a return on investment within a few years, two to five years in India; five to 15 years in Europe.[28]

A recent global review of research and practice in the application of downdraught cooling has shown that it is technically and economically viable in many parts of the world, but to date has largely been applied to non-domestic buildings. However, the same study has shown that the potential market for applying these techniques to residential buildings is even larger than for the non-domestic sector. This chapter reviews the first residential application of PDEC in Europe.[29]

Participation in the Solar Decathlon Competition provided an opportunity to explore the contribution PDEC can make to providing summer-time occupant comfort in a high-performance house as part of a broader passive environmental strategy. The house was erected and tested in Madrid in June as part of the SDE competition and exhibition. The PDEC System in the house was evaluated for the week of the competition in Madrid (19 – 26 June 2010).

The house utilises PDEC to maintain comfort temperatures during the summer season in Madrid, Figure 2.14.33. Nozzles positioned at the top of the double-height space generate a mist of water that evaporates in warm external air drawn through the roof light, Figure 2.14.36. Evaporation of the water cools the air, generating a plume that drops into the dining area and then divides, part flowing through the living room and exiting via a window on the

south wall. The remainder flows through the kitchen, absorbing heat from any appliances that are operating and exiting via a window in the north wall. Operation of the system, including automatic actuators attached to the windows and roof-light, were designed to respond to measurements of external and internal temperature and humidity via a control system. Unfortunately, it was not possible to complete the installation of the roof-light actuators and wiring, or the PDEC control system, in time for the start of the competition on the 18 June. The PDEC system was therefore controlled manually, with the occupants increasing or reducing the rate of cooling according to their perception of how warm they felt. Ventilation was therefore entirely driven by natural forces (buoyancy and wind), and was not augmented by mechanical extract from the kitchen.

The system makes use of a novel nozzle design, by Ingeniatrics-Frialia, of Seville, Spain (www.frialia.com), that combines the motive energy from a pressurised water circuit with a compressed air flow, Figure 2.14.28. This provides the desired level of atomisation of the water flow and avoids the creation of drips when the nozzles start and stop. The system requires energy to drive a pump and small air compressors, to run an ultraviolet water treatment cell, and to operate the window controls. Peak power requirement is approximately 700 W, but this varies with the number of nozzles in operation. There are eight nozzles and peak water consumption is 8 litres/h if run continuously. To run the system for an average of 5 h/day would therefore require 40 litres of water and 3.5 kWh of electricity. The system is therefore not entirely passive in operation.

Seasonal strategies: the house is designed to operate under three distinct seasonal modes, which are based on an analysis of the climate data for Madrid. Summer: during the hot, dry summers in Madrid, maximum daily temperatures can frequently be above 35°C. The protection of glazed openings from the high direct solar radiation is essential. Night-time temperatures

Fig. 2.14.30 The Nottingham House almost complete on site in Madrid

can drop below 20°C, providing an opportunity for convective cooling to be exploited. During the day, PDEC may potentially achieve thermal comfort most of the time, provided that solar heat gains can be minimised and there is sufficient thermal capacitance to stabilise temperatures internally. Plotting data for Madrid on a psychrometric chart, Figure 2.14.35, reveals that during the summer period thermal comfort may be achievable by evaporative cooling alone, even with dry bulb air temperatures above 35°C. This is because the external air is so dry typically below 30% relative humidity in the afternoon. At night, convective cooling will be achieved by promoting buoyancy-driven natural ventilation, pre-cooling the interior before sunrise the next day, Figure 2.14.36.

The shading of exposed perimeter openings is provided by a woven stainless steel mesh, keeping high altitude summer sun out whilst allowing low altitude winter sun to penetrate. Solar gains are also minimised by the high-performance envelope (U-value of roof 0.13 W/m² K, U-value of walls 0.1 W/m² K). Infiltration heat gains are minimised by reasonably 'air-tight' construction and by providing a lobby 'airlock' entrance. Solar gains are further reduced by using the photovoltaic panels to shade the roof, and therefore reduce roof surface temperatures. It was postulated that this combination of strategies would remove the need for conventional cooling. The results of subsequent monitoring are discussed below.

Autumn and spring: During autumn and spring, mild external temperatures, mean external temperatures of 15 – 16°C in May and October will potentially allow the internal air temperature to be brought within the comfort zone by controlling the rate of natural ventilation. Occupant control of window openings should enable the regulation of natural ventilation to remove any heat gains during the day, while set to 'trickle' ventilation at night to provide minimum fresh air. On warm days, evaporative

cooling may be required occasionally, although due to the short monitoring period this has not been evaluated as part of this study.

Winter can be cool, with temperatures rarely dropping below freezing, and generally rising above 10°C during the day. The high-performance envelope will minimise fabric heat losses, and a combination of fabric air tightness and the provision of a lobby 'airlock' will minimise infiltration heat losses. Most of the glazed openings (53%) are oriented to the south to capitalise on the significant potential for beneficial passive solar gains. The combination of passive solar gain and internal heat gains coupled with a high-performance building envelope are likely to reduce the residual heating requirement to well below 15 kWh/m², the Passivhaus standard for heating energy. Top-up heating for this residual heating load will be provided by a ground source heat pump arranged to preheat ventilation supply air.

Testing and monitoring methodology: in order to establish the feasibility of applying PDEC to the Nottingham House, a prototype was constructed and tested during the summer of 2009 at the University of Seville in collaboration with Asociació n para la Investigació n y Cooperació n Industrial de Andalucí a (AICIA) and Frialia. The objective was to characterise the performance of the prototype and to establish its applicability in the climate of Madrid. Additionally, in order to establish the airflow characteristics of the house, computational fluid dynamics (CFD) analysis was also undertaken by AICIA. For details of the prototype, the test results and CFD analysis carried out by AICIA.[30]

The final-version PEDC Prototype, as built in the house, has eight misting nozzles located at a high level within the central atrium. These misting nozzles generate evaporatively cooled air into the central double-height space, which in turn promotes the air flow to first-floor bedrooms and to the ground floor, from where it is

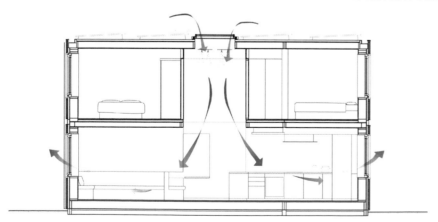

Fig. 2.14.31 Section A-A during a Madrid summer day

Fig. 2.14.32 Four PEDC nozzles in the top of the atrium of the Nottingham House

Nottingham House: Responsive Adaptation + Domestic Ecology

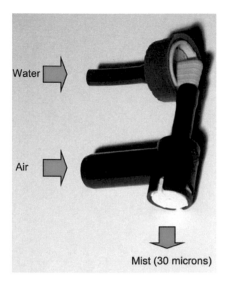

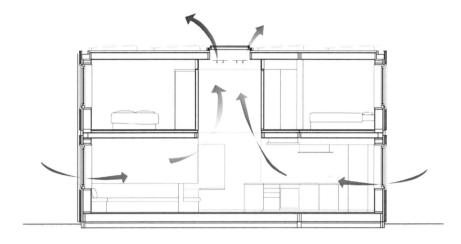

Fig. 2.14.33 Atomising PEDC nozzles designed by Ingeniatrics-Frialia

Fig. 2.14.35 Section A-A showing summer night-time air flow

exhausted via window vents at the perimeter. The nozzles can be switched on or off in pairs, enabling the system to respond to changes in temperature and humidity. The system is made from widely available components, and demonstrates an affordable alternative to conventional air-conditioning. In order to assist with the operation of the PDEC system, and to gather data relating both to its performance and to the performance of the house as a whole, five synchronised Tinytag data loggers instrumented with dry bulb and relative humidity sensors were used. These were set to record every 60 seconds and were located inside in the living room, kitchen and bedrooms. The external sensors were located beneath the photovoltaic (PV) modules on the roof to shade them from direct solar radiation. The back of the PV modules have a silvered surface creating a ventilated low-emissivity environment. The results from the Tinytag data loggers are shown in Figures 2.14.37 – 2.14.40.

Preliminary results - Monitored data: the installation of the PDEC pipework and nozzle array, compressor, hydraulic and electrical cabinets was completed and tested in the Nottingham House in

Madrid on 16 June 2010. Logging of dry-bulb air temperature and relative humidity in three locations in the house and externally (in the shade), ran from 2pm on 19 June to 5pm on 28 June. During this period the weather became warmer than it had during the construction phase of the competition. The external daily maximum shade air temperature rose from 30°C on 20 June to 44°C on 24 June.

During this whole period, in the absence of an automatic control system, a decision was made to keep window and roof-light openings open 24 hours a day to promote night-time convective cooling and to allow ventilation during the day. In spite of the fact that control of the PDEC system was therefore very simple, the record of logged temperature and relative humidity demonstrates that comfortable conditions were obtained for much of the time, Figure 2.14.37. The data also indicated that there was an opportunity for the PDEC system to reduce temperatures further at other times if the Solar Decathlon Competition rules had permitted it to be operated for longer periods during the day. The high-performance building fabric, the triple-glazed windows and the care taken to minimise solar heat gains all have a major impact on reducing the risk of overheating. It may also be the case that the use of high-density Gyproc Rigidur panels internally contributes to stabilising internal temperatures in what is essentially a lightweight building.

It is interesting to note that there is an approximate 4 hour time-lag between the peak external air temperature, about 2pm, and the peak internal air temperature, about 6pm, which reflects the thermal characteristics of the building envelope. However, it is also evident that without the PDEC system internal air temperatures would have risen well outside internal comfort conditions. From the recorded data it can be observed that when the PDEC system was activated, it promoted a rapid reduction in

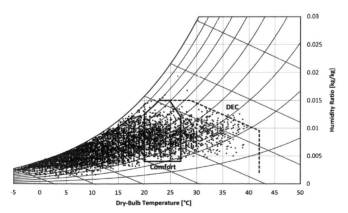

Fig. 2.14.34 Psychrometric chart showing annual hourly average climate data for Madrid, with Givoni's (1994) boundaries for comfort and direct evaporative cooling

temperature within the house. This can be seen particularly well on 22 June, when PDEC was operational after about 2.30pm for approximately 15 minute intervals until about 9pm, maintaining the living room temperature at or below 26°C when the external temp was 38 – 40°C.

For the next two days the external air temperature rose well above 40°C and the impact of switching the PDEC system on and off became even more pronounced. On 23 June, Figure 2.14.38, the PDEC system was not switched on until 1pm, by which time the internal temperature had risen to 27.5°C. With intermittent operation of the nozzles between 1pm and 3pm, the nozzles were on for about 50% of the time, the internal temperature was stabilised, and after 3pm when nozzles were left on continuously, the living room temperature dropped below 26°C, while measured external shade air temperature was about 40°C. When the system was switched off again for the evening public visit (5pm – 9pm), the living room temperature can be seen to rise again, until a peak of 28°C is reached at 8pm. Had the PDEC system been run consistently, and if the house had not had to cope with large numbers of visitors, it is likely it would have held the temperature below 26°C all day. It can be concluded that in a typical house the evaporative system could run until 8pm keeping the indoor temperature below 26°C. The ideal switch-off hour is thus when in door temperature is equal to outdoor temperature. It is important to note that during these extremely hot, dry days, the internal relative humidity did not rise above 65% during the day, and much of the time it was below 50% indicating potential for further evaporative cooling, Figure 2.14.37.

It is also interesting to note that while it was anticipated that the PDEC system would primarily serve the ground floor, the temperature and relative humidity in the main bedroom followed the pattern in the living room fairly closely, and there was not the level of stratification that had been anticipated. This may be because cool air was being caught by the balcony and passed through the open door of the main bedroom, before exhausting

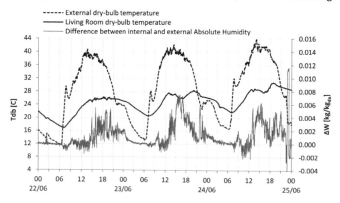

Figure 2.14.36 Internal (living room) and external dry bulb and wet bulb temperatures, 22-24 June 2010, for the Nottingham House, Madrid

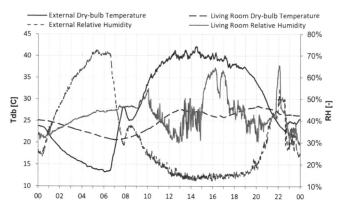

Figure 2.14.37 Internal and external dry bulb temperature and relative humidity, 23 June 2010, for the Nottingham House, Madrid

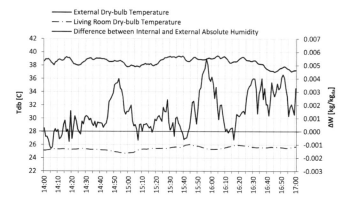

Figure 2.14.38 Measured dry bulb and absolute humidity during the operating period of the PDEC system on 22 June 2010

via the open bedroom window. Operation of the PDEC system took place within the context of the SDE competition and was dictated by two differing requirements. Part of the competition was judged on the ability of the house to maintain a time-averaged internal temperature between 23°C and 25°C, for which PDEC was the sole active strategy used. The other requirement was the energy balance of the house, which was judged on surplus PV generated electricity, and which was impacted negatively by operation of the PDEC system.

It is important to observe that the house provided significant protection from the extreme daytime conditions prevailing outside, most of this through passive means alone. The combination of solar protection (both against direct gains through glazing and indirect gains through the fabric), the heavily insulated envelope, the presence of thermally heavyweight internal finishes and opening the building up to utilise night cooling served to limit temperature rises within the space. This also meant that the need to use the PDEC system to control excessive temperature rises was limited and the period of operation was commensurately small. A schematic of the assumed psychrometric process for PDEC operation is shown in Figure 2.14.40, while Figure 2.14.39 shows the data collected during the operation period on 22

June. Rises in the internal absolute humidity of the ground floor living area can be observed when the system was switched on and depressions in the internal dry bulb temperature can be seen to occur in response. For a detailed analysis of the results of the testing of the PEDC Prototyping in the Nottingham House at the Solar Decathlon Completion please see Passive downdraught evaporative cooling: performance in a prototype house.[31]

Occupants' response: during the course of the competition week students were tasked with guiding visitors around the house, and responding to their questions. Although limited to a maximum of six people at any one time, the students on duty were rotated and so over the week about 30 students, staff and observers spent extended periods of time in the house and experienced the PDEC system operating. Visitors' comments were broadly favourable: "Overall I was really impressed by the system. It's difficult to say how it could be improved as it wasn't operating fully and the manual control and filling of the tank did hinder its performance. However, when it was switched on, its effects were instant, even from parts of the house I didn't expect to feel it, and it seemed to do an excellent job at lowering the temperature of the entire house."[32]

Nearly everyone agreed that the least satisfactory aspect of the PDEC system was the noise from the nozzles. There was a very noticeable hissing induced by the compressed air. One of the students commented: "If the nozzles could be far quieter and less of an eyesore then I think it could be more successful. Noise from the nozzles definitely needs to be addressed, as at its present level it would probably inhibit take-up of the system."[33]

Evaluation of the PEDC Prototype

Measured data from the Nottingham House during the competition week of the Solar Decathlon in Madrid (19 – 27 June 2010) demonstrate that the combination of a high-performance building envelope, night-time convective cooling and PDEC can deliver comfortable conditions throughout the house, even when maximum external temperatures exceed 35°C. The data also indicated that there was significant potential for further evaporative cooling, and that this is most likely to be achieved by automatic control of the misting system. Three main factors limit the period of potential over-heating to the late afternoon and early evening when PDEC is operated:

- Very low U-values (≤ 0.1 W/m² K) and effective shading to all openings minimise external heat gains.

- Night-time convective cooling contributes to low internal start temperatures each morning (20 – 22°C).

- The observed time lag between peak external and internal temperatures of 3 – 6 h. This may be due in part to the use of high-density gypsum fibreboard (Rigidur) panels internally.

The operation of the nozzles is very effective in limiting any further rise in internal air temperature, which is kept within acceptable limits throughout the house, except for 1 to 2 hours at the hottest time of day. At times the internal temperature was 16°C below external dry bulb air temperature. Such a significant temperature depression can only be achieved by evaporative cooling when the external wet bulb temperature is extremely low. There is no significant stratification within the house, which may be ascribed to the effect of the internal 'balcony' catching and directing the cooled air into the bedrooms. The requirements of the competition limited the overall height of the house, which meant that a supply air tower could not be included. However, results from the week of the competition suggest that the absence of an inlet tower is no impediment to the successful integration of a PDEC system within a two-storey house. In spite of this very favourable result, the addition of an inlet tower could improve control over the supply air, and potentially increase air volume flow rate, and thus effective cooling. It might also simplify access for maintenance.

While manual control is clearly a viable option, this requires close occupant involvement and it is likely that performance would have improved had automated control of nozzles and window actuators been operational. This would require the monitoring of both internal and external temperatures and relative humidities as well as wind speed and direction. The latter would assist in avoiding stack reversal when wind pressures are unfavourable. Noise from the nozzles was regarded as unsatisfactory by many of the student occupants. This is one of a number of product development issues that need to be addressed. There is also potential to improve the CoP of the system through the use of variable speed compressors or an air receiver to avoid the stepped response of the present design. This may be further refined by controlling the water supply down to the level of individual nozzles, rather than pairs of nozzles as in the present design.

While the data set is limited, these results suggest that PDEC can provide a viable alternative to conventional air-conditioning

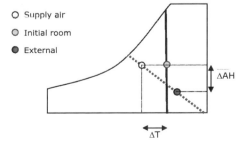

Figure 2.14.39 Schematic of the assumed psychrometric process for PDEC operation

for housing in central and southern Spain, and in other hot, dry regions of the world. Although the system components are widely available and competitive with conventional cooling systems, take-up in the residential sector will require further product development if it is to be successful. Take up for residential applications is also likely to be slow until more systems have been installed. Our Design and Research Team is seeking the application of this approach to a demonstration house, new build or existing) with an occupant family to determine occupant reaction to PDEC over a cooling season.

Conclusion

The house requires no conventional heating as it has a building fabric with a U-value below 0.1W/m²K and triple glazed windows with a U-value of 0.5 W/m²K. It has been re-assembled on University Park in Nottingham as a permanent home that achieves Code for Sustainable Homes Level 6, and is currently undergoing Passivhaus accreditation. The Nottingham House has been designed as a family home with an inviting spatial quality and inventive details. Further, it has been designed as a response to the poor quality production of current mass house builders. It represents an achievable 'zero carbon' home in the context of the current debate about definitions of 'zero-carbon' and the UK Government's commitment to this being mandatory for all homes in Britain by 2016. In essence, the Nottingham House is a prototype built of bespoke elements and components many of which are not yet currently available in the UK. Throughout the project there was a conflict between an essentially experimental construction and absolute deadlines. The opening dates for Ecobuild and Solar Decathlon were finite and non negotiable. Thus, time was of the essence - a constraint that the construction industry eschews for good reason, unless it is essential for the client or build typology.

The Nottingham House Design and Research Team is working on the market viability of the constructional system that has been designed to create homes in climatic conditions throughout Europe. The UK Government's Housing Minister John Healey MP on visiting the Nottingham House at Ecobuild observed, " I think it is priceless. It is a demonstration of new ideas and how they can be put into practice ... in the long term we need to build to this standard, across the board".[34]

The Nottingham House is a situated domestic ecology that fulfils Feenberg's recommendation to design to create appropriatable technology.[35] Almost nothing is more important in peoples' lives than their home and home life. In the twenty first century we have the technology and knowledge to construct a much higher standard of housing, which delights and serves humanity well.

Nottingham HOUSE Project

Client, Constructors and Researchers: Department of Architecture & Built Environment [ABE], **Consultant Architect:** Marsh Grochowski Architects, **Consultant Engineer:** Dewhurst Macfarlane and Partners, and **Principle Sponsor:** Saint-Gobain [Isover]. **ABE Research, Design and Assembly Team:** Mark Gillott: Project Director, Brian Ford: Environmental Design, Guillermo Guzman Dumont: Communications, John Ramsay: Assembly Coordination, Lucelia Rodrigues: Interiors, Michael Stacey: Tectonics and Assembly, and Robin Wilson: Mechanical and Electrical Services. Chris Dalton, Ben Hopkins and Rachel Lee: Designers [RIBA Part 2 Students], with assembly primarily by BArch/MEng, Second/Third Year RIBA Part1/CIBSE Students.

Notes

1   Exhibited at Prototyping Architecture, Nottingham

2   For further information on PEDC see Brian Ford et al eds., The Architecture & Engineering of Downdraft Cooling: A Design Sourcebook, PHDC Press, 2010.
     [move notes to the end of the chapter]

3   Professor of Architecture and Design through Production The Bartlett School of Architecture, UCL

4   Nottingham HOUSE (Home Optimising the Use of Solar Energy)

5   Robert Stern - The Economics of Climate Change: The Stern Review, 2007, Cambridge University Press. The Stern Review was published by the UK Government in 2006, this reference provides the paperback book of this review, as a stable source.

6   AIROH [Aircraft Industries Research Organisation on Housing], 1944, re-assembled at Museum of Welsh Life - St Fagan's, near Cardiff. For more information please see Michael Stacey, Aluminium Pioneers, Cwningen Press, 2013

7   See P. Fjeld, Sverre Fehn: The Pattern of Thoughts, Monacelli Press, 2009 or I. Helsing Almaas, [Ed.] Sverre Fehn: Projects and reflections, Arkitektur N., 2009

8   For the full project credits please see the end of the chapter, just before these endnotes.

9   This single ply PVC membrane supply by Sarnafil is fully recyclable.

10   Future Builds with Aluminium, Case Studies curated and written by Michael Stacey see http://greenbuilding.world-aluminium.org/en/home.html

11   40year guarantees are available on Super Durable grades of Polyester Powder Coating, underwritten by extensive testing.

12   Depending on these results the house may prove to be carbon natural, but not capable of reclaiming its own embodied energy in the short term. The testing will establish whether the Nottingham House is Low Carbon or Zero Carbon Home.

13   Jean Prouvé, [Ed. Huber B. and Steinegger J-C.] Jean Prouvé, Artermis, 1971, p173

14   The full menu was included in the Project Specification, please see Sat Bains, Too many Chiefs only One Indian, Face, 2012.

15   Ben Hopkins in an email to the authors, August 2013

16   Ibid

17   C Pout and E R Hitchin Future environmental impacts of room air-conditioners in Europe. Building Research & Information, 37(4), 2009 pp. 358–368.

18   N Bowman, K Lomas and M J Cook, Passive downdraught evaporative cooling 1. Concept and precedents. Indoor and Built Environment, 9(5), 2000, pp. 284–290

19   L E Thomas and G Baird, Post-occupancy evaluation of passive downdraft evaporative cooling and air-conditioned buildings at Torrent Research Centre, Ahmedabad, India, Proceedings of the 40th Annual Conference of the Architectural Science Association ANZAScA, 2006, pp. 97 – 104.

20   B. Givoni, Passive and Low Energy Cooling of Buildings, Wiley,

Figure 2.14.40 John Healey MP being interviewed outside the Nottingham House at Ecobuild

Figure 2.14.43 The Nottingham House during the Solar Decathlon Competition

Figure 2.14.41 Detail of the completed Nottingham House in Madrid, Stainless Steel Woven Solar Shading, ThermoWood Cladding, with Grey Aluminium Windows and Channels

New York, NY, 1994.

21   N Bowman, K Lomas and M J Cook, Passive downdraught evaporative cooling 1. Concept and precedents. Indoor and Built Environment, 9(5), 2000, pp. 284–290

22   R Schiano-Phan, Environmental retrofit: building integrated cooling in housing, Architectural Research Quarterly, 14(1), 2010, pp 139–151.

23   Brian Ford and C. Diaz, Passive downdraft cooling: hybrid cooling in the Malta Stock Exchange, in Rethinking Development: Are We Producing a People Oriented Habitat?, Proceedings of the PLEA Conference, Santiago, Chile, 2003

24   Brian Ford, R Schiano-Phan and E Francis, The Architecture & Engineering of Downdraught Cooling: A Design Sourcebook, PHDC Press, London, 2010.

25   Ibid

26   Brian Ford and K. Cairns, Market assessment of passive downdraught evaporative cooling in non-domestic buildings in Southern Europe, Proceedings of the 3rd European Conference on Energy Performance & Indoor Climate in Buildings, EPIC, Lyon, France, 2002, Vol. 2, pp. 505 – 510.
      Brian Ford and R. Moura, Market Assessment of Passive Downdraught Evaporative Cooling in Non-domestic Buildings in Southern Europe. Final Report, 2003, ALTENER II Project on 'Solar Passive Heating and Cooling', European Commission-DG Research, 2003 (available at: http://www.phdc.eu/ uploads/ media/ALTENER_1_Final_report_extract.pdf)

27   Ibid

28   Ibid

29   Ibid

30   J M Salmeron, S Alvarez, J Sanchez, B Ford and M Gillot, Analysis of a PHDC (passive and hybrid downdraft cooling) experimental facility in Seville and applicability to the Madrid climate. International Journal of Ventilation, 10(4), 2012, pp. 391–404.

31   Brian Ford, et al., Building Research & Information 40(3) Routledge, 2012, pp 290 – 304

32   Recorded by Brian Ford and Ben Hopkins on site

33   Ibid

34   Recorded on video at Ecobuild by Guillermo Guzman, Communications Director of the Nottingham House Team.

35   Andrew Feenberg, Questioning Technology, Routledge, 1999

2.15 To-and-Fro Table

NEX

Fig. 2.15.2 To-and-Fro Table, designed by NEX

Architect:	NEX
Materials:	Solid walnut with an iron free glass top
Fabricators:	Metropolitan Works
Exhibit:	To-and-Fro Table and 1:10 stereolithography models of the To-and-Fro Table[1]

The To-and-Fro table is designed to expand the range of communication between users through a sophisticated arrangement of material and structure. As verbal communication accounts for only a small part of how people interact, the To-and-Fro table facilitates more open full body communication with certain individuals while remaining discreetly hidden to others. Like the reciprocating back and forth of a good conversation, the table is made up of a field of delicate wooden fins that vary To-and-Fro in relation to each other and interlock to form an intricate lattice. The lattice appears mostly transparent to those sitting either diagonally or opposite the viewer while the table is rendered mostly opaque by those situated further away. While the variable transparency of the table leads to more engaging interactions, it also contributes to the atmosphere of the place it dwells within. Through the creation of complex patterns of light and shadow the piece is able to actively contribute to the space by entering into its own conversation with its surroundings.

Fig. 2.15.3 Stereolithography 1:10 scale model of To-and-Fro Table, designed by NEX

Extensive use of prototyping was made during the design and product development process. Multiple 1:10 scale stereolithography models were used to evaluate early design options. Jointing was tested at 1:1 scale in different wood species and using different drilling bits. The table is designed from individual components that are precisely machined on computer numeric controlled [CNC] routers, which are then hand assembled by skilled craftsmen. The table is made from solid walnut with an iron free or water white glass top. Initial full-scale tests led the practice to choose walnut wood for the entire piece. It is strong and sufficiently densely grained to accept a high level of detailed cutting for fine edges in the design and there it reduced the likelihood of the material warping while it was machined. Nonetheless warping proved to be a significant challenge to address. The fins were six millimetres thick, and the first prototypes distorted in plane as the fibre tensions in the wood were altered by the cutting process. To solve this, we switched to making the fins from a solid walnut laminate pressed from three two millimetre thick layers. The reciprocal pinwheel structure works at two scales – first at the scale of the component fin, and also the scale of the full length and width of the table. The larger scale provided some additional structural stability. More importantly, it allowed us to compartmentalise the assembly process into discrete bays, which maintained control over tolerance creep. A final full-scale prototype was machined on a 5 axis CNC machine and assembled by craftsmen. The table was assembled by one skilled cabinetmaker over about three days. The completed piece demonstrates that while the variation of the transparency of the table can enable more nuanced social exchange, it is also produces a piece of furniture that actively contributes to the atmosphere of the space it is placed within by creating complex patterns of light and shadow when it is simply lit from above.

Notes

1   Exhibited at Prototyping Architecture, Nottingham

Fig. 2.15.4 Underside of the finished table, designed by NEX

Fig. 2.15.5 Final adjustments

2.16 Times Eureka Pavilion

NEX

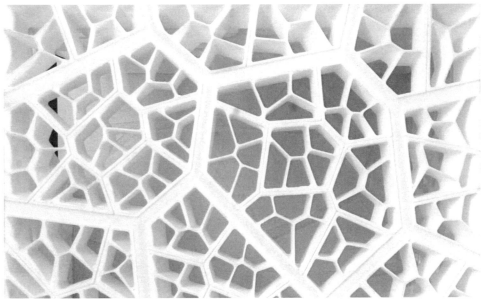

Fig. 2.16.2   Stereolithography model of the Times Eureka Pavilion

Architect / Designers:	NEX and Marcus Barnett
Materials:	Laminated Lumbar and recycled translucent polypropylene
Fabricators:	Blumer Lehman
Location:	Royal Botanic Gardens, Kew
Exhibit:	Stereolithography models of the Times Eureka Pavilion and a 1:1 Cell from the structure of the Times Eureka Pavilion[1]

This temporary garden and pavilion was designed by NEX in collaboration with Landscape Designer Marcus Barnett, and the brief was to explore the significance of plants to science and society. Commissioned by the Times Newspaper and Royal Botanic Gardens, Kew, the Times Eureka Pavilion, 2011, is an award winning structure. In the garden, all plant species were chosen to reflect their medicinal, commercial and industrial uses in everyday life. Based on previous work the practice knew the pavilion would be ideal for prototyping an architectural experiment. 'Freed from the performance requirements of weather tightness, environmental servicing and durability, which designers must address in larger buildings, a pavilion can become an experiment in new arrangements of material, space, and effect.'[2] Further, the explicit interest in the brief of the intersection between science and nature afforded the chance to explore the distinction between the natural and artificial in an architectural space. Designing in the context of Kew Gardens also offered the opportunity to consider the proposal in relation to the history of the pavilion typology, which is well represented within the gardens. What is striking about these existing pavilions is the importance of their silhouette as incidents set in an eighteenth century

Fig. 2.16.1   A 1:1 Cell from the structure of the Times Eureka Pavilion

pleasure garden landscape in the style of Capability Brown. When occupied by the viewer, they function as a meditative destination that frames the picturesque landscape.

For the Times Eureka Pavilion, the practice was interested in subverting these two qualities of the typology. Instead of a strong silhouette we wanted to enmesh the project in its surrounding environment, through its siting and the texture of its envelope. By creating a route through the structure the intention was to form part of a thoroughfare rather than a destination. Finally, desired experience was for the inside to be more like a filter than a frame – to create an envelope that was porous, rather than filled with discreet openings, to filter the sounds and smells on the air while still offering shelter. The design prototype of the deep surface became immediately instrumental in this context, and the knowledge acquired of working with wood during the prototyping of the To-and-Fro table suggested it was the best material to use. Using the prototype of the To-and-Fro table as a precedent, the design of the pavilion explored the use of recursion as a generative process to evolve a three dimensional structure. The technique of recursion is the process of repeating actions or objects in a self-similar way in successive steps, and in this case at different scales. The development of the system is governed by a series of rules that define local structure without determining overall form in advance. Such mathematical growth processes offer an interesting alignment between computation and nature by producing unique and non-repeating instances of form that obey consistent rules of formation.

The practice used two recursive approaches in the Times Eureka Pavilion. The first experiments used a Lindenmeyer System (L-system) algorithm to generate a two dimensional pattern that was then wrapped over a 3D bounding box of the pavilion envelope. Versions of this were iterated many times using different values (initial length of the branches, number of branches branching out in every generation, range of angles between branches). While this exploration revealed a basic arrangement of the primary structure, we discovered it was difficult to control directional bias and it could not create smaller scale venation patterns between branches. In architectural terms, it tended to fix the pattern at a particular scale that made the structure appear too literal, meaning that there was a direct correlation between the scale of the branching in the pavilion and the scale of the branching in the trees in the surrounding garden. This was something to be avoided, thinking that it would be more interesting for users to experience the patterns of plant biology at an unfamiliar scale. To make this shift the practice began looking at techniques that could allow us to mimic patterns of venation[3]. Though not a mathematical model of biological process, eventually Voronoi procedures to subdivide the surface envelope

Fig. 2.16.3 Times Eureka Pavilion, designed by NEX [above]

Fig. 2.16.4 Times Eureka Pavilion, designed by NEX [left]

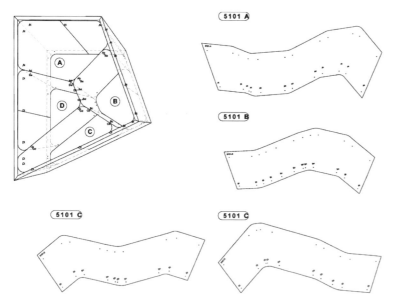

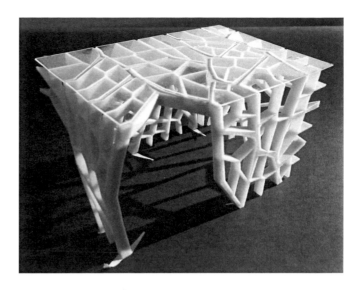

Fig. 2.16.5 Entrance to the pavilion [left]

Fig. 2.16.6 1:50 scale model of Times Eureka Pavilion, designed by NEX [right]

were selected. The process of division was recursive at three scales; the first division produced 21 cells of primary structure with 140mm beams; the second iteration produced 126 cassettes with 20mm thick walls. The final iteration produced 586 cells that would be made from recycled translucent polypropylene.

The virtue of this approach was that it allowed us to establish a rule based process that constantly expressed differentiation at each scale and in each unit. Every cell was unique, just as you find in a biological system. A further level of spatial complexity was introduced by projecting the cell geometry to a single central point inside the pavilion to extrude the depth of the walls. While the aim of this was to produce a visually and environmentally more dynamic space, reinforcing the concept of movement through the structure, it also significantly increased the technical and manufacturing complexity of the timber elements. To be economically viable the entire structure had to be manufactured using a digital workflow and file to factory processes. For the timber structure, the 3D model constituted the full construction documentation, and it contained all dimensional and jointing information. The model was machined on a five CNC saw machine using FSC certified spruce. The primary structure was machined from block laminated lumbar, and the cassettes were cut from 20mm block boards, which was dimensionally stable and resistant to warping when cut. The cut boards were secretly screwed so that when assembled there were no visible fixings. Working tolerances for machining and assembly of all pieces was set at 2mm to ensure a tight fit of elements and to expedite on-site assembly. Intensive use of physical prototypes began with 1:10 scale prints and progressed to 1:5 and full-scale cassettes.

The geometry of the infill cells were individually unfolded at cut from standard recycled polypropylene sheets using a CNC blade cutter. Each cell was numbered and reassembled on site with its nearest neighbours before being inserted into the cassette. The total site assembly time was four days. In the completed space quality of the patterning across the walls, floor and ceiling of the structure produced a powerful sense of occupying a biological structure. In operation the pavilion continued to mimic water transfer in plant biology. Rainwater literally runs of the roof infill cells into the main capillaries, down the walls and into the ground.

Notes

1   Exhibited at Prototyping Architecture, Nottingham

2   Alan Dempsey and Yusuke Obuchi, Nine Problems in the form of a Pavilion, AA Press: London 2010.

3   Adam Runions & Martin Fuhrer, et al. Modeling and visualisation of leaf venation patterns, http://algorithmicbotany.org/papers/venation.sig2005.pdf

2.17 Topology Tests - Digital Grotesque

Michael Hansmeyer and Benjamin Dillenburger

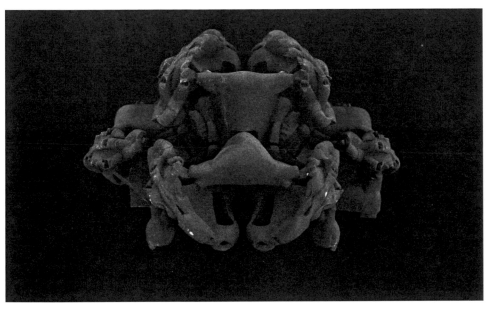

Fig. 2.17.2 Topology test print of a Digital Grotesque Capital

Architect:	Michael Hansmeyer and Benjamin Dillenburger[1]
Materials:	3D print – Silicate and binder
Fabricators:	Voxeljet AG
Location:	Test assembly at ETH Zurich
Exhibit:	Two topology tests of Digital Grotesque[2]

New materials and fabrication methods have historically led to radical changes in architectural design. They have indeed been primary drivers in its evolution. Today, additive manufacturing heralds a revolution in fabrication for design. Yet in architecture, this technology has up to now been limited mostly to small scale models. Digital Grotesque takes additive manufacturing technology to a true architectural scale. Not a small model is printed, but the actual room itself. Digital Grotesque presents a fully immersive, solid, human-scale enclosed structure with a perplexing level of detail. Its geometry consists of hundreds of millions of individual facets printed at a resolution of a tenth of a millimeter, constituting a 3.2m high, 16m² large room.

The synthesis of additive manufacturing and computational design is particularly promising. Algorithms can produce an architecture with details at threshold of human perception, and these forms now can be printed at the scale of sand-corns. There is no longer a cost associated with complexity, as printing a highly detailed form costs the same as printing a primitive cube. Nor is there a cost for customisation: fabricating highly individual elements costs no more than printing a standardised series. Ornament and formal expression are no longer a luxury - they are now legitimised.

Fig. 2.17.1 Digital Grotesque, Design development physical render, digital silicate print

Fig. 2.17.3 Sand removal and cleaning after printing

Fig. 2.17.4 Printed space - grotto part 1

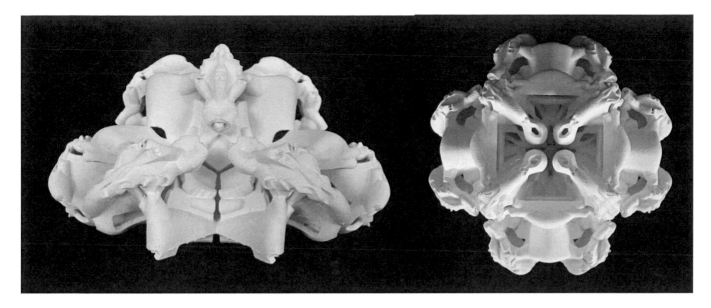

Fig. 2.17.5 Prototype or typology test of a Digital Grotesque Capital - elevation and plan

In the Digital Grotesque project, we aim to create an architecture that defies classification and resists reductionism. We explore unseen levels of resolution and topological complexity in architecture by developing compositional strategies based on purely geometric processes. We use algorithms to create a form that appears at once synthetic and organic. The design process thus strikes a delicate balance between the expected and the unexpected, between control and relinquishment. The algorithms are deterministic as they do not incorporate randomness, but the results are not necessarily entirely foreseeable. Instead, they have the power to surprise. Instead, they have the power to surprise. As a fictive narrative space, the Digital Grotesque project is less concerned with functionality than with the expressive formal potentials of digital technologies. It examines new spatial experiences and sensations that these technologies enable. As such, Digital Grotesque is a lavish, exhilarating space, full of details at the threshold of perception, waiting to be discovered and spurring one's imagination of what is yet to be created. .[3]

Notes

1   Michael Hansmeyer and Benjamin Dillenburger are both architects and programmers who explore the
         use of algorithms and computation to generate architectural form, based in the CAAD group
         at ETH's Architecture Department, Zurich.

2   Exhibited at Prototyping Architecture, Cambridge, Ontario

3   Research for the Digital Grotesque project was carried out at the Chair for CAAD at the Swiss Federal
         Institute of Technology (ETH) in Zurich and all components were printed by Voxeljet AG. The first part of
         the grotto is a commission by FRAC Centre for its permanent collection

2.18 Passion Façade

Antoni Gaudí and Mark Bury

Fig. 2.18.2 Computationally designed colonnade, The Bones of Christ, superimposed into the context of the West façade of Sagrada Família Basilica

Architect: Antoni Gaudí and Mark Bury[1]

Materials: Local Sandstone

Stonemason: Jordi Barbany, Granits Barbany

Location: Barcelona

Exhibit: Digitally printed 1:25 model of part of the Passion Façade

The design and construction of the Sagrada Família Basilica by the Catalan Architect Antoni Gaudí (1852 – 1926) is a process that has involved physical modelling and prototyping at all scales throughout its 130 year progress. The only surviving formal evidence for the Passion design from Gaudí's lifetime is a photograph of a highly charged drawing of the west façade completed in 1917. The Passion, or west, façade of Sagrada Família Basilica faces the setting sun and is concerned with the passion of Christ, and the events surrounding his crucifixion and resurrection. However, the façade has remained incomplete, and the church has yet to be crowned with a colonnade of Gaudí's unique and powerfully organic columns. The colonnade is said to represent the extended rib cage of Christ on the cross, the space celebrates the life of the saints and forms the cave-like entrance to the tomb of the risen Christ.

Despite being worked over for a long period, there had been no consensus that any of the previous models produced were the appropriate representation of the colonnade in the photograph of the original drawing so design stopped. Modelling and interpretation commenced again in the recent post digital period. However, with no surviving restored scale plaster models from Gaudí to refer to, prototyping both at scale and at 1:1 became a crucial part of the process. A simplified schema was developed for the colonnade, each column became a hyperbolic paraboloid with roots and branches arranged around a hyperboloid of revolution trunk. Design iterations proceeded initially around superimposition of different designs over the original photograph, and subsequently through discussion around rapid prototyped plaster versions of the colonnade. Many versions of the model were printed and mounted at scales ranging from 1:100 to 1:25. At 1:25 it was possible to test important views of the façade including from the park and the street.

Notes

1   Architect Director and Coordinator for the Sagrada Família Basilica: Jordi Bonet & Jordi Faulí. Project Architect for the Sagrada Família Basilica: Jordi Coll. Design architects for the Passion Façade completion: Mark Burry and Jane Burry. Technical Architect: Toni Caminal. Documentation architect: Xisco Llabres. Composition of presented material: Michael Wilson, Spatial Information Architecture Laboratory (SIAL), RMIT University.

Fig. 2.18.3 [above] and Fig. 2.18.4 [right] A digitally printed 1:25 model of part of the Passion Façade

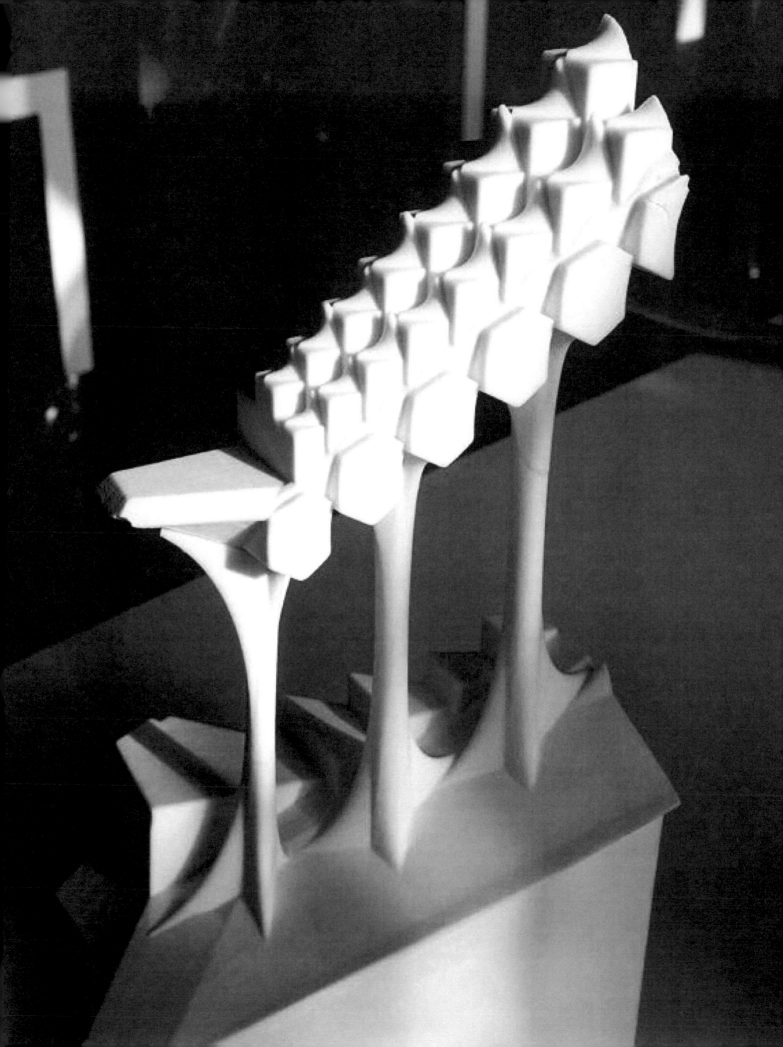

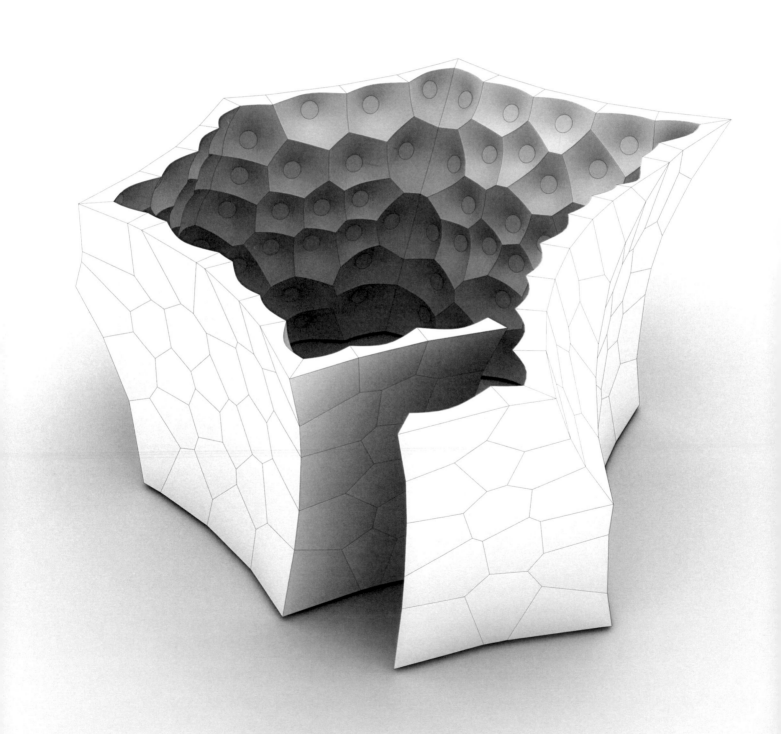

2.19 FabPod

SIAL @ RMIT

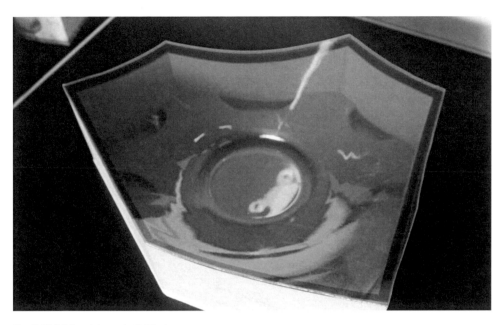

Fig. 2.19.2 1:1 prototype of a FabPod

RMIT Research Team:	Nick Williams, John Cherrey, Daniel Davis, Alex Pena de Leon, Jane Burry, Mark Burry
Invited Researcher:	Brady Peters, CITA, Copenhagen
Materials:	Spun Aluminium Hyperboloid panels (1.5mm thick blanks), formed on a tool CNC fabricated from stacked 35mm MDF sheets, 12mm E0 MDF frame, vacuum formed white translucent acrylic sheet and PET based absorbent material.
Fabricators:	RMIT
Exhibit:	Two 1:1 FabPod prototypes

FabPod combines research into the sound diffusing properties of hyperbolic surfaces, the problem of semi-enclosed meeting areas within open plan settings and the use of digital modelling and mass customised CNC prototyping. The exhibited prototypes are part of continuing research addressing acoustic performance and full-scale fabrication. The first iteration of this research was developed in 2011 for the Responsive Acoustic Surfacing (RAS) Cluster at the Smartgeometry workshops held in CITA, Copenhagen. It was initiated in response to anecdotal evidence from musicians that the newly completed interior of Gaudí's Sagrada Família Bassilica has a surprisingly diffuse acoustic. While techniques for evaluating reverberation and absorption of sound are well developed, the diffusion of sound is a more emergent area of research.

Fig. 2.19.1 Digital model of a prototype meeting facility

2.19.3 The geometry of the FabPod is derived from research conducted into the sound scattering properties of hyperboloids - inspired by Gaudí

2.19.5 The FabPod creates a semi-enclosed meeting area within an open plan office setting, RMIT

Fig. 2.19.4 A prototype meeting facility

Fig. 2.19.6 The FabPod exhibited

Initial research outputs from the design and testing of surfaces have been extended in this more complex brief. Based on a series of geometric and fabrication constraints, a digital workflow has been developed to allow for the quick proposal of form, geometric articulation and material distribution. These design proposals can be digitally simulated to understand acoustic performance and easily fed back into further design iterations. Acoustic performance acts as a design driver. This process is being applied to the construction of full-scale proposals to rigorously test the flexibility and sophistication of the digital systems as well as the fidelity of the fabrication techniques. Importantly, this allows for further layers of feedback from the physical to the digital, demanding that the digital model best abstract the behaviour of the physical and meaningfully enhance the design process.

Fig. 2.19.7 A prototype meeting facility

2.20 Loblolly House Prototype

KierenTimberlake

Fig. 2.20.2   Loblolly House viewed from the Northwest, architect KieranTimberlake

Architect / Designers:	KierenTimberlake
Materials:	Bosch Rexroth Aluminium Extrustions and basic connectors; Timber and ply wall/floor/roof cartridges; Prefabricated cedar rainscreen.
Fabricators:	Bensonwood
Location:	Chesapeake Bay, Maryland
Exhibit:	1:1 Prototype of Loblolly House

The thousands of parts, which make up a building are collapsed into a few dozen off-site fabricated assemblies that are simply attached to an extruded aluminium frame on-site, to make this house. Located on a barrier island off the coast of Maryland's Chesapeake Bay, Loblolly House seeks to deeply fuse the natural elements of its site to architectural form. Positioned between a dense grove of loblolly pines and a lush foreground of saltmeadow cordgrass and the bay, the architecture is formed about and within the elements of trees, tall grasses, the sea, the horizon, the sky and the western sun that define the place of the house. Timber foundations minimise the footprint and provide savannah-like views of the trees and the bay, and the staggered boards of the east facade evoke the solids and voids of the forest.

Loblolly House proposes a new, more efficient method of building through the use of building information modelling (BIM) and integrated component assemblies. The frame, comprised of Bosch Rexroth aluminium framing, is bolted together as opposed to welded, creating a

Fig. 2.20.1 Loblolly House Prototype being assembled by Peter Curry

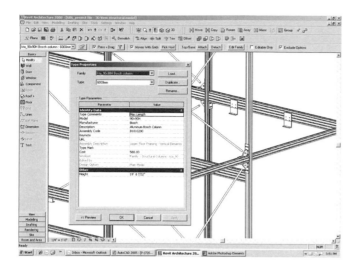

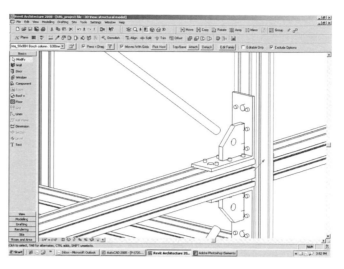

Fig. 2.20.3 Building information model built for the Loblolly House – showing the extruded aluminium frame

Fig. 2.20.4 Component Details of the Loblolly House BIM

structural system for the house which can be disassembled without affecting the capacity of beam and column components to be reconnected. The bolted scaffold serves as a frame into which off-site fabricated kitchen, bathroom and mechanical blocks, and floor and wall cartridges are inserted without the use of permanent fasteners or wet connections. Upon disassembly cartridges and blocks are removed as whole units and column/beam scaffold sections are unbolted.

Loblolly House preserves embodied energy with the easy disassembly and reassembly of its essential elements. The disassembly and redeployment potential is evident in the detailing and quality craftsmanship of the energy intensive scaffold, blocks, cartridges, and service spines. This ensures a design-for-disassembly strategy where the components with the highest embodied energy can be disassembled and redeployed with a minimal loss of energy.

'Loblolly House is not only a statement in favour of a more ecological approach, it is an essay in prefabrication that exemplifies KieranTimberlake's engagement with craft, industry and manufacturing. The new techniques they utilise include, scaffolding, blocks and cartridges.'[1] Loblolly House gains its authenticity from the integration of space, structure and layered environmental systems.

Notes

1   Professor Michael Stacey, Introduction, in Kieran, S., Timberlake, J., eds. Loblolly House: Elements of a New Architecture, Princeton Architectural Press, pp.10-12.

Fig. 2.20.6 Structural connections at the entrance to the glass footbridge

Fig. 2.20.5 Loblolly House being assembled by Laura Gaskell at Prototyping Architecture Exhibition, Nottingham

Fig. 2.20.6 Scoond-level dining and living area, with one section of the adjustable facade open

2.21 Zoid

Yves Ebnöther

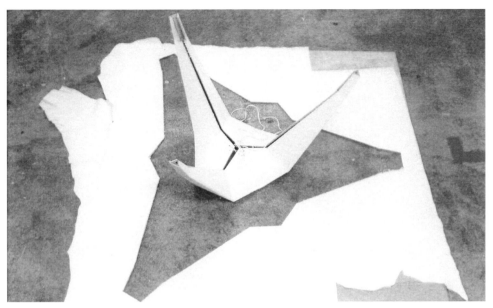

Fig. 2.21.2 Leather and ply prototype used in the design development of Zoid

Designer: Yves Ebnöther, ETH, Switzerland

Materials: Folded Aluminium

Prototype Fabricators: RAPLAB D-ARCH, ETH Zurich, Switzerland

Production Fabricators: Georg Ackermann GmbH, Germany

Exhibit: Three Zoid aluminum stools - finished in silver, champagne and
gold anodising

Briefing: ' ... to develop an artefact which exemplifies the material potential of sheet metal ... '

Response: '... create a beautiful and sturdy three-dimensional object which is surprisingly folded out of a single flat sheet ...'

Zoid is a prototypical product, which explores the possibilities of small-scale computer-controlled production. Initiated as a showcase project for a steel furniture manufacturer over a decade ago, it was only possible to solve its geometrical issues with the help of advanced parametric software. The project nicely explores the structural and aesthetic potential of folded sheet aluminium. The main challenge lay in the development of the flat cutting pattern, which allows for the stool to be folded from just one piece. While the calculation of the pattern and its production rely on digital processes, the actual folding, the transformation of the flat sheet into a voluminous body, is done by hand.

Fig. 2.21.1 Zoid Folded Aluminium Stools, designed by Yves Ebnöther

2.21.3 Unfolded net pattern.

The driving force behind this was the fascination with a geometrical challenge, paired with a manufacturing method and a versatile material - investigating always under the premise of how little does it take, when exactly is the point reached where the prototype becomes a product? As such, the outcome as a piece of furniture is arbitrary - Zoid is essentially a materialised thought.

Notes

1   Zoid is a registered design (modèle déposée), www.ebnoether. com. Designed and made by Yves Ebnöther, ETH, Switzerland

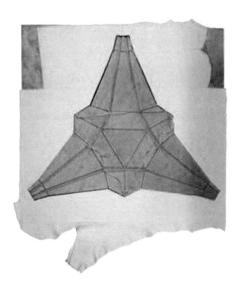

Fig. 2.21.4 Zoid Folded Aluminium Stool, designed by Yves Ebnöther

Fig. 2.21.5 Zoid Folded Aluminium Stools, designed by Yves Ebnöther

2.22 Stressed Out

Sixteen*(makers)

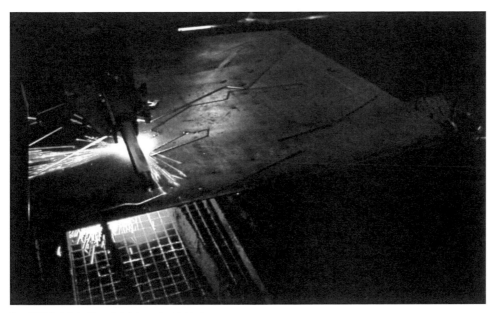

Fig. 2.22.2 Fabrication of stainless steel table top

Architect / Prototypers:	Bob Sheil, Emmanuel Vercruysse and Justin Goodyer
Material:	Stainless Steel
Manufacturing:	Perforations, CNC Waterjet and Folded with Snap Fit Joints
Exhibit:	Stressed Out Table[1]

The Stressed Out Table is designed to reduce a generic form to its minimal essential structure that can be readily manufactured to order. The table-top is made from a single standard size sheet of stainless steel; where cuts, folds and perforations are formed from the maximum amount of available material with a minimum of offcut and waste. The perforation pattern is generated by playing with data results from structural stress analysis that identifies the loading paths of the furniture unit as a structure. A dynamic script was written to determine proximity, shape, and size rules, which carried an equal number of aesthetic decisions to technical feedback. The version in the exhibition is the first and original prototype, for which modifications are continually being developed. Each iteration would be numbered as a prototype in sequence as the design evolves. In the digital age, clearly the unit could be manufactured from anywhere the material and tooling are available. However, as we learnt with this iteration, some instructions can be misread and following its first arrival from the fabricator to the studio (North to South of England), it was sent back to the folding company for correction, for which they happily obliged. We see these narratives as essential information in handing an object over from its makers to its owners, as every object has a story beyond the form, function, and image it serves. The title is a delightful

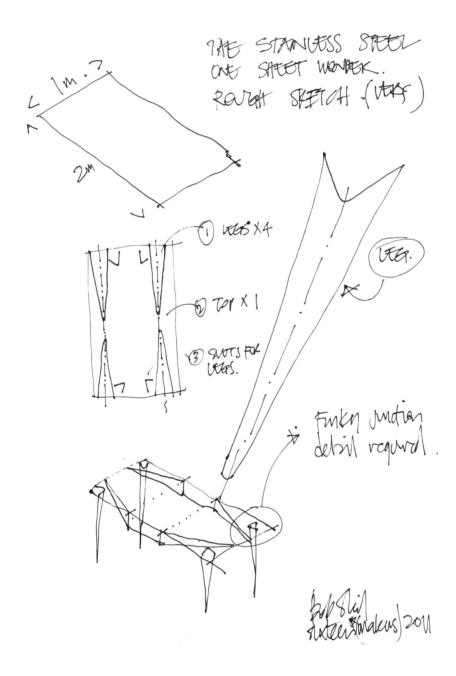

Fig. 2.22.3 Sketch of Stressed Out table by sixteen*(makers)

conflation of a comment on life in London, as sixteen*(makers) are primarily located at The Bartlett, University College London and the use of finite element analysis to optimise the form of the table. Stressed out was first shown in 2011 at Testbed 1 Gallery London at *Turning the Tables*, an exhibition curated by Yale Reisner and Sir Peter Cook.

Fig. 2.22.4 Structural stress analysis identifies the loading paths of the furniture as a structure

Fig. 2.22.5 Stressed Out Table by sixteen*(makers) exhibited at Testbed 1 Gallery, London

De-Fabricating Protoarchitecture
Bob Sheil[2]

Fig. 2.22.6 'Manufacturing Protoarchitecture 1'. In the foreground, early components of the '55/02' shelter by sixteen*(makers) in collaboration with Stahlbogen GmbH. In the background components of more everyday fabrications by Stahlbogen. For the former, precise assembly of the digital model was not a project objective, for the latter, it is a quality upon which the business depends. Materials: Steel

Fig. 2.22.7 'NW Projection: 55/02 Kielder 07.03.10 1643 hrs'. Partial scan of shelter 55/02 at Cock Stoor, Kielder Forest and Water Park, Northumberland, UK. 3D survey carried out by ScanLab Projects.

'Tools provide possibilities, from these possibilities we discover advantages, advantages become a convenience, and convenience can too easily become a convention. There are alternatives: rather than supporting just the more efficient execution of conventional tasks, tools can encourage new ways of thinking. The creative use of a tool should include opportunities for the designer to embed his own design logic within that tool. Such customisation should be recognised as a key aspect of design creativity.'

Robert Aish[3]

Introduction

How can a contemporary architect or maker distinguish between the drawn and the made? Through an examination of my body of work with sixteen*(makers) this chapter in Prototyping Architecture will exercise and examine this contemporary dilemma in practice and pedagogy.[4] Reflecting on a series of underlying issues associated with building things from digital data, a discipline that many in the construction industry are still grappling to master. Someone who is a master of this technology is the author of the quote above, Robert Aish. Apart from his pedigree as a graduate of Industrial Design at the Royal College of Art, where he studied under David Pye, his Ph.D. in Human Computer Interaction from the University of Essex, his career as a senior engineering software developer with Arup, Rucaps, Intergraph, Bentley, and now Autodesk, and his role as a consultant for many of the world leading practices and universities, it is his early experience in the shipyards of Gdansk where he managed information generation for the fabrication and assembly of hull components that strike me as a formative reference behind these remarks. It is such underlying knowledge and tacit experience in the physical and tactile that informs the basis of this paper and the work it refers to.

Set within the context of design and fabrication tooling of ever increasing definition and adaptability, the ideas this paper shall explore are:

- The status of the dynamic and adaptable digital design model in relation to the physical results that are built from it.

- The status of the resulting physical assembly as an architectural prototype, and

- The difference between the drawn and the made.

Further reinforcement of this discourse is drawn from and refers to the publication *Protoarchitecture: Analogue and Digital Hybrids* (Wiley July 2008),[5] and a forthcoming title *High Definition: Zero Tolerance in Design and Production* (Wiley January 2014).[6] Each of these publications seeks to examine parallel and immediate developments both in practice and research that present new challenges to established methodologies in design and fabrication. The former title explores the beginnings of a recent period in architectural history (circa 2000-2007) where a significant and growing proportion of experimental design was not exclusively colonised by computational processes or computational theory. The rose tinted glasses of the computational age were slipping off, and a hybrid world; dense with the feedback of unpredictable, inconsistent, and unexpected results was readdressed as a defining ingredient in making architecture. The term Protoarchitecture has been adopted to reflect

Fig. 2.22.8 Sheil, R. (ed). Protoarchitecture: Analogue and Digital Hybrids. (78). Architectural Design. London: John Wiley & Sons. (2008) ISBN-10: 0470519479, ISBN-13: 978-0470519479

work that is part real, part ideal, part resolved, and part in progress. It also recognises propositions that are prompted by a compatible interest in analogue and digital techniques and thus parallel constructs of the physical and the virtual. Protoarchitecture captures work that does not conform to type, is exceptional, experimental, and transgresses habitual practice in representation with that of making. Examples of work argued in this context include amongst others that by the Founder of the Centre for Architectural Structures and Technology (CAST) at the University of Manitoba, Professor Mark West,[7] the products and environment of La Machine in Nantes led by Pierre Orefice and Francois Delaroziere,[8] Strandbeests by Theo Jansen,[9] Prosthetic Mythologies by Kate Davies and Emmanuel Vercruysse of Liquidfactory, and Robotic Membranes by Mette Ramsguard Thompson of the Centre for Information Technology in Architecture (CITA) at the Royal Academy of Fine Arts Copenhagen. Each of the presented works not only portrayed an alternative and critical approach to practice, but an alternative and critical role for the designer as an active participant in the work's production.

Six years on, *High Definition: Zero Tolerance in Design and Production (Jan 2014)* is exploring subsequent developments in design tooling and practice. Central to this forthcoming publication is an examination of Light Detection and Ranging Technology (LIDAR)[10] in architecture; Presently capable of capturing distances up to 6000m in radius (or more if launched from airborne positions) and generating 3D point clouds to an accuracy of less than 1mm, such tools offer unprecedented accuracy for the development and interrogation of design strategies before, during and post production.[11] With its roots in the automotive production industry, and applications in crime forensics, mining and marine engineering, mechanical verification, medicine and landscape, the use of 3D scanning instrumentation in architectural design opens up entirely new avenues of understanding and engagement with the complexities of context, form, behaviour and volume that heretofore have been crudely approximated, or poorly grasped. As the designer's array of digital tools to propose and make their ideas has become significantly enriched in recent decades, the component of armoury that has remained out of step with potential has been the means to navigate, embed and verify design outcomes as they emerge in context.

LIDAR technology has begun to transform this problem. Without such tools, the exploitation of greater levels of precision, complexity, and dynamic composition in design representation, is curtailed by unmatched resources in execution and delivery. Today, through affordable 3D LIDAR technology and it facilitation of high accuracy data capture, this gap is narrowing.[12] Complex design propositions in a number of file formats may be tested and developed within three dimensional point cloud files that are accurately referenced into real environments. Likewise, built work may be scanned and cross referenced to the design information from which it was produced, thus offering a clear mapping of the real upon the ideal. Yet to date, the subject of high accuracy, zero tolerance design production has been exclusively published through didactic, scientific and mechanical themes. How does the technology work? How is it used? This publication will explore such themes on a level of creative and speculative critique, that range from its stretch capability to how it challenges the role of the designer.

Residing within the context of adjacent themes on high definition, examples of work to be argued in this context include the self-assembly works of Skylar Tibbets at MIT, information production, flow and procurement at Gehry Technologies, and the boundaries of surveillance technology explored by Andy Hudson-Smith at the Centre for Advanced Spatial Analysis, UCL, and others who will be referred to later in this paper. Running as a critical subtext is a discussion on the role and value of zero tolerance as a design and fabrication standard. Negotiating zero tolerance asks us to define an appropriate proximity to high definition technology within an industry still very far removed from the laboratory facilities of its automotive or aeronautic cousins.

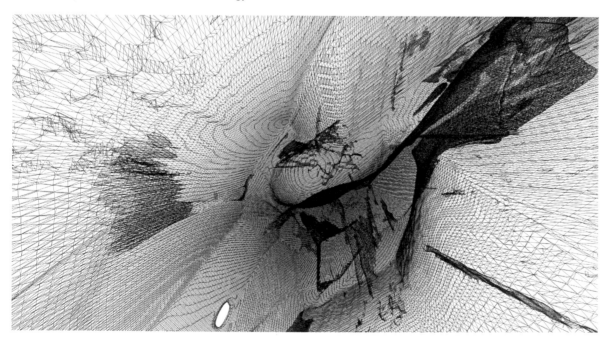

Fig. 2.22.9 'Subverting the Lidar Landscape' by Matt Shaw (Bartlett School of Architecture MArch Unit 23, 2007-09). The point cloud image of a speculative building component is captured from a 3D laser scanner. Material defects and unseen anomalies are detected by the scanner and appear in the point cloud as digital noise. We have yet to fully understand the behaviour of real materials in digital space. Materials: Polymers, grease, hardwood, gelatin and steel.

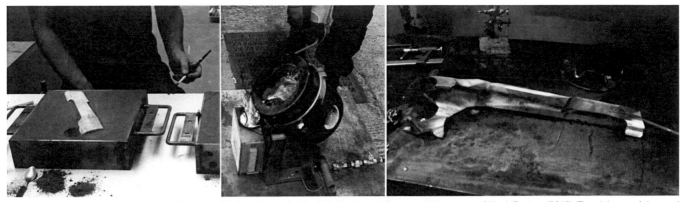

Fig 2.22.9 'Incisions in the Haze' from the Prosthetic Mythologies project by Kate Davies and Emmanuel Vercruysse of LiquidFactory (2012). The alchemy of the sand casting is magical. The foam form is buried in sand, packed down and engulfed in its cocoon, molten metal is poured into it, dissolving and replacing the foam - transfiguring it - when the form boxes are opened a fiery hot object shrouded in smoking burnt black sand emerges. Materials: Sand, Aluminium, Gas.

'There is a great deal of mythology associated with craft – and with professional practice generally.'

Peter Dormer – *The Art of the Maker* (1994)[13]

Not To, but Through

Over the past three decades computation in architecture has developed an array of powerful tools for the development and evolution of geometric complexity. It has also provided the design and construction industry with additional tools and processes that modify the protocols and connectedness of visualisation, production and procurement.[14] Yet crossing the material threshold raises significant questions regarding; the objective of digital information as an instruction to make, the subsequent status of the built work being generated, and the difference between simulation and fabrication. Prior to the adoption of computer-aided design (CAD), architectural drawings were made using cumbersome tools that had not changed in any radical sense for more than 2,000 years. Other than the evolution of more precise instruments and more stable materials on which to draw, the standard toolset of the architectural designer remained remarkably consistent until the late 20th century. For the architect who has wished to break from tradition, one of the greatest challenges has been to transcend the limited possibilities of these tools and understand the difference between design propositions that are possible to make but difficult to draw, or possible to draw and difficult to make.[15] Lurking within this equation was intent, a design intent that existed between the drawing and the artefact, and one that relied upon conversation with other disciplines, trades and experts to be fulfilled as a physical entity.[16] Implicit information on the specific production tools that might be used to make the design, or how such tools should be used, maintained, deployed or controlled, was limited.

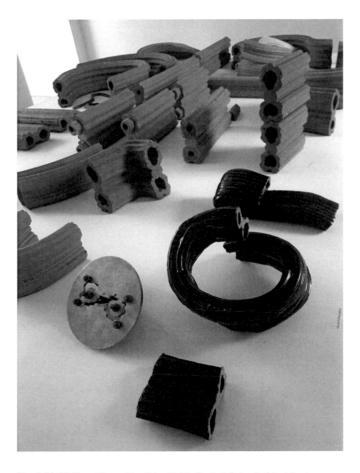

Fig. 2.22.10 'Terra Therma' by Peter Webb (Bartlett School of Architecture MArch Unit 23, 2008-10). Ideas and materials are metaphorically and literally extrapolated from a site in North London and developed as prototypical building components for a space of variable temperature and humidity. The elements are extruded through a digitally controlled variable jig. Materials: London Clay

Only in instances such as the illustrated profile of soft joints, or the geometry and materiality of a specific mould and surface for casting, might visual information alone and the technique of how the desired result be made become synthesised. If not conveyed in this way, or augmented in specification clauses, decisions on production tooling were placed in the domain of the fabricator who took responsibility for the selection of appropriate tooling, standards, craft, durability, use, appropriateness of specific material samples, finish, delivery, and so on. In this context, it was understood that the architectural drawing as an instruction to make was highly constrained and limited, and that its primary focus was to define and secure the required outcome while allowing essential room for negotiation on how this was achieved. For the architectural design to be made, other drawings, such as shop drawings, were required as a rehearsal to making. The nature of this exchange has been significantly altered by CAD/CAM, the fusion of drawing and manufacturing technologies that plug design information with the production equipment that makes what is described. Despite the many advanced levels of capability, this technology provides, its potential to release design constraint, open new frontiers, and extrapolate results not previously achievable has the potential to bypass many of the essential transactions between design and making that are incorporated in the exchange between either field of expertise. Thus not only has the architectural drawing altered its role as a carrier of design information, so too has the architectural model, the prototype and the speculative construct. The neat divisions that once commissioned, sequenced and qualified these key productions are converging, and the degree of cross-fertilisation between each mode of representation provided by digital tooling has generated a turbulent network of information flux.

The transposition of the performance of physical materials into a computational realm that subsequently decants what is explored back into a physical realm is a sequence of challenging translations. In the first instance it seeks to identify a direct relationship between the performance of digital and physical matter, and secondly it seeks to interpret highly complex, dynamic and living systems as a template for form generation. Quite apart from the inevitable selectivity involved, such an approach has the potential to reduce architectural production to a systematic selection exercise devoid of the immeasurable and immaterial qualities that make it more than the sum of its parts.[17] It is the manner in which design information allows for indeterminacy and anticipates the possibility of how it can be made that make it work in the form of a built artefact. The skill in describing architecture before it is built is to make design information that anticipates, rather than dictates, how it is translated through time, site, materials, fabrication processes, assembly and use, and to understand the difference between the first prototype and the last.

One of the potential problems facing the age of digital fabrication is its heightened reliance upon data made by experts with a lot of experience in representation, geometry, form, and the illustration of materials, but less with experience in how things are made or perform. Unless the designer is located in the place of production and is at least a witness to on site decisions on issues such as tool paths, machine rates, material orientation, and makeability, the integrity of their information is a risk. And without such critical links, the built artefact is at risk of becoming no more than a physical render of a projected image where the exploration of its performance as a construct ceased at the point of simulation. With the exception of highly simplistic or linear tasks such as mono material 2D cutting or 3D printing, the jaded phrase file to factory is a overly simplified term. A more accurate and helpful

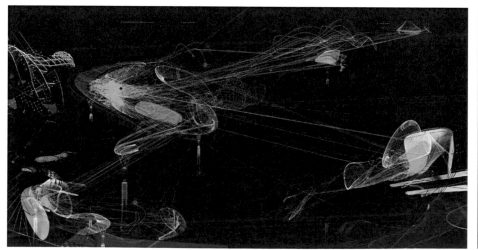 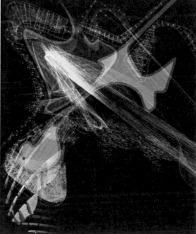

Fig 2.22.11 'Spaces of Uncertainty – The Augmented Instrumentalist' by Emma Kate Matthews (Bartlett School of Architecture MArch Unit 23, 2010-11). Composite model, acoustic simulation, and sound perspective of a small listening chamber for a proposed performance space on the Venice Moses Barrier. Design as a hybrid of digital representation, physical representation, manufacturing data, sound clips and environmental simulation. Materials: Steel, concrete, air.

term to describe the communication of data between designer and manufacturer might be file through factory. The key change conveys more clearly how the journey is not entirely one way, nor does it cease to evolve at the moment it is transferred from the former to the latter.[18] These arguments have been further developed as an idea of persistent modelling by Phil Ayres at CITA..[19]

The Birth of the Protoarchitect

Constraints of any kind have long provoked designers both positively and negatively, but as the means to describe design escalates and expands, and the imagination of form, language and complexity is stretched, the question of what conceptual strategies inform the making of a design has become increasingly ambiguous. Key to ensuring that design concepts acknowledge manufacturing constraints is the need to remain critically aware of the difference as well as the similarity between drawn and made things, and how both are produced. Digital manufacturing processes have nevertheless injected a lot more freedom in the domain of the designer, and ideas that might have remained as an experimental esquisse in a previous age are being manifested in physical form to levels of fabrication

completeness previously in reserved for the finished article.[20] Such early resolution presents the work in a category beyond conventional notions of the prototype, but outside conventional notions of building. They are, I would argue, protoarchitectures of a particular kind; constructs that seek to test, validate, or exhibit speculative design propositions that have emerged through digital investigation of the visual and theoretical; as well as the technical for example structural performance or practical for example workmanship. Such protoarchitectures provide a form of translated architectural evidence between the digital to the material, and as a consequence, exist as a form of proof of concept for research and design questions that lie beyond the artefact on view.

These steps are further enriched by the resurgence of 1:1 built artefacts being produced at an increasing number of leading architectural research centres and schools of architecture around the world. The past decade has witnessed an incremental surge of investment in digital fabrication equipment by these organisations; including in some cases the commission of new prototyping laboratories or new forms of shared and expanded

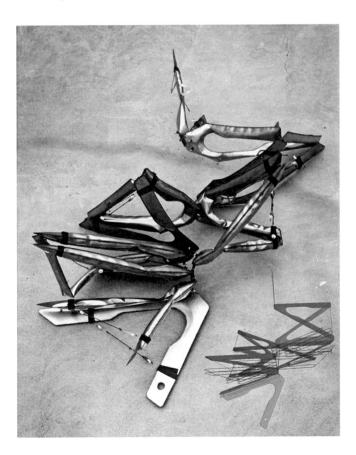

Fig. 2.22.12 'Digital Material' from the Persistent Model Project by Phil Ayres (2010). Materials: Steel, Air

Fig. 2.22.13 'Hear, Here' by Ric Lipson (Bartlett School of Architecture MArch Unit 23, 2007-09). A digitally prefabricated protoarchitecture that tests acoustic properties of a large scale listening ear. Materials: Plywood, glue, paint.

Fig 2.22.14 'Manufacturing Protoarchitecture 2'. The fully assembled '55/02' shelter at the factory of Stahlbogen GmbH in Blankenburg, prior to dismantling, finishing and delivery to site. Materials: Steel

facilities with other parallel disciplines, such as civil engineering or computer science. Some have been additionally facilitated by establishing new facilities upon existing traditional workshops, where the experience and inventories of analogue conventions are informing hybrid disciplines, cultures and practices. In parallel to the development and analysis of design information in simulated environments, such fabrication environments are refuelling the visual and visionary exploration of experimental architecture through the essential gains of self-production. Central to the significance of this resurgence are two ingredients, firstly co-production, that is the making of protoarchitecture by either by designers in collaboration with technical colleagues, or multi-disciplinary staff who operate in both realms, and secondly the location of design practice within the place of production.[21] With both components in place such actions and facilities have the capacity to respond to clear requirement for new hybrid disciplines within the construction industry across design, fabrication, computation, and project management. Such new roles will also lead to strengthening the new relationships that are emerging between academia, practice and industry, triggered by the same shifts in technology.

For the Protoarchitect set within this context, the as-built speculation provides critical feedback and essential verification unattainable in representation alone. Evidence obtained on how the work operates as a feasible and conceptual construct is derived by cross-referencing physical and digital tectonics, and by measuring how closely the built work resembles both the intent and embedded information of its digital master. Difference between both realms is a measure of its transformation through production, where the cause may not always be clear. This is of particular significance when specific claims are made for the status of the built work in relation to methodology of representation, technique, or associated generative rules that

are transferred by its digital master. In this context, if an evident difference between the digital and the physical is not recognised, the resulting construct can only be regarded as a reality of a very exclusive kind; a beta-reality that is stage managed to demonstrate theoretical challenges in design, but not in manufacture, use, occupation or context. Where it is implied in particular that materials are synthesised as physical and digital matter,[22] one could assume that the palette of architectural materials selected for the physical construct should be capable of matching the behaviour of its avatar and visa versa. With the many challenges such an approach presents, this paper will now looks at a number of recent projects that cross the digital and analogue threshold where the difference between drawing and making is a defining principle of the work explored.

De-Fabricating 55/02

Adopting a built work as a test bed for these ideas, the 55/02 shelter in Kielder by sixteen*(makers) and Stahlbogen GmbH, was captured in 3D LIDAR one year post completion. As previous texts record,[23] the shelter was designed as an oscillation of design decisions made in drawn and fabricated format at Stahlbogen's factory in Blankenburg. Although substantially digitally fabricated, the as built shelter carried many decisions that were made on the shop floor without being recorded on the digital design file. Some of these decisions involved component removal, others component augmentation or adjustment, where judgement varied between the practical and the visual, and also the work's identity. Key to understanding why such changes relate to the points above, is that all were made by the co-authors of the digital design file, who were also co-makers of the work, and they were decisions solely informed by the built work as it evolved, not decisions dictated by the drawing that preceded it.

This practice was adopted from the very beginning of the shelter's fabrication, notably on decisions surrounding the number, proximity and geometry of folds in the shelter's sheet steel skin.[24] Had the facility of scanning been available at these stages, rather than post completion, many further decisions might have been effected. In the first instance, availability of 3D scan data for the chosen site rather than the GIS mapping (which was supplied) would most certainly have influenced primary design decisions such as site configuration, proximity to existing trees, footings layout, and more specific referencing to immediate context. Yet the availability of the technology soon after completion still offered scope to extract lost, hidden or new information, and to gain a deeper understanding on the utilisation of scanning technology as a design tool. For detailed description of LIDAR technology, how it functions, and is controlled, see Vosselman, et al, 2009, or Bryan, et al 2009.[25] For additional insight into the role of representation in developing 55/02 see Sheil 2012.[26]

The scans that were subsequently captured and processed

by ScanLAB Projects[27] were developed through the following illustrated steps. Through each step, this paper will conclude by examining the most significant consequences for design and fabrication strategies provided by the information acquired, and speculate on implications or revisions that might be adopted in future design or fabrication strategies now that technology is readily available. In the first instance, developments on how the data has been analysed and visualised stem from a single visit to site in 2010. Similar to the manner in which LIDAR technology is deployed in forensic work[28], capturing was fully executed without clear expectations on what the data would be used for, or indeed what it would reveal. In this regard, capturing is a pure exercise in the comprehensive recording of high definition geomatic data that is tied into accurate positional coordinates, the greater the saturation of information the greater the scope for later analysis. To following steps illustrate the exercise, which was carried out by ScanLAB Projects, who also advised on the key insights described.

001 Data Acquisition

The image shows the placement of reference geometry and markers within the scene. Markers were placed to be visible from as many scan locations as possible, and 6-7 markers were visible from any singular capture point to provide redundancy and cross checking within the reference network. In future, such markers could be embedded within the built fabric as discrete permanent tags, and thus behave as design life registers as the work is made, transported, assembled, installed and used. Positioning of such built-in tags may be reverse calculated to optimise later capture, thereby potentially easing the task of attaching applied reference marks on site.

002 Post Production of Data

Scan data, including imported RGB values for every point in the cloud, is then passed through conversion software to produce a series of discrete point cloud models that are subsequently stitched together to produce a single cluster by snapping reference geometries. External geo-localisation of the data then places the cluster within a global context and a digital clone of the built work is generated. At this point the model has exportable value as a surveyed, visualisation and interrogative tool in both 3D & 2D as animated or still imagery, or vectorised data. The Digital clone has clear value as an accurate record of the built work, but also as the data is rich in definition, it introduces value to the clone as a visually explorable and spatial record of the construct. In this regard, such data and its various visualisation exports has currency as a rich 3D archive and verification tool, allowing later changes or removals to be compared against the 'original' built work. Examples of such applications are present in the museums and collections industry where the stable conservation of objects as well as spatial organisation has particular relevance.

Fig. 2.22.15 Data Acquisition.

Fig. 2.22.16 Post Production of Data.

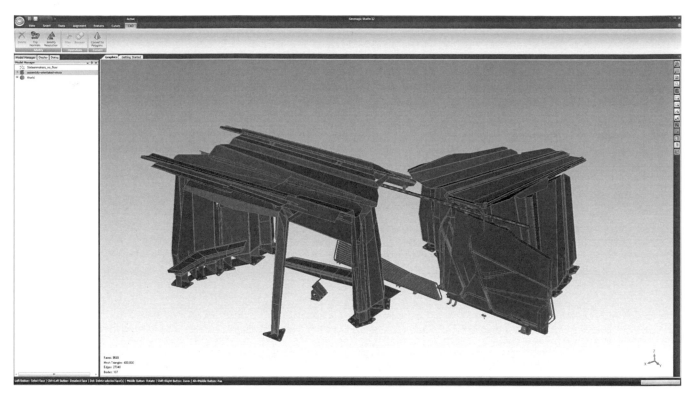

Fig. 2.22.17 Import Digital Fabrication Model

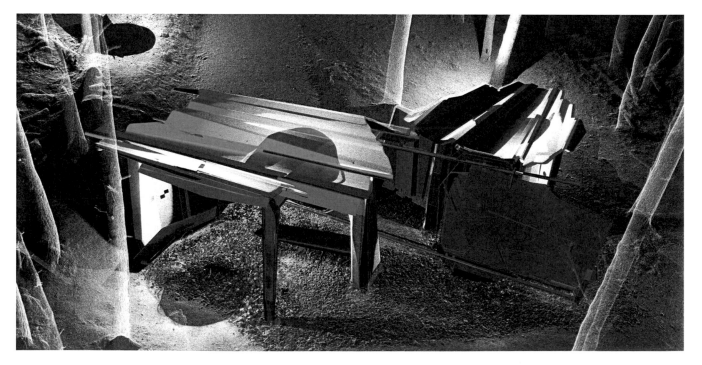

Fig 2.22.18 Alignment of Data

Fig 2.22.19 Alignment of Data

003 Import Digital Fabrication Model

Although designed and made for amongst other purposes as a critique of design and manufacturing integration, the making of 55/02 reflects many of the challenging issues facing the construction industry on information flow and verification, albeit on a small scale. Whereas for 55/02 such bureaucratic hurdles were turned into a creative advantage for its hybrid and resident designer/makers, the industry at large faces a continuous challenge in grasping the multitude of unrecorded changes or amendments that are common to complex projects. Underpinning this cycle of continual verification of the as-built back to the as-designed is the stringent requirement to build the design that was agreed with planning and building control authorities prior to construction. Cross referral of as-built data as captured through 3D scanning to BIM data clearly offers an option on whether to concede or adjust these constraints. The next step in this sequence therefore is to import the final CAD model and 3D point cloud model into an environment where both may be superimposed.

004 + 005 Alignment of Data

This set of images show CAD data and Scan data aligned to each other where best fit algorithms refine the position of the whole assembly based on sub-sampling the data sets. Where 55/02's vermilion colour shows at full strength, the surfaces of both models are aligned. Ghosted areas highlight non critical misalignment in some of the tank areas and roof elements, either component by component, or chunk by chunk. As a purely speculative exercise, none of these faults have any significance in the performance, functionality or quality of the shelter, and

an exact fit was never set as a requirement in the first place, however the data clearly has value in establishing the presence of difference between the digital model and the final assembly. Clearly additional observations could have been recorded had the shelter been scanned and verified against the digital model as it was first fully assembled in the factory. In this case, it would therefore have been possible to attribute where differences originated in journeys between design data, prototyping, fabrication, factory assembly, transport and site assembly. In the construction industry, we are not fully accustomed to the protocols of precision manufacturing, where it is common practice to tag components with a host of information, including the identity of the fitter (e.g. Rolls Royce engine assemblies). However, mapping of 3D scan data upon BIM modelling is beginning to roll out in the construction industry[29], and will soon be a regular exercise in updating design files against verified as built data.[30] There are of course at least two ways this asset may be utilised. One, it may focus entirely on the notion that difference = fault, and fault = claim. Alternatively, it may offer a complex and cumbersome industry with the tools to accommodate design decisions through the production of the work. This route would of course reach all the way back to concept design and subsequent immediate stages where a speculative proposition is locked into an expected final delivery. To date parametric design models have offered considerable flexibility in allowing for mass customisation or precision manufacturing prior to the point of production, and to some extent during production. However, progressive feedback from LIDAR data upon design and production modelling now offers greater capability to absorb difference as a regular rather than irregular occurrence.

006 Deviation of Assembly

This slide illustrates a transposition of deviation calculations shown upon the CAD model alone. It more clearly highlights any areas of conflict or disparity. In this instance the spectrum spans from red to grey, signifying elements of perfect match to those of total absence. In the case of the latter, components shown in grey were either taken out or substantially reconfigured between the saving of the final CAD model and the assembly of the final construct. Referring to earlier comments above on the embedding of registration marks as a built in array, equally such marks may be deployed to facilitate calibration and alignment of construct assembly, and furthermore, may be associated with new technologies in material marking[31].

007 Deviation of Component

The final step in this sequence illustrates alignment analysis for individual components. Again, in this instance errors are non-critical, but the information offers feedback to the manufacturer and designer in much the same way that a prototype should. It provides heretofore unavailable data that refines knowledge on the scope of tolerances in the production process. In many instances such difference is neither technically nor aesthetically significant, however even when it is, the capacity to identify and measure difference between the design and the artefact is a portal to many potential divergences between authorship and responsibility, intent and execution, and meaning to materiality.

Zero tolerance: Consequence or Conclusion

Zero tolerance in digital manufacture is both theoretically and practically achievable, however the construction industry must negotiate its expectations on how valuable such accuracy is. Rather than seek finite calibration between the drawn and the made, such tooling as described above aught to be used for continuous renegotiation on their differences. If for no other reason, acknowledging the gap between both disciplines respects the immeasurable and vital contribution of the craftsman. This paper therefore concludes that the status of the dynamic and adaptable digital design model in relation to the physical results that are built from it, is one of adaptability and facilitation, and conditions that must remain open to the design opportunities that reside in manufacture and production. It concludes that the status of the resulting physical assembly is an architectural prototype, perhaps better identified as protoarchitecture, and the difference between the drawn and the made is a rich territory for collaborative and creative engagement.

Notes

1   Exhibited at *Prototying Architecture*, Cambridge, Ontario
2   Professor of Architecture and Design through Production The Bartlett School of Architecture, UCL
3   Director of Software Development Autodesk Platform Solutions in Bob Sheil & Ruairi Glynn, (ed.) *FABRICATE - Making*

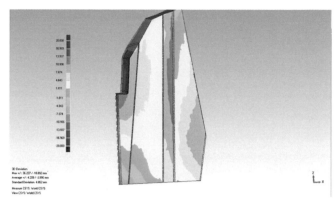

Fig. 2.22.20 Deviation of Assembly

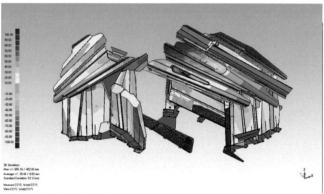

Fig. 2.22.21 Deviation of Component

Digital Architecture (PB) Toronto: Riverside Architectural Press. ISBN-10: 1926724186; ISBN-13: 978-1926724188

4   Developing a set of ideas that first appeared in a short article in the *Material Computation i*ssue of Architectural Design in February 2012. It came about through an invitation by the publisher to pose a counterpoint to the issue's overarching themes, and was framed at that time as piece entitled *Distinguishing between the Drawn and the Made.*

5   Sheil, Bob (ed). *Protoarchitecture: Analogue and Digital Hybrids.* (78). Architectural Design. London: John Wiley & Sons. (2008) ISBN-10: 0470519479, ISBN-13: 978-0470519479

6   Sheil, Bob. (ed). *High Definition: Negotiating Zero Gravity.* Architectural Design. London: John Wiley & Sons. (2014)

7   Mark West, *The Fore Cast* in Bob Sheil (ed)., *Manufacturing the Bespoke: An AD Reader.* London: John Wiley & Sons.

8   Froncoise Delarozière, & Claire David, *Le Grand Répertoire : Machines de Spectacle*

9   See Jansen, Theo. *The Great Pretender* 010 Publishers Amsterdam (2007)

10   G. Vosselman & H-G. Mass, *Airborne and Terrestrial Laser Scanning*, Whittles, Caithness, 2009.

11   Emitting upwards of 100,000 pulses per second LIDAR technology involves a scanning and ranging laser system that produces pinpoint accurate, high-resolution, topographic maps. The original technology has been in existence for 20-30 years, but the commercial applications for LiDAR generated topographic maps have only developed within the last decade. Today the entire process of airborne laser mapping is highly automated from flight planning, to data acquisition, to the generation of digital terrain models.

Fig. 2.22.22 Manufacturing Protoarchitecture 3'. Setting out jigs lie on site prior to commencement of final assembly of the 55/02 shelter. Such physical tools are entirely derived from the digital file that generates the architectural assembly, and thus act as 'difference' verifiers.

The basic components of a LiDAR system are a laser scanner and cooling system, a Global Positioning System (GPS), and an Inertial Navigation System (INS). Information obtained from Airborne 1 (http://airborne1.com/). See also USGS Center for LIDAR Information Coordination and Knowledge.

12   In 2009 3D LIDAR scanners cost in the region of £100k, today compact units are available for £20k.

13   Peter Dormer, *The Art of the Maker: Skill and Its Meaning in Art, Craft and Design*, Thames & Hudson (1994) p14.

14   Branko Kolarevic, *Architecture in the Digital Age: Design and Manufacturing*,Taylor & Francis, 2003

15   Bob Sheil, Transgression from drawing to making, *Architectural Research Quarterly* Vol.9(No.1), 20-32. Cardiff. Cambridge University Press, 2005

16   David Pye (1964 & 1968) and Peter Dormer (1994) – *The Art of the Maker: Skill and Its Meaning in Art, Craft and Design*

17   Stephen Gage, *The Bespoke as a Way of Working*, not a Style in Bob Sheil, (ed)., *Manufacturing the Bespoke: An AD Reader.* London: John Wiley & Sons, 2012

18   Mark Burry, *Models, Prototypes and Archetypes* in Bob Sheil, R. (ed)., *Manufacturing the Bespoke: An AD Reader.* London: John Wiley & Sons. 2012

19   Phil Ayres, *Persistent Modelling: Extending the Role of Architectural Representation,* Routledge, 2012

20   Charles Walker, and Martin Self, *Fractal, Bad Hair, Swoosh, and Driftwood* in Bob Sheil, (ed)., *Manufacturing the Bespoke: An AD Reader.* London: John Wiley & Sons.

21   See Bob Sheil and Nick Callicott, The Point of Production, pp.75-110, in *55/02 A sixteen*(makers) Project Monograph.* Bob Sheil (ed)., et al., Riverside Architectural Press, 2012

22   Achim Menges, *Material Computation: Higher Integration in Morphogenetic Design,* Architectural Design. London, Wiley, 2012

23   Bob Sheil, *A Manufactured Architecture in A Manufactured Landscape* in Architectural Research Quarterly Cambridge University Press, Vol.13, No.3/4, 2009

24   Bob Sheil,(ed.), *55/02 A sixteen*(makers) Project Monograph.* Toronto: Riverside Architectural Press, 2012

25   See endnote ix or Bryan, Blake, Bedford, Barber & Mills *"Metric Survey Specifications for Cultural Heritage"* (2009), English Heritage

26   Bob Sheil, *Ways of Seeing, Ways of Doing*, in *55/02 A sixteen*(makers) Project Monograph*, Riverside Architectural Press, 2012, pp.75-110

27   ScanLAB Projects is run by Matthew Shaw and William Trossell, both of whom have backgrounds in architecture and fabrication. http://www.scanLABprojects.co.uk/

28   http://www.faroasia.com/products/laser-scanner/sea/forensics-and-accident-scenes.html

29   Thomas Graabæk (of BIM Equity) lecture at Confluence Symposium at CITA, Royal Academy of Fine Art Copenhagen. https://vimeo.com/55766548

30   Thomas Graabæk (of BIM Equity) lecture at Confluence Symposium at CITA, Royal Academy of Fine Art Copenhagen. https://vimeo.com/55766548

31   See Signature Materials Project at the Institute of Materials, Minerals and Mining.

32   An earlier version of this essay appears in Michael Stacey, ed., *Prototyping Architecture: The Conference Papers*, Riverside Press, 2013, pp. 420-239

2.23 Bones

Barkow Leibinger

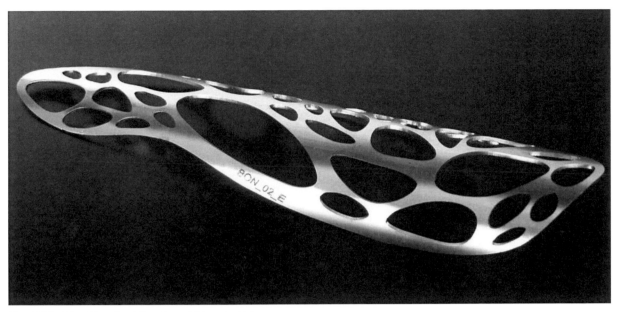

Fig. 2.23.2 A Revolving 3D cut Bone from stainless steel tube

Designer:	Barkow Leibinger
Materials:	Stock tubes of stainless steel
Fabricators:	Trumpf
Exhibit:	CNC machined stainless steel circular hollow sections - Bones

'How do tools (more elaborately defined as emerging technologies or techniques) drive our architecture? Tools shape materials that make forms, not the other way around.' Regine Leibinger and Frank Barkow[1]

A fragment from *An Atlas of Fabrication* is exhibited in Prototyping Architecture – the Bones. The technique is 3D Cutting (Revolving). Stock tubes of stainless steel have been CNC cut, bilaterally, symmetrically or randomly. With an ornamental and performative intent, these components of Barkow Leibinger's architecture can become, sunscreens for glass facades or elements in a rotating dynamic façade. Barkow Leibinger's Berlin-based practice can be characterised by the interaction of practice, research and teaching. Their interdisciplinary, discursive attitude allows their work to expand and respond to advancing knowledge and technology. Recent projects include a gatehouse and factory-campus event space in Stuttgart Germany and the TRUTEC Office Building in Seoul. Current research projects have focused on revolving laser cutting; CNC-cut translucent concrete formwork; façade systems, pre-cast concrete and ceramic elements. Digitally tooled materials no longer accessorise construction but contribute to essential components including skins and structures. Their research folds into ongoing construction projects focusing on a 'trickling down' of these technologies informing the construction of everyday building types including office buildings, factories and pavilions. This method favours expanding building systems leading to formal, phenomenal, physical and material effects.

'The exhibition, installation and mock-up are instrumental in offering an alternative to the enduring and troubling gap between representation (historically models and drawings) and building.'

Frank Barkow[2]

Notes

1   Regine Leibinger and Frank Barkow, *An Atlas of Fabrication*, AA Publictaion 2009, p. 1.
2   Frank Barkow, *Revolutions of Choice in* in Michael Stacey, ed., *Prototyping Architecture: The Conference Papers*, Riverside Press, 2013, pp. 412-419

Fig. 2.23.4 CNC machined stainless steel Bones – from Barkow Leibinger's Atlas of Fabrication

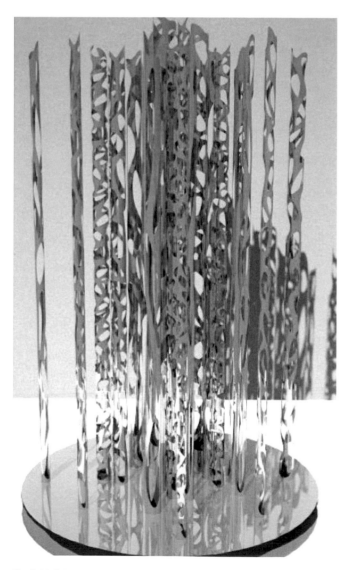

Fig. 2.23.3 Bones, as dis[played at the Venice Bienalle

Fig. 2.23.5 Nomadic Garden

2.24 Thames Water Tower

Michael Stacey[1]

Fig. 2.24.2 Thames Water Tower by Brookes Stacey Randall Fursdon

Architect:	Brookes Stacey Randall Fursdon
Engineer:	Atelier One
Materials:	Hand Polished Sand Cast Stainless Steel, Mild Steel Core, Stainless Steel Sheet and Curved Toughened Glass, Dark Grey Anodised Aluminium and Polycrystalline Silicone Photovoltaic (services not listed).
Fabricators:	Charles Henshaw & Sons
Location:	Holland Park, London
Exhibit:	Thames Water Tower: wooden pre-prototype for form approval, the timber pattern of the sand casting and the stainless steel cast prototype for approval of the production batch.[2]

This inventive tower of glass and stainless steel is a prototype for an environmentally responsible and responsive building. It was built to house a surge pipe on Thames Water's ring main; an unseen marvel of hydro engineering serving all of London. The tower celebrates this otherwise invisible achievement with an amplified electronic barometer in the centre of Holland Park Roundabout, London. The project was realised through the research and application of new technologies. The tower is clad with sophisticated, purpose-designed suspended glazing supported by bespoke stainless steel sand castings. All water is fully recycled within the tower. The polycrystalline solar cells of the vane assembly generate energy to power the barometer's pumps. It is the first public building in London to be powered by photovoltaic. The Thames

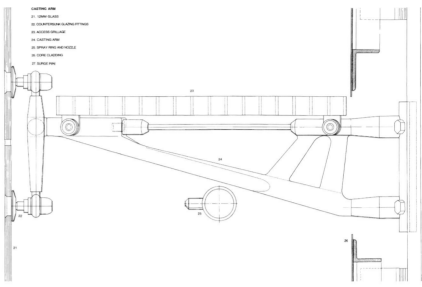

Fig. 2.24.3 Thames Water Tower - pre pattern timber prototype

Fig. 2.24.4 Brookes Stacey Randall Fursden's integrated casting detail of the Thames Water Tower

Water Tower demonstrates engineering excellence and contributes to London's public realm. Contemporary responses included, 'such is the inspirational nature of the tower that the panel felt its qualities transcended the question, is it sculpture or architecture?' RIBA Award. 'It is one of the most successful pieces of public art in Britain' Hugh Pearman, Sunday Times.

The exhibit comprises a hand fabricated wooden pre-prototype prepared by Charles Henshaw & Sons from Brookes Stacey Randall's working drawings, for form approval by the architect. The sand casting mould, which includes the methoding to successfully feed the stainless steel into the casting during casting and cooling. The first cast grade 316 stainless steel prototype is also displayed. The weight of this casting is 13.34kg. It has been hand polished because the final castings are in the very damp environment of the enclosed barometer, conditions similar to a casting used in a marine context.

'Foundries are a fascinating cross between Dante's Inferno and a wonderland of lost components. These satanic mills offer considerable technical opportunity to an inquisitive architect or engineer. Casting is an affordable route to the reintroduction of craft into the building industry in the form of a reliable and repeatable manufacturing process, based on the skill of the die or pattern maker, the inventiveness of the architect/engineer and the expertise of the foundry. Castings are a good example of the application of batch production, to match the particular requirements of a building project.' Michael Stacey[3]

Fig. 2.24.5 Thames Water Tower, Shepherds Bush, London

Fig. 2.24.6 The timber pattern of the sand casting

Fig. 2.24.7 Hand polished stainless steel cast prototype for approval of the production batch

Fig 2.24.8 Thames Water Tower base detail. The stainless steel clad base houses all of the services of the tower

Notes

1   Michael Stacey founding partner at Brookes Stacey Randall
    Fursdon, 1987, set up Michael Stacey Architects in 2004.
2   Exhibited at Prototyping Architecture, Nottingham and
    Cambridge, Ontario.
3   Michael Stacey, Component Design, Architectural Press, 2001, p.
    65.

2.25 Quantum Cloud

Anthony Gormley

Fig. 2.25.2 Rapid prototype nodes for Quantum Cloud, printed wax and LOM

Artist:	Anthony Gormley
Engineer:	Elliott Wood
Materials:	Wax and Cast Steel
Rapid Prototyping:	Department of Mechanical Materials and Manufacturing, University of Nottingham and Casting BSA
Location:	Greenwich, London
Exhibit:	Anthony Gormley's fractal marquettes, wax printed rapid prototype of node, investment cast steel node, finished by galvanising.

Commissioned to celebrate the new millennium outside the Dome at North Greenwich. Anthony Gormley's vision for the Quantum Cloud was a man in a fractal cloud. He insisted the sticks or cords of the structure did not have clumpy space frame nodes. This is where, for Elliott Wood the challenge began. The creation of a node that could deal with the variations in relative angles and rotations was a key factor in the success of this project. There was no repetition of the joints making the use of normal casting techniques impractical. Every one of the 364 nodes was unique. Spherical joints that could be designed to facilitate the degrees of freedom required were not visually acceptable. The members had to be joined seamlessly with minimal evidence of jointing at any of the connections. 'Rapid prototyping was essential in the delivery of the sculptors vision of a human in a metallic cloud'.[1] Rapid prototyping enabled 364 unique nodes to be produced directly from the computer model. Three-dimensional solid models were generated using the geometry of the overall three-dimensional model. These were produced using Multi-Jet Modelling (MJM) and Laminated Object Manufacturing (LOM). These two processes use wax and paper respectively to create the sacrificial patterns. The patterns were cast using a lost wax process; also know as investment casting, by BSA.

Due to the cost of stainless steel, carbon steel was adopted and then galvanised after the fabrication and casting process. The connections to all of the tetrahedral units had to be welded to achieve full moment connections between the elements. Grade A4 steel was adopted for the castings as this had a low carbon content to enable site welding to be carried out without the need for preheating. These were then galvanised after casting and the connections were ground back locally to allow the welding to be carried out on site.

Notes

1   Michael Stacey, Component Design, Architectural Press, 2001, pp.181-182.
2   Exhibited at *Prototyping Architecture*, Nottingham

Fig. 2.25.3 Investment cast steel node produced from one of 364 unique node geometries [above]

Fig. 2.25.4 Investment cast steel node produced from one of 364 unique node geometries [below]

Fig. 2.25.5 Casting the lost wax ceramic moods at BSA [right]

Fig. 2.25.6 Robot dipping the wax forms in a zircon sand mix at BSA [below]

2.26 Nasher Sculpture Center

Renzo Piano Building Workshop[1]

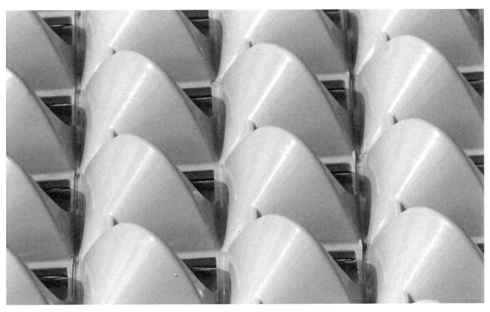

Fig. 2.26.2 The polyester powder coated cast aluminium solar shading components form the unique shading of the Nasher Sculpture Center

Architect:	Renzo Piano Building Workshop
Engineers:	Arup
Materials:	Lost wax and cast aluminium
Location:	Dallas, Texas, USA
Exhibit:	Digitally printed wax prototype and a polyester powder coated cast aluminium solar shading component[2]

The Nasher Sculpture Center, designed by Renzo Piano Building Workshop, is one of the few institutions in the world devoted to the exhibition, study, and preservation of modern sculpture. It consists of a 5,000m² building and a two-acre garden. From the outset, the project was conceptualised as a synthesis of nature and building. The building is made of parallel stonewalls, which create the gallery pavilions. Each pavilion is enclosed by low-iron glass facades and a roof that permits a 150m long unobstructed view corridor from the street, through the building, and across the length of the garden. These attenuated perspectives have created an effect of transparency and lightness.

The cast aluminium shells form the unique shading of the Nasher Sculpture Center's bespoke glass roof. Each shell plays an important part in creating an environment with optimum conditions for displaying sculpture by successfully filtering direct light that could degrade the works on display. The result is a spectacular naturally lit environment. The design team at Arup worked closely with architect Renzo Piano to deliver this matrix of day light blockers. The result is

Fig. 2.26.1 A gallery of the Nasher Sculpture Center bathed in daylight

an eye-catching roof composed of over half a million aluminium shells. Each shell weighs a mere 40g and is precisely cast in aluminium at the correct angle to exclude the direct rays of the sun whilst maximising and precisely controlling daylight as the sun tracks across the Dallas sky. Shade is critical for a glazed roof gallery in an area like Dallas where the sun is so intense. The form for the roof shading was found by using equations to chart the sun's path through the course of the day. In-house rapid prototyping was used to produce a 1:1 prototype of the solar shading cells, in wax.

Alistair Guthrie, Arup Director noted: "After projecting the sun's path specific to the gallery site, we then designed the shells and roof in a way that enabled Piano's ambition to create the thinnest possible roof. The design ensures that the gallery enjoys excellent daylight but excludes direct sunlight. What's unusual about this project is that the roof was cast in aluminium straight from the drawing board to production using original computer programming data." [3]

Notes

1   Unlike many architects Renzo Piano Building Workshop make their drawings freely available on the practice website - www. rpbw.r.ui-pro.com

2   See *The Future Builds with Aluminium*, http://greenbuilding.world-aluminium.org/home.html, where the case studies are written and organised by Michael Stacey

3   Exhibited at *Prototyping Architecture*, Nottingham

Fig. 2.26.3 Digitally printed wax prototype of the shading shells

Fig. 2.26.4 A gallery of the Nasher Sculpture Center bathed in daylight

NEW MATERIALS AND TECHNOLOGIES

ADDITIVE MANUFACTURED VIOLIN

It is every violin maker's dream to produce an instrument to rival the sound of a Stradivarius and researchers at The University of Nottingham are trying to do just that... using Additive Manufacturing technology. Dr Joel Segal has teamed up with EOS GmbH to produce a laser-sintered violin, which has been in development in the Engineering Faculty over the past year. EOS produced a body made from Alumide® (aluminium filled polyamide) using one of their advanced laser-sintering systems, the EOSINT P390. The University provided the ancillary components including: tuning pegs, strings and bridge. Professor John Dominy assembled the violin at specialist manufacturer Carbon Concepts.

Laser-sintering is an Additive Manufacturing technology. Any three-dimensional geometry can be built effectively and flexibly, without any tools, laborious milling path programming or casting process. As a prerequisite, 3D CAD geometry data has to be available. During production, the 3D CAD model is sliced into layers, topographically. EOS's innovative laser-sintering technology then builds the required geometry layer by layer. The energy of a laser solidifies powder-based materials, for example plastic, metal or foundry sand. The laser-sintering process allows for the production of several different parts in one single build.

A typical application of Alumide® is the manufacture of stiff parts of metallic appearance for applications in automotive manufacture, for example: funnel tests or parts that are not safety relevant, for tool and injecting and moulding, small production runs, for illustration models of metallic appearance and aged structures, to name a few. An advantage of Alumide® is low tooling costs; machining is possible, if apart metal can be used, different effect. Surfaces of parts made of Alumide® can be finished: grinding, polishing or coating.

RESEARCHERS: Manufacturing Research Division, Faculty of Engineering, University of Nottingham.

MATERIALS AND PRINTING: EOS GmbH

MANUFACTURER: Carbon Concepts

3.1 Additive Manufactured Violin

Joel Segal and EOS GmbH

Fig. 3.1.1 Additive Manufactured Violin, digitally printed by The University of Nottingham in collaboration with with EOS GmbH

Researchers / Designers:	Manufacturing Research Division, Faculty of Engineering, The University of Nottingham
Materials:	Alumide® (aluminium filled polyamide)
Fabricators:	EOS and Carbon Concepts
Exhibit:	The Additive Manufactured Violin and conventional bow.

It is every violinmaker's dream to produce an instrument to rival the sound of a Stradivarius, researchers at The University of Nottingham are trying to do just that, using additive manufacturing technology. Dr Joel Segal has teamed up with EOS GmbH to produce a laser-sintered violin, which has been in development in the Engineering Faculty during 2012. EOS produced a body made from Alumide® (aluminium filled polyamide) using one of their advanced laser-sintering systems, the EOSINT P390. The University provided the ancillary components including; tuning pegs, strings, and bridge. Professor John Dominy assembled the violin at specialist manufacturer Carbon Concepts. A carbon fibre violin researched and designed by the same team is also illustrated.

Process Laser-sintering is an additive manufacturing technology. Any three-dimensional geometry can be built effectively and flexibly, without any tools, laborious milling path programming or casting process. As a prerequisite, 3D CAD geometry data needs to be designed. During production, the 3D CAD model is sliced into layers, topographically. EOS's innovative laser-sintering technology then builds the required geometry layer by layer. The energy of a laser

Fig. 3.1.1 Additive Manufactured Violin, digitally printed by The University of Nottingham in collaboration with with EOS GmbH

Prototyping Architecture   207

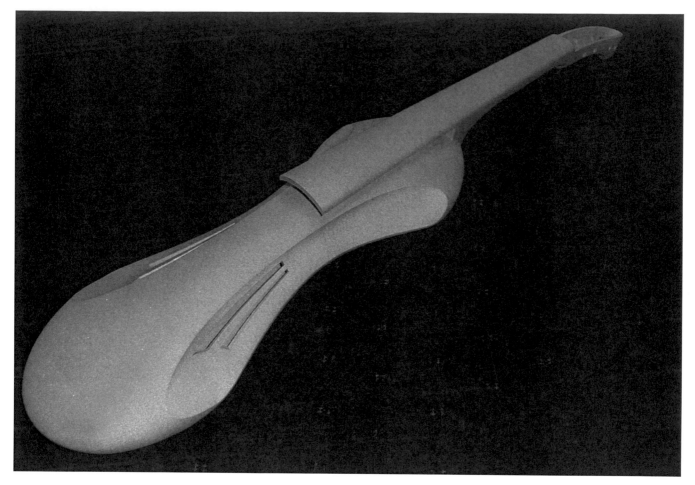

Fig. 3.1.3 Alumide® digitally printed violin body

solidifies powder-based materials, for example plastic, metal or foundry sand. The laser-sintering process allows for the production of several different parts in one single build.

Material

A typical application for Alumide® is the manufacture of stiff parts of metallic appearance for applications in automotive manufacture, for example wind tunnel tests or parts that are not safety critical, for tool inserts for injecting and moulding small production runs, for illustrative models of metallic appearance and jig manufacture, just to name a few. An advantage of Alumide® is that low tool-wear machining is possible, if apart needs to be milled, drilled or turned. Surfaces of parts made of Alumide® can be finished by grinding, polishing or coating.

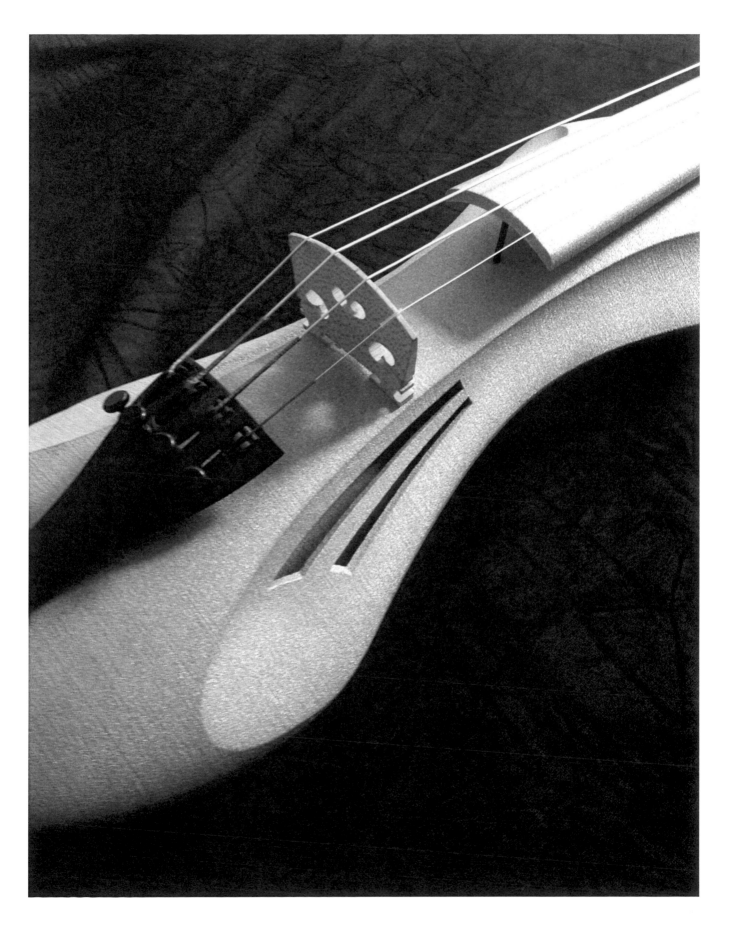

Fig. 3.1.4 Alumide® digitally printed violin body with bridge and strings

3.2 Additive Manufacturing

Additive Manufactured Research Group

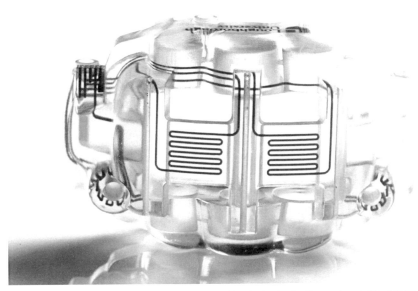

3.2.2 An additive manufactured component incorporating electronic circuitry, produced at the EPSRC Centre for Innovative Manufacturing in Additive Manufacturing

Researchers / Designers: EPSRC Centre for Innovative Manufacturing in Additive Manufacturing at The University of Nottingham

Materials: Selected laser melted Titanium 6Al-4V – exhibit example only

Fabricators: Printed at The University of Nottingham

Exhibit: Topology optimised structural component three-dimensionally printed using Titanium 6Al-4V, with a selective laser melting process[1]

Additive Manufacturing (AM) is the direct fabrication of end-use products and components employing technologies that deposit material layer-by-layer. It enables the manufacture of geometrically complex, low to medium volume production components in a range of materials, with little, if any fixed tooling or manual intervention beyond the initial product design. The EPSRC Centre for Innovative Manufacturing in Additive Manufacturing at the universities of Loughborough and Nottingham is a new nucleus of research activity focused on next generation multifunctional AM technology. The fundamental and translational research carried out within this world-class Centre will help shape the future national and international AM research agenda. Through technological expertise and research professionalism, the EPSRC Centre's activities will enable UK companies to achieve and maintain leadership in the commercial realisation of the next generation of AM technology.

Notes

1   This is the AMRG exhibit at Prototyping Architecture, London and Cambridge. A wider range of AM components were displayed during the Nottingham stage of this exhibition.

Fig. 3.2.1 Algorithmically optimised titanium 6AL-4V aerospace part digitally printed by Selected laser melting

3.3 Nematox II
Additive Manufactured Node for Façade Construction
Holger Strauss

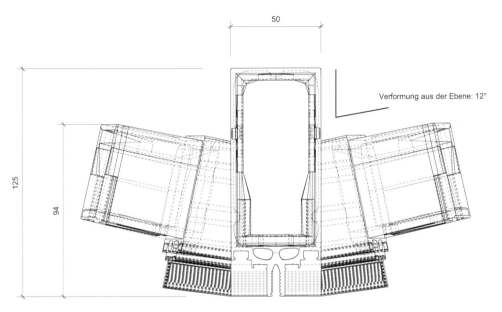

50

Verformung aus der Ebene: 12°

125

94

Fig. 3.3.2 Nematox II -a digitally printed aluminium node CAD drawing

Researchers / Designers: Holger Strauss and Ulrich Knaack[1]

Materials: Selected laser melted aluminium

Fabricators: Kawneer-Alcoa

Exhibit: Nematox II - a digitally printed aluminium node in a Kawneer-
                           Alcoa curtain walling assembly

The context for the development of Nematox II is the technological progression of building envelopes in the twentieth and early twenty first century, Nematox II seeks to address the geometric complexity of many contemporary façades by digitally printing an integrated node. Additive Manufacturing (AM) offers a path to seamlessly integrate this complexity into a directly printed aluminium component. By digitally merging the mullion and transom of the curtain walling, all the deformations and joints of the members within a façade system are virtually planned, checked and prepared for AM production. Digital planning and digital fabrication eases the difficult details in the production shop and on site, requiring simple 90° cutting of extrusions providing pre-planned geometric precision. Nematox II nodes are digitally printed in aluminium. It is the first component arising from the change in construction engineering logic resulting from the application of Additive Manufacturing. This major advance was generated by the collaboration between ConstructionLab in Detmold, Germany and the global systems company Kawneer-Alcoa as part the *Influence of Additive Processes on the development of façade constructions* initiative. Additive Manufacturing is no longer on a technology transfer wish list, it is available as part of the repertoire of the contemporary construction industry.

Notes

1   Dipl.-Ing. Holger Strauss, Prof. Dr.-Ing. Ulrich Knaack, Delft Technical University, Delft, Netherlands, Façade Research Group, TU Delft and University of Applied Sciences – Hochschule Ostwestfalen-Lippe, Detmold, Germany.

Fig. 3.3.1 Nematox II -a digitally printed aluminium curtain walling node

3.4 Energy Bag

Seamus Garvey[1]

Fig. 3.4.2 Seamus Garvey and colleagues with fully inflated Energy Bag prototype

Researchers / Designers:	Professor S. D. Garvey and Dr. A. J. Pimm.
Materials:	Polyester reinforced fabric with structural aramid tendons and a butyl rubber bladder
Fabricators:	Thin Red Line Aerospace, Chilliwack, Canada[2]
Collaborators:	E.ON, EMEC and Thin Red Line Aerospace
Location:	Orkney, United Kingdom
Exhibit:	The fully inflated Energy Bag prototype[3]

The Energy Bag™ is a flexible containment for storing compressed air underwater. The ultimate motivation is to store energy. The cost of the Energy Bag is below £50/m³ and this is almost independent of water depth. The energy stored depends strongly on water depth. At 600 metres depth, it takes only 60 cubic metres to store 1 MWh. The Energy Bag serves to hold the air down while the water itself becomes the pressure vessel keeping the air compressed. The optimum size of Energy Bag is around 20 metres in diameter. The bag seen here is 5m in diameter and has been trialled successfully underwater in Orkney. Up take of Energy Bags is presently being considered by several different companies. They will be used as economical energy stores in conjunction with farms of offshore wind turbines to smooth out the intermittency of the output from those machines, and to enable electrical power to be delivered to land when required, rather than simply when the wind blows. On some islands the Energy Bags already make economic sense. Gran Canaria is one excellent example. There, electricity is presently

Fig. 3.4.1 The empty Energy Bag prototype being recovered form the North Sea

Fig. 3.4.3 Diver preparing to enter the water to service the Energy Bag, Orkney

generated using expensive diesel fuel shipped to the island. Onshore wind power is a relatively cheap power source but some means must be found to reconcile energy supply and demand. This adventurous concept has been pioneered at The University of Nottingham.

Notes

1 Seamus Garvey is Professor of Dynamics & Director of the Rolls-Royce UTC in Gas Turbine
  Transmission Systems, Faculty of Engineering at The University of Nottingham
2 Funding from E.ON International Research Initiative
3 Exhibited at *Prototyping Architecture*, Nottingham – simply due to its size.

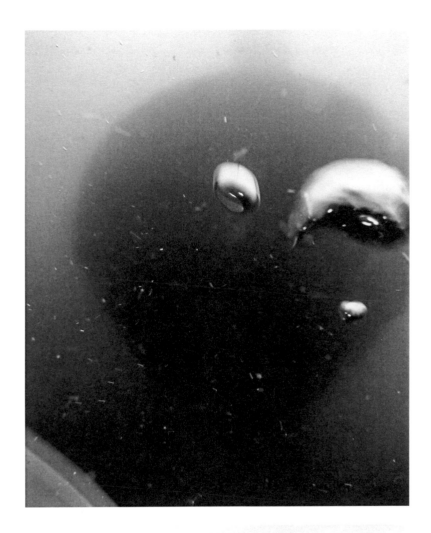

Fig. 3.4.4 The Energy Bag prototype being tested underwater off Orkney

Fig. 3.4.5 Diver entering the water to examine The Energy Bag prototype underwater off Orkney

3.5 Plumen 001 Low Energy Light Bulbs

Plumen

Fig. 3.5.2 Plumen 001 low energy light bulbs

Researchers / Designers:	Plumen
Materials:	Bent glass tubes, PBT and Copper
Fabricators:	e3light Group
Exhibit:	10 No. Plumen 001 low energy light bulbs illuminating the tables providing a brief contemporary of metal forming from sand castings to additive manufacturing of aluminium and titanium.[1]

The Plumen 001 is the world's first designer energy saving light bulb. The energy saving light bulb is a neglected, yet inspiring invention. It uses 80% less energy than the traditional incandescent light bulb, keeps down electricity bills and is better for the environment. It also lasts around 8 times longer. Despite this, people tend to buy them out of moral obligation. To some the problem is the light they give off, to others it is the way they look. Both can be solved. Plumen believe the answer is in the design. Make the bulb attractive and people will spend a bit more enjoy a better quality of light and a design they appreciate every day.

Glass tubes can be bent in many different shapes, so why are there thousands of manufacturers but only three designs? Plumen aims to address this problem. The excellence and elegance of the Plumen 001 Bulb was recognised by the Award of Brit Insurance Design of the Year 2011. The Plumen 001 is the first of, many products that will show that light bulbs can be efficient and beautiful at the same time.

Notes

1   Exhibited at *Prototyping Architecture*, Nottingham and Cambridge, Ontario

Fig. 3.5.1 Plumen 001 low energy light bulbs illuminating the tables providing a
brief contemporary of metal forming

SCHÖCK ISOKORB®

Schöck

einfach besser bauen

Schöck Bauteile GmbH
D-76534 Baden-Baden
Tel. +49/7223/967-0

Zugelassen vom
Deutschen Institut für
Bautechnik, Berlin
Zulassungs-Nr.
Z-15.7-240

Typ KS 14

h = 180 mm

218190/1

3.6 Schöck Isokorb: Structural Thermal Breaks

Eberhard Schöck

Fig. 3.6.2 Schöck Isokorb structural thermal break for in situ concrete to concrete construction details

Engineer / Inventor:	Eberhard Schöck
Materials:	High-density polystyrene units and micro stainless steel fibre-reinforced concrete cores, with stainless steel reinforcing bars
Fabricators:	Schöck Bauteile GmbH [Schöck UK Ltd.]
Exhibit:	Schöck Isokorb KXT structural thermal break for in situ concrete-to-concrete construction; Schöck Isokorb KS structural thermal break for in situ concrete to steel construction; Schöck Isokorb KST structural thermal break for all steel construction.

If an element of a component, cladding system or structure starts in a warm interior and is in direct contact with the outside or another element that is, then a thermal or cold bridge has occurred. There are two primary risks posed by cold bridges; energy loss and the risk of condensation or damp. Energy loss or dramatic thermal outflow will result in excessive heat and energy consumption, firstly by negating the thermal efficiency of the building and secondly by increasing the chance of a dew point forming within the construction, thus causing condensation and interstitial condensation. Structural thermal breaks are a key point in every building and they require detailed consideration from both the architect and the structural engineer. Schöck Isokorb's thermal breaks make this process easier, because they transfer sheer forces and continuous bending moments to concrete slabs while reducing thermal conductivity. Achieving this through the use of high-density polystyrene units and micro stainless steel fibre-reinforced concrete cores. This combination makes the units strong enough to transfer loads and maintain full structural and thermal integrity. Schöck welds stainless steel to mild steel reinforcement to protect against any corrosion or condensation that may occur within the units.

Fig. 3.6.1 Schöck Isokorb structural thermal break for in situ concrete to steel construction

3.7 QbissAir

Trimo

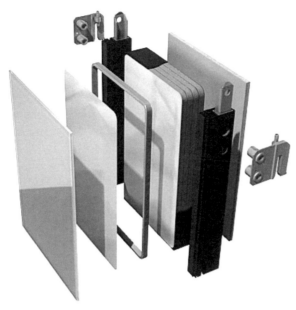

3.7.2 Digital Model of the layer construction of the transparent option with the QbissAir system

Researchers / Fabricators: Trimo Dd. of Slovenia

Materials: Glass and air

Exhibit: 1:1 Wall assembly incorporating QbissAir's range of clear, translucent and opaque modules

QbissAir is a unitised total wall system designed to maximise the internal floor space of a building by being up to three times thinner than traditional façades. It comprises opaque, translucent and transparent modules, which are designed to self-span between the floor slabs of a building. Each module consists of an inner and outer skin that incorporates internal insulation chambers of still air. The system is designed so it can be installed from inside the building, eliminating the need for external access. QbissAir is a modular façade system, which demonstrates how the science of thermodynamics can be used to produce a highly insulated product with low G-values and minimum air leakage, whilst maintaining a minimal wall thickness. In other words, it elegantly provides a high performance and low carbon building fabric.

A key feature of the design of QbissAir is its excellent thermal performance, which is achieved by controlling the thermodynamics of the system rather than using solid insulation materials. QbissAir is a range of clear, translucent and opaque modules of identical thickness, which can be installed from inside the building. A QbissAir glazed facade can achieve a U-value of 0.35w/ m^2 k and a G value of 0.1 at an overall thickness of 133mm. Acoustic performance averages 45db and air tightness is 1.2 m3/ m2/hr @50 Pa. Also unique to the system is the incorporation of structural members within the modules, eliminating the requirement for a secondary support

Fig. 1.7.3 QbissAir transparent unitised cladding system

Fig. 1.7.4 QbissAir transparent unitised cladding system including opening lights

structure such as a curtain wall. The external skin is normally glass [enamelled, translucent or transparent] but a range of alternative materials and finishes are also available. The system is manufactured using structural glazing technology, therefore no external frames or caps are necessary. When installed, QbissAir provides a flush internal and external face with no intermediate mullions or transoms. The joints between modules are sealed with 20mm recessed gaskets.

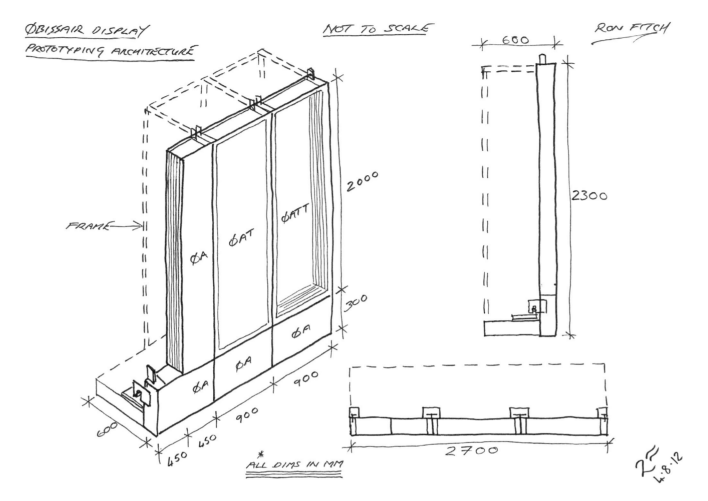

QBISSAIR DISPLAY
PROTOTYPING ARCHITECTURE

NOT TO SCALE

RON FITCH

FRAME →

ØA ØAT ØATT

2000

300

ØA

ØA ØA ØA

600

450 450

900

900

2700

600

2300

* ALL DIMS IN MM

2.
4.8.12

Fig. 1.7.5 Sketch showing QbissAir transparent unitised cladding system

3.8 A Brief History of Glass Corners

Cantifix Ltd

Fig. 3.8.2 1:1 Four corners prototype - A Brief History of the Glass Corners at Prototyping Architecture Exhibition, Nottingham

Researchers / Designers:	Cantifix Ltd
Materials:	Key exemplar: UV bonded double glazed corner unit
Fabricators:	Cantifix Ltd
Exhibit:	1:1 Four corners prototype - A Brief History of Glass Corners[1]

Evolution is the gradual development of something into a better form. When used to describe materials the implementation of an evolutionary process must combine knowledge and experience with available new technologies. Cantifix has been building glass structures for over 26 years. It has positively driven the development and use of many new technologies in the direction its customers demand. Architecture has always embraced the use of glass in buildings, and new production techniques allowed larger panels to be available, for example, the standard maximum size of laminated glass is now 6000 x 3210mm, glass began to define the buildings we live and work in.

The last 20 years has seen a rapid growth in the processes of toughening, laminating and coating of glass, which has increased the possibilities and potential of new markets. Glass is now available to everyone at both large and small scales, such diversity puts greater emphasis on good detailing. Cantifix has developed the Invisible Corner, an all-transparent double glazed corner units, as the next logical stage in glass construction. Applying knowledge and experience of structural glazing to modern technology, the Invisible Corner combines two panels to effectively form a single piece of glass, which can be put together to form a sealed double-glazed unit - creating a practically undetectable corner with a standard U-value of 1.5 W/m²K.

Fig. 3.8.1 Invisible double-glazed glass corners, by Cantifix.

Fig. 3.8.3 - 4 example of site applied silicone bonded corner

"The Invisible Corner has assured the future of transparency, allowing freedom of design and creating striking and technically beguiling enclosures and façades" Charlie Sharman, Cantifix Ltd.

Notes

1   Exhibited at *Prototyping Architecture*, Nottingham

Fig. 3.8.5 - 7 Invisible double-glazed glass corners, by Cantifix. An elegant approach to the Modernists vision of blurry the boundary between house and garden without sacrificing comfort and thermal performance.

TECHNOLOGY TRANSFER

4.1 Range Rover 2012 All Aluminium Body Shell

Jaguar Land Rover

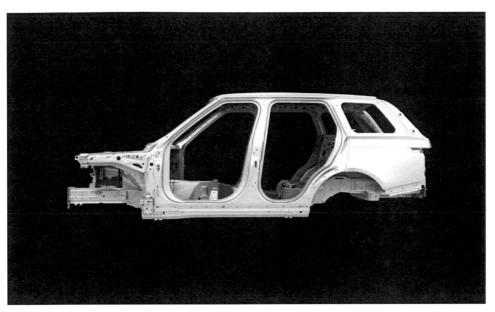

Fig 4.1.2 The Range Rover 2012 All Aluminium Body Shell

Researchers / Designers: Mark White, Chief Technical Specialist – Body Engineering, Jaguar
                            Land Rover - Product Development

Materials: Aluminium sheet – 6000 series, 5000 series, Aluminium
                            Extrusions, 14 Aluminium Castings, 2 magnesium castings PHS /
                            HSS Steel[1]

Fabricators: Jaguar Land Rover

Exhibit: The prototype structure of 2012 Range Rover all-aluminium body
                            shell[2]

The Range Rover 2012 has been designed and fabricated with an all-aluminium body, it was launched by Jaguar Land Rover [JLR] in September 2012. Designed and engineered in Britain, it is the world's first SUV with a lightweight all-aluminium body. It achieves a weight saving of 420kg when compared with the previous model, which is the equivalent to the weight of five average adults. This third generation of JLR light weight vehicle architecture combined with improved aerodynamics, results in an increase in fuel efficiency of over 20% - significantly reducing the carbon footprint of owning a SUV. It uses up to 50% recycled aluminium and is a high-profile example of potential technology transfer from other industries. JLR has built on its own past experience of developing all aluminium body structures, including the XJ Jaguar, the first volume-production car to use an all-aluminium monocoque chassis.

There is a competitive EU road map for carbon reduction in the European Car Industry, Mark White, JLR's Chief Technical Specialist – Body Engineering, observes 'in Europe there is now an agreed [car] industry roadmap to reduce emissions by 3% per year over the next 20 years'.[3] This is undertaken collaboratively with outcomes being shared by the major car manufacturers but is competitive as how the savings are achieved remain specific to each manufacturer. Perhaps this is a better model for the construction industry rather than the prescription of Code for Sustainable Homes or Passivhaus standards.

The development of the new Range Rover took very significant R&D investment by JLR. The use of virtual testing reduced the R&D carbon footprint by 320kg of CO_2, by saving 750 Kilometres of testing. However, over 300 physical prototypes were produced in the development of the new Range Rover. Key components that deliver the 420Kg weight saving, nearly half a metric tonne, are:

-        Aluminium body and aluminium closure parts;
-        Aluminium intensive suspension and sub-frames;
-        Magnesium castings (Cross car beam & front end carrier);
-        Composite plastic upper tailgate;
-        Aluminium brake callipers;
-        And an aluminium space saver wheel.

The aluminium components are 40% lighter than steel equivalent parts saving 190kg in weight. Based on market research, JLR sought to keep the image of the existing Range Rover, whilst improving performance beyond fuel economy, including the clearance angles for off road journeys. In essence, the Range Rover 2012 is a mimetic design, underscored a great technical inventiveness.

Notes

1   See Figure 1.57 Introduction –, in Michael Stacey, ed., *Prototyping Architecture*, 2013, p. 37
2   Exhibited at *Prototyping Architecture*, Nottingham
3   Mark White, *Why does the European Car Industry need Light Metals to survive in a Sustainable World*, in 11th INALCO Conference 2010, *New Frontiers in Light Metals*, Katgerman L. and Soetens F., eds., IOS Press, 2010 , p. 23.

Fig 4.1.3 XJ Jaguar, the first volume-production car to use an all-aluminium monocoque chassis